Blessed by Bosasa

Blessed by Bosasa

Inside Gavin Watson's state capture cult

ADRIAAN BASSON

Jonathan Ball Publishers
JOHANNESBURG AND CAPE TOWN

All rights reserved.

No part of this publication may be reproduced or transmitted, in any form or by any means, without prior permission from the publisher or copyright holder.

© Text 2019 Adriaan Basson
© Published edition 2019 Jonathan Ball Publishers

Originally published in South Africa in 2019 by
JONATHAN BALL PUBLISHERS
PO Box 33977
Jeppestown 2043

ISBN 978-1-77619-002-7
ebook 978-1-77619-003-4

Every effort has been made to trace the copyright holders and to obtain their permission for the use of copyright material. The publishers apologise for any errors or omissions and would be grateful to be notified of any corrections that should be incorporated in future editions of this book.

Twitter: www.twitter.com/JonathanBallPub
Facebook: www.facebook.com/JonathanBallPublishers
Blog: http://jonathanball.bookslive.co.za/

All images courtesy of Media24, unless otherwise credited.

Zapiro cartoons © 2019 Zapiro. Originally published on Daily Maverick. Re-published with permission. For more Zapiro cartoons visit www.zapiro.com

Cover design by publicide
Design by Triple M Design

Set in 11/15pt Minion Pro Regular

To Vernie Petersen and every other whistleblower
who died of a broken heart.
Your struggle was not in vain.

Contents

Acronyms and abbreviations x
Cast of characters xii
Infographic: Love me tenders xiv

Preface xvii

PART ONE: Genesis
1. The first fight 3
2. Getting hooked on Bosasa 6
3. Meet the Watsons 9
4. 'I sold my company to the ANC' 16
5. The forgotten comrade 20
6. 'We need to make money. The struggle is over' 26
7. Betrayal 31
8. Selling out 35
9. Old networks, new money 38
10. 'Oh Lord, won't you buy me a Mercedes-Benz?' 43
11. Connecting the dots 48
12. The smoking gun 50
13. Richman 52
14. Smoke and mirrors 55
15. Red flags 58
16. Gambling with state money 60
17. Mti resigns 63
18. The smoking bazooka 67

19. The Mbeki links 70
20. Crash and burn 74
21. Enter the Cobras 77
22. #BosasaLeaks 82
23. Burner phones and death threats 86
24. Protecting my sources 94

PART TWO: Depravity
25. The 'affair' 99
26. Let us pray 106
27. The Donald Trump of Krugersdorp 113
28. Sex on the desk 118
29. The k-bomb 120
30. Rape and death 125

PART THREE: A good comrade
31. The Mitchells Plain Youth Movement 131
32. Into the lion's den 135
33. Petersen's secret dossier 139
34. 'Shona Malanga' 142
35. Stranger things 147
36. The fear 153
37. 'Something must break' 158
38. Comradely betrayal 162
39. Departing 168

PART FOUR: Atonement
40. The unlikely snitch 177
41. From the Guptas to the Watsons 181
42. Monopoly money 186
43. The little black books 192
44. A stuffed Louis Vuitton bag and a charge sheet 198
45. Braai packs and birthday cake 205
46. Green, black and gold (and food parcels and cash) 209

47. The chef who sold his Ferrari 215
48. Enter the Ramaphosas (by Kyle Cowan) 224
49. The curtain falls 230
50. 'We were prostitutes' 236
51. The wounded buffalo 239

Epilogue 242

Acknowledgements 248
Author's notes 250
Notes 252
Index 271

Acronyms and abbreviations

ACSA	African Correctional Services Association
ACTT	Anti-Corruption Task Team
AFU	Asset Forfeiture Unit
AGO	African Global Operations
ANC	African National Congress
ANCWL	ANC Women's League
BEE	Black Economic Empowerment
BEMS	Bosasa Empowerment and Management Services
CCMA	Commission for Conciliation, Mediation and Arbitration
CIA	Central Intelligence Agency
Cope	Congress of the People
CP	Conservative Party
DA	Democratic Alliance
DCS	Department of Correctional Services
Kwaru	KwaZakhele Rugby Union
LFCC	Little Falls Christian Centre
MEC	member of the executive committee
MK	uMkhonto weSizwe
MP	member of parliament
NDPP	National Director of Public Prosecutions
NDZ	Nkosazana Dlamini-Zuma
NEC	national executive committee
NGO	non-governmental organisation

NIA	National Intelligence Agency
Nicro	National Institute for Crime Prevention and the Reintegration of Offenders
NP	National Party
NPA	National Prosecuting Authority
OAU	Organisation of African Unity
POB	public-office bearer
PSC	Public Service Commission
SAA	South African Airways
Sacos	South African Council on Sport
SACP	South African Communist Party
SAHRC	South African Human Rights Commission
Sanef	South African National Editors' Forum
SAPS	South African Police Service
SARS	South African Revenue Service
Saru	South African Rugby Union
SBDC	Small Business Development Corporation
SIU	Special Investigating Unit
SSA	State Security Agency
TRC	Truth and Reconciliation Commission
UDF	United Democratic Front
UMNO	United Malays National Organisation
WWF	World Wrestling Federation

Cast of characters

THE BOSASA BOYS

Gavin Watson   Danny Mansell   Angelo Agrizzi   Joe Gumede

Papa Leshabane   Andries van Tonder   Frans Vorster   Sesinyi Seopela

THE ANC WOMEN

Nosiviwe Mapisa-Nqakula   Nomvula Mokonyane   Hilda Ndude

THE COUNSELLOR	THE 'MISTRESS'	THE SPY BOSS	THE ZUMA FIXER

Denise Bjorkman	Lindie Gouws	Gibson Njenje	Dudu Myeni

THE PRISON BOYS

Ngconde Balfour	Linda Mti	Patrick Gillingham

THE SLEUTHS   THE PRESIDENT'S SON

Willie Hofmeyr	Vernie Petersen	Andile Ramaphosa

Love me tenders

Between 2003 and 2018 Bosasa and its subsidiaries were awarded government tenders worth over R12.2 billion by these 18 departments and entities.

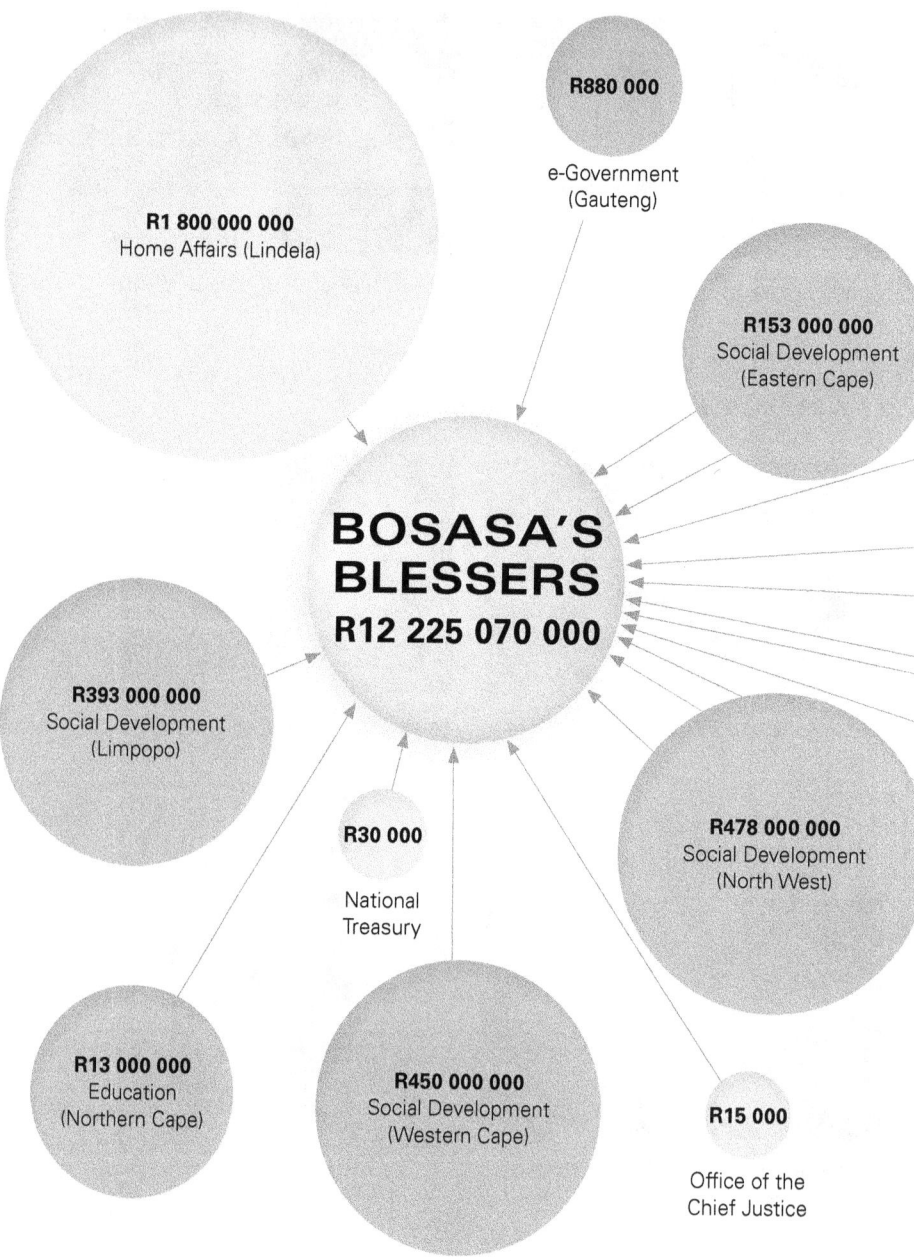

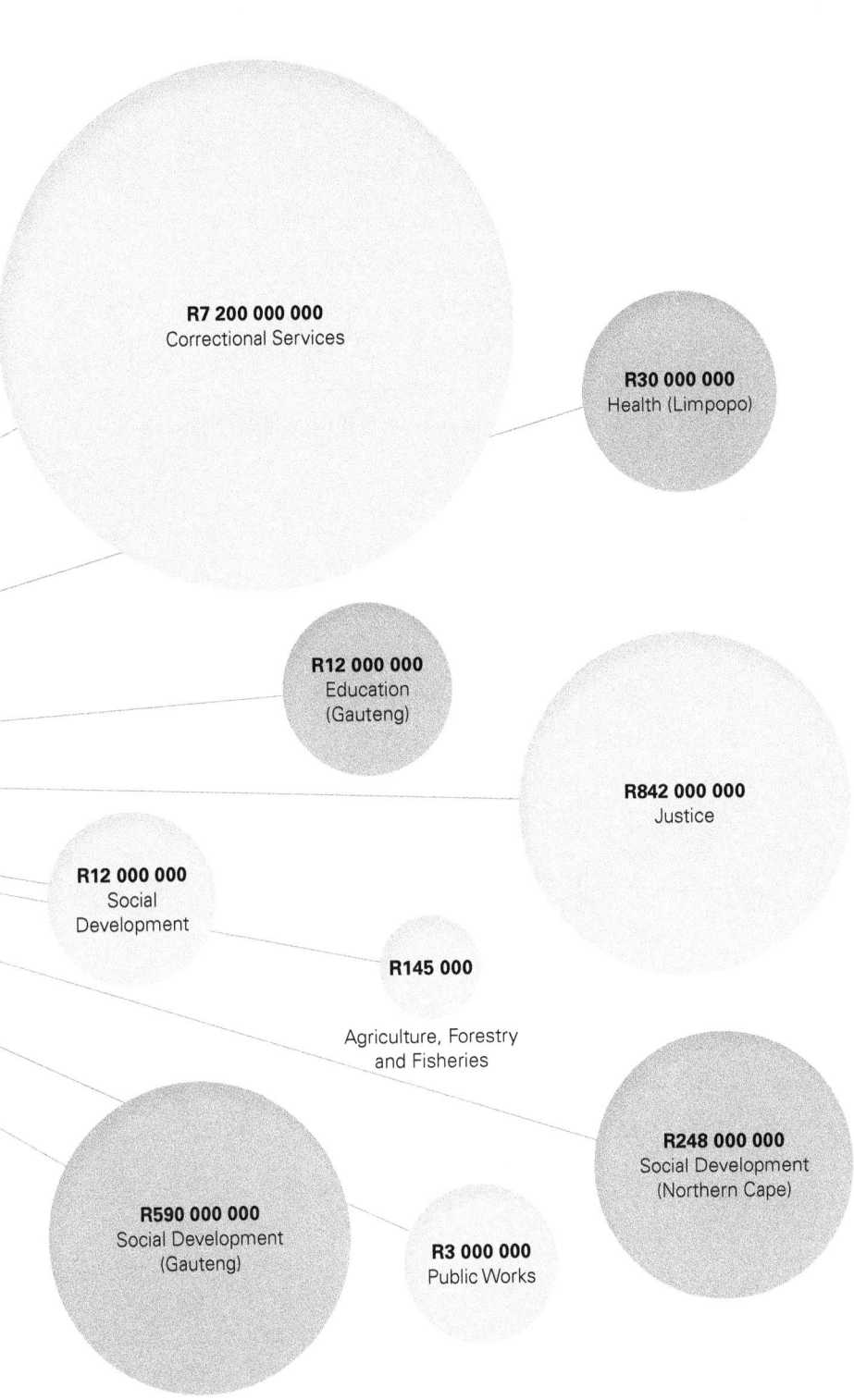

> 'YOU WILL BE BLESSED WHEN YOU
> COME IN AND
> BLESSED WHEN YOU GO OUT.'
>
> Deuteronomy 28:6
>
> engraved on a brass plaque at the entrance to Bosasa's Mogale Business Park

Preface

When the Italian chef-turned-fixer Angelo Agrizzi started spilling the beans on Bosasa in January 2019, I'd been investigating the company for 13 years. What had started out in 2006 as just another story about prison-tender irregularities had grown into the biggest threat to President Cyril Ramaphosa's 'new dawn', which was built on promises of clean governance and anti-corruption arrests.

Agrizzi's captivating revelations meant 'state capture' was no longer limited to former president Jacob Zuma and the Gupta family. Alongside Agrizzi, Bosasa CEO Gavin Watson – one of the Watson brothers who'd fought in the liberation struggle in the 1970s and 1980s – became a household name for South Africa's chattering classes. Suddenly the African National Congress (ANC) was on trial and the story to which I'd dedicated more than half of my working life as an investigative journalist was threatening to bring down the governing party – and its president.

A few weeks before the May 2019 general election, the ANC was polling less than 50% of the popular vote. Pollsters and researchers who actively tracked the factors influencing the vote identified the Bosasa revelations as the main reason why thousands of potential ANC voters looked set to take their crosses away from Ramaphosa's party.

The full extent of Bosasa's capture of not only the correctional services department but the entire ANC ultimately contributed to making it impossible for Ramaphosa and the ANC to cross the 60% threshold they'd hoped for. The ANC finally ended on 57.5% of the national vote, the lowest by Africa's oldest liberation movement since it had come to power under Nelson Mandela in 1994.

In November 2018 Ramaphosa admitted he'd received a R500 000 donation from Watson to his 2017 campaign fund for the ANC presidency. A few weeks into his term as state president, Ramaphosa's detractors inside and outside of the ANC turned the spotlight on this matter. It was clear that Bosasa had become the millstone around Ramaphosa's neck.

In July 2019 Bosasa threatened to derail Ramaphosa's new-dawn tenure when Public Protector Busisiwe Mkhwebane found that the president had violated his oath of office by not declaring to Parliament Watson's gift. Mkhwebane, who'd become the main protagonist in the fightback against the Ramaphosa administration, used the Bosasa donation as the launch pad from which to mount a full-out attack on Ramaphosa's campaign funding and integrity.

On the morning of 26 August 2019, just before dawn, as the net started closing in on him and he was trapped between the ANC's warring factions, Gavin Watson drove at high speed into a concrete pillar outside OR Tambo International Airport in Johannesburg. His death on the scene sparked a bitter battle over the legacy of a good comrade who'd gone rogue.

The question on everyone's lips was: what secrets was Watson taking with him to the grave?

In this book, I try to answer this question as far as possible. Who exactly were Gavin Watson and his facilities-management company in Krugersdorp that threatened to bring down Ramaphosa's Thuma Mina[1] project?

The story of Bosasa is not of one company or tender that was awarded corruptly by a comrade to his crony; it's the story of how corruption engulfed a once-proud liberation movement and turned freedom fighters into self-serving parasites. It's the story of how political connectivity and noble BEE policies were abused to enrich a new political elite and prop up the ANC at the expense of the poor. It's the story of how honest comrades who stood in the way of looting and plunder were crushed. And it's

PREFACE

the story of how religion was used to create a state capture cult in which loyalty and fear trumped human rights and the rule of law.

It's a story that must now be told.

Adriaan Basson
September 2019

PART ONE

Genesis

1

The first fight

I've only been in one fist-fight in my life. It was 1996 and I lived with my family in a very modest neighbourhood called Witpoortjie[1] on the border between Roodepoort and Krugersdorp on the outskirts of Johannesburg's West Rand. My parents were both teachers and tried their very best to protect me and my two sisters from the social ills of growing up on the wrong side of the tracks, as Witpoortjie certainly was in those days. They largely succeeded and bless them for that.

Roodepoort, and Witpoortjie in particular, was politically a very conservative place. My father was deemed a liberal for helping the National Party (NP) in the 1992 yes/no referendum[2] and for not using the k-word. The NP was actually the opposition in Roodepoort, with the right-wing Conservative Party (CP) – a breakaway from the NP by Andries Treurnicht and other NP leaders who deemed PW Botha too liberal – always coming out tops in the whites-only elections. (An oom called Jurg Prinsloo, a staunch CP member, was the main political honcho in town, and later represented the party in Parliament. Much to my surprise, Advocate Prinsloo SC would years later resurface as Jacob Zuma's legal counsel in his failed attempts to sue the media for defamation.)

The white West Rand of the 1980s and '90s wasn't a place for sissies. You played rugby, had a girlfriend (or two), smoked Peter Stuyvesant from the age of 14, started drinking brandy and Coke when you turned 16, and received your first motorbike, a 50cc Suzuki, Yamaha or Kawasaki, on your

16th birthday. Disputes were resolved with fists. On Sundays you went to church to repent. Push repeat.

Despite my relatively large physique, I was terrible at rugby. That pretty much zeroed my chances of having a girlfriend. I preferred tennis, sang in the school choir and wrote for the school newspaper. I didn't smoke until I was 18 and had my first brandy and Coke at university. My father refused to buy me a motorbike after seeing one too many of his pupils in hospital with brain damage after writing off their bikes.

So I was pretty much a social outcast and needed to do something to increase my social capital. Want a recipe for disaster? Throw more than 30 testosterone-charged 15-year-olds into a woodwork workshop for an hour with very little supervision. That's when the fist-fight happened. I can't exactly remember what Martin – who was much smaller than me but unbearably irritating – did to push me over the edge, but it was probably something like flicking my ears from behind or trying to trip me, things that nowadays we call bullying.

The other boys formed a circle around us and dared us to a barney. My 'security advisor', a boy with much more fighting experience than me, suggested that we do it after school, outside the school premises, to prevent us all from landing up in the principal's office. Deal.

I was prepped on the art of war and given a small wooden block to clench in my fist for extra impact. My only reference to fighting at that point was watching copious amounts of WWF wrestling on TV and the odd local boxing match featuring guys like Pierre Coetzer, Johnny du Plooy and Dingaan Thobela.

Hoërskool Bastion was located on the edge of Witpoortjie, in the last street of the neighbourhood. From the rugby fields you had a clear view of the mine dumps to the west – the remnants of when gold was discovered under this barren earth in the late 19th century, leading to the establishment of Johannesburg, the city of gold. The winters were dry, and the school grounds and adjacent veld were yellow between March and October. Beyond the high school walls was a big piece of veld bisected by a large stormwater pipe. We were warned by our teachers that the pipe was used by satanists as a place to slaughter cats and burn candles and stuff.

THE FIRST FIGHT

On the other side of the veld was Chamdor, an industrial area hosting meat packers, large hardware warehouses and building-equipment vendors. Some of my friends' parents worked in Chamdor as factory workers, drivers and builders. To the south of Chamdor was Kagiso, a township carefully established far enough from 'white' Witpoortjie that we never had any business to do there. Apartheid spatial planning was extremely effective on the West Rand in keeping black and white apart.

North of Chamdor were more fields and mine dumps, interrupted by Main Reef Road, which ran through Krugersdorp to Randfontein. My dad drove the school bus for extra money and travelled this road every day to pick up children at the famous Uncle Harry's roadhouse in Randfontein. On his way there he would pass a small, insignificant street called Windsor Road; from his viewpoint on Main Reef Road he would've seen only a few mining hostels and oak trees to the right. Ten years later, these would've been complemented by huge blue, yellow and red signs with the words 'Bosasa', 'Sondolo IT', 'Phezulu Fencing' and 'Kgwerano' painted on them.

The entrance to Windsor Road was a ten-minute drive by car or motorbike from the scene of my first and only fist-fight.

It was a horrible experience and I had no idea how the fight was supposed to start. All I remember is that Martin klapped me in the face and I retaliated, punching him with a fist clenching that little wooden block. It must have worked because Martin didn't turn up for school the next day. Nobody ever challenged me to a barney again but I felt dirty and guilty, and was relieved to go back to the school choir and newspaper.

Walking away from the scene of that crime, I had no idea that a much bigger fight with the residents of 1 Windsor Road awaited me ten years down the line.

2

Getting hooked on Bosasa

'Have you heard of a company called Bosasa? They're selling TV screens to correctional services at R26 500 a pop.'

That's how Bosasa first appeared on my radar, in March 2006 – and then what should have been just one more story about a dodgy tender became a personal mission for me. I wanted to know and expose everything about Bosasa: the corruption, the crooks and creeps behind the name, and how prayer meetings were used to establish a state capture cult in the very unlikely location of the far West Rand.

In 2006 the term 'state capture' wasn't yet part of our political lexicon. We pretty much had the arms deal scandal, Tony Yengeni[1] and Schabir Shaik, but nobody knew it was possible to actually steal an entire state department, government or even president.

My first real exposure to what we now call state capture was during the marathon corruption and fraud trial of Shaik, Zuma's financial advisor, in Durban in 2004-2005. This trial introduced me to the dark side of the ANC: the money-laundering and crime networks of the exile years that had continued to operate under the new democratic dispensation. I also learnt for the first time that it was at the nexus of politics, money and crime that the biggest corruption happens, and that I should shift the focus of my work there.

Covering the Shaik trial gave me great insights into the ANC's murky relationship with business and money. The Shaiks were active in the ANC's underground struggle, which involved peddling information and moving money in all sorts of interesting ways to fund the fight against apartheid. After 1994, governing a state under law, some in the party found it difficult to adapt and play by the new rules. Instead of fighting apartheid, the ANC now had to fight elections, which required them to find millions of rands for posters, buses, food parcels, rallies, tents, speakers and, most importantly, T-shirts – thousands of T-shirts. A number of post-democracy scandals featuring the ANC involved party funding of election paraphernalia like T-shirts, food parcels and rallies.

I found Shaik's candid evidence about the ANC's early attempts to copy the Malaysian model of party funding fascinating. Testifying in his own defence, Shaik told the Durban High Court in 2004 that he and the first post-apartheid ANC treasurer-general, Thomas 'TT' Nkobi (after whom Shaik's companies were named), visited Malaysia after 1994 to study the Bumiputera model of affirmative action. Bumiputera means 'son of the soil' and refers to indigenous Malay people who believed they were sidelined by the British colonists in favour of Chinese people before Malaysia's independence in 1957.[2] The ruling United Malays National Organisation (UMNO) party introduced affirmative-action policies that included giving UMNO direct shareholding in private companies that benefited from state contracts.

Shaik, then helping Nkobi and the ANC to reconfigure the party's finances away from foreign-donor funding, was excited by this prospect of filling the ANC's coffers with dividends from government contracts. But after Nkobi's death in 1994, and in particular after then Deputy President Thabo Mbeki strongly opposed the idea (it would have amounted to corruption under South African legislation – something Mbeki realised), the model suffered a premature death.

Instead of the ANC as a party, Shaik continued to cut Jacob Zuma in on his deals. Zuma had been elected national chairperson of the ANC in 1994; he was elected deputy president of the ANC in 1997 and appointed deputy president of South Africa in 1999.

In June 2005 Shaik was found guilty of corruption and fraud, with the judge stating in his verdict that there was overwhelming evidence of a corrupt relationship between Shaik and Zuma.

Durban-based Shaik wasn't, of course, the only opportunistic businessman who cut his teeth in the struggle against apartheid and thought he'd won the lottery when the ANC took over the levers of power after the 1994 elections. A few hundred kilometres to the south, in the windy city of Port Elizabeth, Gavin Joseph Watson was making similar plans to monopolise the state with the assistance of his brothers and struggle friends in government.

It was a phonecall from journalist Carien du Plessis[3] in March 2006 that alerted me to Watson and what he was up to. Calling from Media24's newspaper-strewn parliamentary office on Plein Street, Carien told me that Bosasa was selling TVs to the Department of Correctional Services (DCS) at a jaw-dropping price. 'The Watson brothers are involved,' she told me.

Carien was working for *Die Burger* in Parliament at the time, and covered the correctional services portfolio committee, the oversight committee in Parliament that keeps tabs on the department's budget, as part of her beat. We'd often joke that it was only the two of us, and maybe three or four other people, like members of parliament (MPs) Dennis Bloem and James Selfe, who were interested in the DCS.

In a crime-ravaged country like South Africa, most people unfortunately had little sympathy with prisoners or the way our prisons were run. Despite the fact that most prisoners will eventually be released and walk among us again, most South Africans have a lock-them-up-and-throw-away-the-key attitude when it comes to criminals. This makes it much easier for prison employees and service providers to get away with dodgy deals – most people literally just don't care.

3

Meet the Watsons

Very few people have a neutral view of the Watson brothers. They have a complicated history, and it's not uncommon for the words 'heroes' and 'crooks' to feature in conversations about them and their past.

Famous for refusing to play whites-only rugby under apartheid, Gavin, Valence, Ronald (Ronnie) and Daniel (Cheeky) Watson attract strong opinions from most South Africans – negative or positive, depending on who you ask. (There's also a sister, Sharon, who's married to a Bosasa service provider and featured in the hearings of the Zondo Commission, which was established in August 2018 to investigate allegations of state capture.)

The family grew up on farms in the Eastern Cape towns of Kommadagga, Alicedale and Somerset East. Their father, Dan, a farmer and lay preacher, later started a clothing store in Port Elizabeth. Dan and his wife Bobbi taught their children that all people are equal and that you should 'love thy neighbour as thyself'.[1]

Vusi Pikoli, a former National Director of Public Prosecutions (NDPP), remembered the Watsons from his struggle sports days in the Eastern Cape in the 1970s. 'We got to know them when they joined the KwaZakhele Rugby Union [Kwaru] ... which was part of the South African Council on Sport [Sacos] under the late Hassan Howa. Our mantra then was "no normal sport in an abnormal society". Dan "Cheeky" Watson, who was a Springbok triallist, deserted Doctor Danie Craven's establishment rugby and was regarded as a rebel for joining an African rugby union playing in the townships.² His brothers, Valence, Gavin and Ronnie, weren't as good or prominent [at rugby] as Cheeky.

'Their involvement in black rugby subsequently led to their political involvement against apartheid and hence their association with the ANC. So I knew them even before I left for exile [in the 1980s] to formally join the ANC.' And Pikoli remembered that the Watsons 'had always been in business since the apartheid days'.³

But since democracy in 1994 the family had been in the news for all the wrong reasons – being in business with the infamous Brett Kebble,⁴ running the crooked Bosasa, bullying SA Rugby into including Cheeky's son, Luke, in the Springbok squad⁵ ... Their legacy as anti-apartheid warriors who'd gone up against their own people in defence of human rights had almost evaporated, and their family name had become synonymous with ANC corruption and state capture.

By the beginning of 2019 both Gavin and Cheeky had been implicated in crimes of corruption, fraud and money laundering. Valence had all but disappeared from the South African business landscape, and he and Ronnie had just had their plans to develop a massive wind farm in the Groot Winterhoek mountains near Uitenhage in the Eastern Cape scuppered by environmental concerns.

Australian journalist Kristin Williamson wrote a book about the Watson brothers titled *Brothers To Us – The Story of a Remarkable Family's Fight Against Apartheid*.⁶ Reading the book 22 years after it was published in 1997 made for fascinating insights into the personalities of the brothers, particularly Gavin, the main protagonist in the Bosasa story. I was told by Bosasa employees that Gavin Watson always had copies of the book in his office, next to copies of the Bible. He would hand out copies of *Brothers To Us* to his colleagues to read. 'Interestingly, he always kept the book away from his children,' Angelo Agrizzi told me.⁷

Williamson's book chronicles the Watsons' upbringing as farm children in the rural Eastern Cape and how they became politically active through their refusal to play whites-only rugby. Valence and Ronnie were the most politicised of the brothers, while Cheeky was the sporty one, and Gavin ran Dan Watson American Imports, the family's clothing business. 'Gavin, the self-appointed leader, was dominating and forthright. He said what was on his mind without considering whether feelings might be hurt,' Williamson wrote of the man who saw himself as head of the family, and who would decades later be described as 'narcissistic' and 'a bully' by his Bosasa colleagues.[8]

The clothing business helped to fund the ANC's activities in the Eastern Cape, and Ronnie and Valence were recruited by uMkhonto weSizwe (MK), the ANC's armed wing, to destabilise townships and infiltrate trade unions.[9] The brothers' commander in MK was Linda 'Richman' Mti, the Eastern Cape ANC leader who would years later be central to claims about Bosasa's corruption in the DCS. 'Richman told them that his mother always said he would live to see the day when he'd tell a white man what to do. "Now I've got two. My whiteboys!"'[10]

Ronnie Watson – of the four brothers, the most secretive and mysterious – was close to Chris Hani, the South African Communist Party (SACP) leader and MK chief of staff. In 1993, when Hani was assassinated by the Polish anti-communist immigrant Janusz Waluś, a piece of paper with Ronnie Watson's registration number on it was found in the glove compartment of the murderer's vehicle.

Limpho Hani, the SACP leader's widow, told Williamson that after 1994 the Watsons remained in the background. 'They do research. If I need information, Valence will get it for me. They prefer working in the background. We, the new politicians, always know they are there for us.'[11]

The Watsons' first major run-in with the law was their arrest in 1986 on charges of arson, fraud and attempted murder for allegedly burning down their family house in Port Elizabeth to claim the insurance money. At that time the family business was struggling and the state argued that the brothers had conspired to use the insurance claim to settle their debts.

Valence, Cheeky and Ronnie were charged with paying two of their employees and fellow rugby players, Archie Mkele and Geoffrey Nocanda, to soak the house with petrol and set it alight while the Watson family was away on a weekend break; both men had suffered serious burn wounds in the resulting explosion. Nocanda testified against the brothers, while Mkele refused to, claiming he'd been tortured by the police to extract a confession.[12] The Watsons contended that they were the victims of a 'dirty tricks' attack by the apartheid security forces for their allegiance to the ANC.

In 1987 Valence Watson was convicted of arson and fraud by the Port Elizabeth Regional Court, but the conviction was overturned by the Grahamstown High Court later that year.

Three figures from the arson court case would later feature in the Bosasa saga. Mkele and his former wife, Munirah Oliveria,[13] are major shareholders in Bosasa through an entity called Bosasa Empowerment and Management Services (BEMS). This company owns 100% of Bosasa Operations, which later changed its name to African Global Operations (AGO). BEMS is owned by Mela Womans Investments (34%), Mpako Investments (26%), The Employees Trust (22%) and Nzunzo Investments (18%).

According to shareholder documents presented by Angelo Agrizzi to the Zondo Commission, Oliveria owns 100% of Mela, which makes her the single largest shareholder in Bosasa, with 34% equity. The Archie Mkele Business Trust owns 100% of Nzunzo Investments, which gives him 18% control over Bosasa.

Oliveria lives very modestly in her family house in Newton Park, Port Elizabeth. Before Bosasa's contracts with the DCS were terminated in 2019, she managed the St Albans Prison facility for Bosasa. I found it strange that the company's 34% shareholder, who was surely earning millions in dividends from a company that had won government tenders worth over R12 billion, lived such a low-key life and effectively worked as the company's employee. Oliveria's millions were certainly nowhere to be seen: she drove a relatively modest Toyota Fortuner, a far cry from the Ferraris, Porsches, Audis and BMWs of Bosasa's directors in Krugersdorp, and was regarded as a normal employee.

Her ex-husband, Archie Mkele, 'played absolutely no role in Bosasa; we never, ever saw him,' said long-time employee Frans Vorster, who was one of a few *bittereinders* (diehards) who made the transition from the Afrikaner-owned Meritum to the ANC-supporting Bosasa.[14]

Rumour at Bosasa was rife that Mkele and Oliveria had been rewarded through their shareholding in Bosasa for helping the Watsons burn down their house, but the employees had no proof that this was the case, and the Grahamstown High Court ruling of 1987, which avowed the brothers' innocence, stands.

A third person from the arson court case who benefited from Bosasa many years later was Arthur Kotzen, whom Williamson describes as a 'conservative businessman who was managing director of a construction company' from Port Elizabeth. Kotzen had been a key witness for the Watsons, testifying that a few months before the incident he'd offered to buy the Watsons' family home for R700 000; the property was insured for R440 000.[15] 'The Watsons would have made more money by accepting our offer than from the insurance,' he said. 'I don't believe they would have tried to bomb their house. It was a beautiful property. They would have been crazy to bomb it.'[16]

Twenty years after Kotzen's evidence helped to acquit three of the Watson brothers, he was back in the news, this time as the construction partner of a Bosasa project to build a prawn farm called SeaArk at Coega in Port Elizabeth. Of all the Bosasa stories I covered over the years, this one ranks as one of the craziest.

By 2007 Bosasa was cash-flush due to all its state tenders, and Gavin Watson decided to bring out a team of US 'scientists' to build and operate a prawn farm in the Eastern Cape. Watson employed a convicted embezzler, David K Wills, as head of the project to build the 'world's first closed biosecure farming system', according to Bosasa's PR.

Three years, tens of millions of rands and several environmental complaints later, the company was shut down.

Arthur Kotzen had a building company called BuildAll that Watson purchased for R15 million to build the prawn farm. According to Agrizzi, who was chief operating officer and Gavin Watson's 2IC at the time, Kotzen, who died in 2012, was 'a bullshitter of note'. Kotzen was a close associate of Watson's brother Ronnie and Danny Mansell, who'd co-founded Bosasa with Gavin Watson. '[Kotzen] was a building contractor who had two bakkies and a couple of wheelbarrows,' Agrizzi told me.[17]

'Gavin had this thing about having to look after Arthur Kotzen. Ronnie put Arthur in touch with Gavin to build SeaArk. And Gavin decided to buy the company called BuildAll. I queried it. Suddenly, we had to pay R15 million for a company that had two bakkies and a couple of spades and a wheelbarrow. You know what the auditors valued the business for? R600 000. So later on we went through a bad spot, we shut down SeaArk and BuildAll, and I had an argument with Gavin: I told him we needed cash in the business. I said, "You overpaid [for] BuildAll. In my view they should give R3 million back because the project never finalised."'[18]

According to Agrizzi, Gavin Watson allowed him to recoup the money. Attorney Brian Biebuyck called in Arthur Kotzen and he wrote out a cheque for R3 million in the presence of Ronnie Watson. 'Ronnie was with him; he took instructions from Ronnie,' said Agrizzi, with reference to Kotzen's proximity to the family.[19]

Mkhuseli 'Khusta' Jack, an ANC and United Democratic Front (UDF) activist and businessman from the Eastern Cape, was one of a few critical voices in Williamson's book about the Watsons. 'They were the first white people to have a high profile and enjoy celebrity status in the townships amongst black people. But they couldn't manage that fame of theirs,' he said. 'It became very destructive. They started to venture into politics.'[20]

'They were businesspeople,' he continued, and told Williamson about the brothers' overriding need to control. 'The Watsons like having control. They have remote control even now. These guys are bad. They can work with anyone. They're like the Kennedys. They have their own organisation as a family. It's nothing to do with belonging to a political organisation.'[21]

Fanie van Zijl: Good intentions

'I sold my company to the ANC Women's League. It was a strong company. I had a very good idea. I can clearly remember the night I got the idea. It was a beautiful idea that children should not be kept with hardened criminals.'[1]

4

'I sold my company to the ANC'

Fanie van Zijl was arguably South Africa's top (white) athlete in the 1970s. A Springbok middle-distance runner, he was 'almost unbeatable' and an 'amazing strategist' in the 1 000- and 1 500-metre races.[2] He was also a prolific entrepreneur and started several manufacturing and services businesses in Krugersdorp on the West Rand in the 1970s under the umbrella name Meritum.

Van Zijl and his business partner, Jurgen Smith, saw potential in buying up old mining hostels on the West Rand and running them as private lodges, renting out rooms to miners, employees of Telkom and other blue-collar workers. Meritum took over the catering and cleaning of these hostels in the 1980s. The company also took over the catering at mines in Krugersdorp, Randfontein and Carletonville.

Van Zijl contracted a friend, Paulus Vorster, better known as Oom Vossie, who owned a dry-cleaning business in Randfontein, to do the laundry at the hostels. Vorster's son, Frans, who joined Bosasa as head of security (and would become Gavin Watson's go-to man when politicians, government officials or the Watson brothers needed cars or car repairs), recalled, 'At the time I worked as a policeman in Krugersdorp and later as station commander at Tarlton Police Station. We [Meritum] saw a business opportunity – a space to hold foreigners who were arrested.' The West Rand, with its proximity to the gold mines, saw a lot of undocumented foreign nationals being arrested by the police. 'A number of police stations simply didn't have enough space in their holding cells to keep foreigners and feed them. So we started to negotiate with home affairs.'³

Van Zijl had another idea – to establish youth centres for awaiting-trial juveniles, who at the time were kept with adults in the same prison. Driven by a personal belief that children shouldn't be kept with 'hardened criminals', Van Zijl converted some of his empty hostels into youth-friendly prisons. Van Zijl was passionate about his project to remove children from adult prisons 'where they could be sodomised'.⁴

Negotiations took place with the police and the DCS, which had a major overcrowding problem in the early 1990s. A senior prison official called Patrick Gillingham represented the DCS. 'Patrick and my father were good friends; at that stage he [Gillingham] wasn't corrupt,' said Frans Vorster.⁵ As a result, Meritum youth hostel was launched in 1995 as a project with the department of social development; and a year later Lindela opened its doors as the country's first repatriation centre where undocumented migrants awaited determination of their legal status in the country.

In 1996 everything changed. Although black economic empowerment (BEE) wasn't yet an official policy of the ANC government, there was pressure on companies doing business with the government to include black shareholders in their companies and in doing so change the face of business in South Africa. Van Zijl and Smith knew they had to change the ownership structure of the company. Enter the Watsons and a group of ANC Women's League (ANCWL) leaders.

At the centre of the initial introduction was the Small Business Development Corporation (SBDC),⁶ which was started in 1981 by Dr Anton Rupert and his son Johann as a public-private partnership to support small, medium and micro businesses. At the time Jurgen Smith, a co-owner of Meritum, was a senior member of the SBDC, and Eastern Cape businessman Danny Mansell headed up the provincial branch of the corporation. Gavin Watson was looking for new business opportunities after the family's clothing business had folded, and ended up knocking on the door of the SBDC. Mansell helped Watson to assist emerging black businesses in Port Elizabeth. But something went wrong, and Mansell was paid out by the corporation to leave – details about Mansell's sudden departure from the SBDC are sketchy and those who know are either dead or refuse to talk.

Having met Smith during his time at the SBDC, Mansell, Watson and Port Elizabeth accountant Tony Perry put together a bid to buy Meritum. Van Zijl recalls how the three men drove from Port Elizabeth to Johannesburg to discuss the purchase. 'Watson was representing the ANC Women's League. He said, "Let's go to Johannesburg to see the ANC Women's League." When we got there, it was only Nomvula Mokonyane at the meeting. I didn't know her.' At the time, Mokonyane was the Gauteng MEC for agriculture, conservation and environment. 'We concluded the deal. We had a contract. I gave them a big discount. I figured this was my contribution to the ANC.'[7]

But Meritum was never sold to the ANC. The deal was done with Dyambu Operations (which later became Bosasa Operations), a facilities-management company of which Watson and Mansell owned 90% of the shares in equal parts. The other 10% was owned by a group of ANCWL leaders through their company Dyambu Holdings. 'Bosasa was never an ANC front company. Gavin may have wanted it to seem that way, but the ANC never endorsed Bosasa,' said Angelo Agrizzi, who lifted the lid on Bosasa's continuous support of the ANC through donations of money, resources, facilities, food parcels and even birthday cakes.[8]

Agrizzi recalled that Van Zijl and Smith sold Meritum to Watson and co for 'about R6 or R7 million'. Mansell used his payout from the SBDC to buy the shares in Dyambu Operations.

Watson left his family in Port Elizabeth and moved to Johannesburg to be close to the action. Mansell ran Dyambu, and Watson was responsible for marketing. Watson also had a consultancy job with Sun International to help them win casino licences. 'Gavin arrived without a house or a car. He drove plenty of Sun International cars, but he didn't have his own,' Frans Vorster remembered.[9] Agrizzi recalled that Watson essentially 'lived out of his boot'.[10]

Smith stayed on at Dyambu (and then Bosasa) until his death in 2016, but Van Zijl left much earlier. 'Fanie and Doc Smith fought,' Agrizzi explained. 'He [Van Zijl] didn't know Lindela [the repatriation camp] was part of the transaction. He [had] wanted to retain the properties. For years, Smith and Van Zijl never spoke to each other. Van Zijl was still trying to run the business after Watson arrived [as an employee], but Watson would have none of it. There was a major breakdown, there was *snot en trane* [heavy crying]. Watson told Van Zijl to go home and retire and rest.'[11]

It was evident to me that Fanie van Zijl was sad and upset about what had become of the company after he left in the late 1990s. Talking about the allegations of corruption, bribery and state capture levelled against Watson and his peers, he said, 'Why must you do business like this? How much money do you want to make? There are plenty of ways to do honest business.'[12]

5

The forgotten comrade

Hildagarde (Hilda) Nikiwe Ndude should have been a household name in South African politics, like her struggle peers Nosiviwe Mapisa-Nqakula, Baleka Mbete and Nomvula Mokonyane. In the famous picture of Nelson and Winnie Mandela leaving Victor Verster Prison in Paarl on 11 February 1990 with their clenched victory fists in the air, she's there in the middle, behind them, wearing a navy-blue blazer over a green blouse – as the ANC's head of protocol at the time, she graced every major newspaper and TV channel in the world that week.

A UDF veteran, Ndude joined the struggle at a young age as a community activist in what was then the Cape province.[1] Ndude was one of the ANC leaders intimately involved with the organising of Mandela's release in February 1990: she was one of a few people who briefed Mandela that morning on what would await him outside prison, as he prepared to be a free man for the first time in 27 years.

Another person who played a prominent role that day was Brigadier Patrick Gillingham, a senior apartheid-era prison warder in charge of the management of prisoner Mandela. Gillingham was by his side as Mandela signed his exit forms.[2]

On that morning Ndude and Gillingham were on different sides, Ndude representing the 'new' South Africa, Gillingham representing the old apartheid regime. A few years later, both Ndude's and Gillingham's lives would be fatefully impacted by Gavin Watson and Bosasa.

Ndude joined the Western Cape legislature as an opposition ANC member in 1994 after the NP had managed to win the province in the country's first democratic election. At the time she was a senior leader in the ANCWL and served on its national executive committee (NEC). Two years later she was called to a meeting at the home of the Nqakulas in Cyrildene, Johannesburg. The attendance list read like that of a latter-day cabinet meeting, but in 1996 these women were all provincial politicians, MPs or in business: Mbete, Mapisa-Nqakula, Mokonyane, Lindiwe Maseko, Lindiwe Zulu, Nozuko 'Girly' Pikoli, Mavivi Myakayaka-Manzini, Nomatyala Hangana and Makho Njobe. Adelaide Tambo served in an advisory capacity.

According to Ndude, it was Nosiviwe Mapisa-Nqakula's husband, Charles,[3] who introduced the women to Ronnie Watson. And Mapisa-Nqakula herself was introduced to Ronnie by her husband, who'd met him in the ANC underground. 'They worked together and arrived in the country together. He [Ronnie] was very close to Charles and comrade Chris [Hani].'[4]

In his book *The People's War*, Charles Nqakula told how he met Ronnie Watson in 1985 through Hani, then general-secretary of the SACP, at a hotel in Lusaka.[5] Nqakula was impressed by the 'concise and incisive' intelligence reports Watson delivered to the ANC in exile; he had the ability to think ahead and predict the future, wrote Nqakula. According to the book, Ronnie Watson 'worked with Mbokodo [the ANC's security department] cadres such as Linda Mti (Richman) and Lizo Njenje (Gibson Makhanda)'.[6]

Mavivi Myakayaka-Manzini confirmed that the women's initial contact was with Ronnie, not Gavin: 'He was the one in the ANC,' she noted.[7]

'Ronnie Watson is a close family friend. Not was; is,' said Nosiviwe Mapisa-Nqakula – the woman who was minister of two government departments, home affairs and correctional services, from which Bosasa, and by extension the Watson clan, benefited richly. 'He is the godfather to my late son. I am not going to distance myself from Ronnie; he is very close to us.'[8]

But despite the fact that Ronnie was involved in a number of key Bosasa moments, including negotiating with Agrizzi to stay on at the company and not blow the whistle in 2018, Mapisa-Nqakula was adamant that I shouldn't conflate her very close and personal relationship with Ronnie with Gavin Watson's businesses. 'My relationship with Gavin is very different,' she said, and later called it a 'love-hate' situation.[9]

And there's a further link between the Nqakula and Watson families: Mapisa-Nqakula's brother, Siviwe, was head of security at the Post Office when Bosasa Security won a multimillion-rand tender to provide security to post offices around the country in the early 2000s. Angelo Agrizzi told the Zondo Commission, the public inquiry into allegations of state capture launched in 2018, that Siviwe Mapisa and then Post Office CEO Maanda Manyatshe were bribed by Gavin Watson to win the tender. Apart from cash, Watson allegedly also gave Mapisa a Cartier pen and cufflinks during a visit to Dubai; Agrizzi testified to 'how much [Mapisa] appreciated the gift'.

To top it all, Siviwe Mapisa also accompanied Ronnie Watson on hunting trips to his game farm in the Eastern Cape. 'I had to arrange trucks to transport the meat from the Eastern Cape to Mapisa's house in Gauteng at the expense of the company,' Agrizzi testified.[10]

Mapisa-Nqakula was shocked to hear that Agrizzi referred to the meat deliveries as a bribe. Although she, her husband Charles and their grownup children are regular hunters on Ronnie Watson's farm, 'the animals we kill belong to Ronnie, not the state,' she said. 'When we go over the weekend, after we hunt, we leave the meat with Ronnie, who makes sausages and packages the meat. It's then delivered to us. Agrizzi [said] the transportation of the meat was done by Bosasa – I don't know who would transport the meat.'[11]

As to who paid for the meat and its transportation, Mapisa-Nqakula's family's relationship with Ronnie Watson was of such a nature that the notion that it could have been construed as a benefit never even crossed her mind, she said.

Ronnie Watson had told Charles Nqakula and Chris Hani in the early 1990s that the ANC would govern South Africa, but that some leaders of the movement 'would have their characters assassinated, and if the vilification did not lead to them being marginalised, they would be targeted for elimination.'[12] After Hani's assassination, it made sense that Nqakula would have lent Watson an ear, so when Watson asked Nqakula and his wife for an introduction to ANCWL leaders to add a 'feminine touch', in Ndude's words, to the mining industry, they obliged.

Hilda Ndude said that Ronnie Watson told them there were business opportunities in the traditionally male-dominated mining industry. 'He said this was an opportunity for us ladies to organise ourselves into a company.... There was a lot that we [could] do, catering and cleaning at the mining hostels. That's what we would do. We looked at this and said, "We don't know anything about business, and we're not sure that we have time for this because we're in the leadership of the ANC Women's League."'[13]

Mapisa-Nqakula invited Nozuko Pikoli to join Dyambu in the early 1990s. 'The mining industry at the time was going through tough times [and m]any mining companies were getting rid of non-core business activities,' Pikoli said. 'At the same time, many businesses were aggressively pursuing ... black professionals and particularly those who were seen to be active in various capacities in the black community. Businesses were keen on ... sprucing up their image by being seen to have the participation of those from the black community through directorships and some form of shareholding.

'Many of us at the time saw nothing wrong in being part of business now that the environment was opening, so as to learn and one day be a standalone entrepreneur. We were also cognisant that the political organisations did not owe us anything and that at some stage one needed to have an independent source of income.'[14]

Myakayaka-Manzini stressed that the Dyambu Operations deal had nothing to do with the ANCWL. 'We formed it as women who wanted to be part of the economy of South Africa. Our first concern was the issue of migrant labour, which destroyed many families. So when we were approached by a company that was catering for miners, we thought this was a project that could help bring families together. We were dreaming of building houses for miners where family units could be accommodated in decent houses.'[15]

23

Mapisa-Nqakula stressed that it was never intended to be an ANCWL front company, but was a company formed by a group of ANCWL leaders in their personal capacities. 'We were very raw; we had no clue about business,' she said. 'We weren't directors, but shareholders. We were shareholders of a company called Dyambu. The split between operations and holdings only happened later.[16] At the time, Hilda [Ndude] had some personal difficulties and we had to get her out of the Western Cape, so she was appointed CEO of our company.'[17]

While most of the other women remained in Cape Town as parliamentarians, Ndude moved up to Gauteng to run Dyambu from her Sandton office.

Ndude confirmed that the women were mindful that the Dyambu deal couldn't be perceived as the ANCWL getting into business. The company they purchased, Meritum, had contracts to clean and cater in the mines, and they didn't see a conflict of interest with their roles as politicians. 'We clarified that from the onset with Ronnie, when we went into the deal, that we would be individuals, not the ANC Women's League. But Ronnie Watson coaxed them that they shouldn't be shy to use their political influence by saying, "No, man, you guys know how to talk, you are leaders, you'll be able to convince the workers."'[18]

Besides the contracts in the mines, the purchase contract also included the Lindela property, which was positioned at the train station in Krugersdorp. According to Ndude, Ronnie Watson told them they could also get involved at the deportation centre to 'put a feminine touch there.'[19]

The women believed that they were the owners and Gavin Watson the manager of the Dyambu business.

Three years later, in 2000, Gavin Watson told Hilda Ndude to sign a letter that effectively transferred the full ownership in Dyambu Operations – which later became Bosasa Operations – to him.

Today, 19 years later, Ndude believes that Gavin Watson 'stole the company from us.'[20]

Hilda Ndude: Meeting Gavin Watson

'We weren't looking for business opportunities; that was the last thing on our minds. We were a group of friends, colleagues, inside the ANC Women's League. This thing came to us by Ronnie Watson. Ronnie Watson was a member of the South African Communist Party and friends with Charles Nqakula, who was chair of the party. We said to Ronnie [that] there would be challenges. We don't know anything about business; who would run that thing? Ronnie said he [would] bring his brother ... Gavin Watson.'[1]

6

'We need to make money. The struggle is over'

In 2019, 13 years after I first started to write about Bosasa, the company's name was in the headlines again. Angelo Agrizzi, long-time confidant and right-hand man of Gavin Watson, was singing like a bird in front of the Zondo Commission.

The commission had been established on the recommendation of then Public Protector Thuli Madonsela, who'd investigated state capture by the Guptas during Zuma's term as president. She had established several facts about Zuma's proximity to the Guptas and executive decision-making that was outsourced to Saxonwold, the location of the Guptas' family compound in Johannesburg, but had found that it was impossible for her office to investigate the full extent of state capture, and had therefore asked the president, then still Jacob Zuma, to appoint a judicial commission of inquiry. The commission's terms of reference weren't limited to the Guptas, but extended to 'the conduct of any other family, individual or corporate entity doing business with government or any organ of state'.[2] What started out as an inquiry into the Gupta family and its relationship with Jacob Zuma quickly turned into a Truth and Reconciliation Commission for corruption, and the ANC was at the centre of it.

After all that time investigating Bosasa, there was still one thing I could never establish: how had it all begun?

I called Hilda Ndude, a founding member of the company that became Bosasa. I wanted to understand how the deal had come about. How did Dyambu become Bosasa? Was Bosasa supposed to be a front for the ANC

'WE NEED TO MAKE MONEY. THE STRUGGLE IS OVER'

Women's League? How did Gavin Watson enter the company? And how much money did they make?

When I contacted her at the beginning of 2019, Ndude was down and out. She'd just been released from three years' house arrest after pleading guilty to stealing money from the Congress of the People (Cope), an ANC breakaway formed by struggle stalwarts Mosiuoa Lekota and Mbhazima Shilowa after the ANC had recalled Thabo Mbeki as state president in September 2008.

Lekota and Shilowa, the former defence minister and Gauteng premier, respectively, had been outraged that the ANC could elect a corruption-implicated person like Jacob Zuma as its president and remove Mbeki before the end of his term. They formed Cope on the basis that it would be a return to the ANC's founding values.

Ndude agreed with these sentiments and left her political home of many years to join Cope. But she betrayed the new party, and in November 2015 she pleaded guilty to eleven counts of fraud and five of money laundering totalling R1.5 million.[3] Ndude was sentenced to eight years in jail, conditionally suspended for five years, and a further three years of house arrest.

Hilda Ndude's part in the story started in 1996 with the meeting at the Nqakula house in Cyrildene where Ronnie Watson had pitched the idea of a business to a group of naïve ANCWL activists. They would tender for cleaning and catering services on the West Rand's gold mines, he said.[4]

When Gavin Watson and the women of Dyambu took over the company, it already had catering contracts with the Blyvooruitzicht and Leslie gold mines on the West Rand, and this was later expanded to other Goldfields mines in Gauteng and the Free State. The company's first non-mining contracts were for catering at Sasol and security services at the Post Office and Airports Company South Africa.

There were subsequent meetings, which Gavin Watson attended and during which he would outline the planned company and how it would operate. Jurgen Smith, one of the original founders of Meritum Hostels, was also present.

'They were convincing us this is the way to go. We needed to make money, because all our lives we've been involved in the struggle and really we did not have time to work for our families,' Ndude recalled. 'And this was an opportunity for us also to make some money. "Black economic empowerment" and "women" were the buzzwords at the time, so they used that and we never saw anything wrong [with what we were getting involved in] ... The Watsons were the ones who did the original negotiations with the owners because they knew business.'[5]

Gavin was brought in to run the company for the women, Ndude said. They, the women of Dyambu, would be the shareholders, and Watson the manager. 'We designed everything [the company name and branding], and Gavin was going to run the entity for us.'[6]

Nozuko Pikoli confirmed this. 'Gavin Watson was brought in to be the overall manager of all the operational business activities of Dyambu. We needed someone who was knowledgeable about running business. Remember, we inherited businesses already in operation [at] the various mines.'[7]

They decided on the name Dyambu, Xitsonga for 'sun', because it was 'feminine'. Former ANCWL deputy president Mavivi Myakayaka-Manzini, who came up with the name, said she thought of the sun 'which is warm because that's what we wanted to bring, warmth to the miners and their families'.[8]

When it came to the structure of the company, there were three Dyambu entities: Dyambu Holdings, Dyambu Operations and the Dyambu Trust, with 'Ma' Adelaide Tambo as its chair. 'We didn't even think of making money at that time,' Myakayaka-Manzini said. 'We established a trust that was going to ... make sure that whatever we [got] from the business [would] benefit the women, men and children in the hostels.'[9]

The women had big dreams – the Dyambu Trust would ultimately benefit poor women from the Eastern Cape and Limpopo, the two provinces in which most of the original shareholders had their roots. 'We were talking big at the time, even talking about cooperatives of women,' said Mapisa-Nqakula. 'We had big and great ambitions about Dyambu.'[10]

Hilda Ndude became the face of the company. 'We needed to have a woman running the company. You couldn't say this was a women's company, but then have a white man running it. I was asked by the group [the

'WE NEED TO MAKE MONEY. THE STRUGGLE IS OVER'

ANCWL leaders] if I would be keen to leave the [Western Cape] legislature to come out and run this thing,' Ndude said.[11]

Giving up her ANC political career, Ndude left Cape Town politics for a corporate office in Johannesburg. She left behind Mbete, Mapisa-Nqakula, Mokonyane and the other shareholders – all of whom became senior leaders in the ANC and in government – to try and make them some money.

Still firmly under the impression that she and her comrades were the owners of the Dyambu companies, Ndude settled into her office and apartment in Sandton and drove an Audi A6, all courtesy of Gavin Watson.

It didn't take her long to realise something was wrong. The women's only role and purpose at the time was to accompany Watson to meetings with mineworkers to convince them that Dyambu would do a better job cooking for them and cleaning their hostels than the incumbent service provider.[12] When there were fights on the mines, the women would assist by intervening to negotiate peace.

At the same time, articles appeared in the press about the poor conditions at the Lindela repatriation facility, which was part of the facilities purchased from Meritum by Dyambu, and which Dyambu now managed for the department of home affairs. Lindela was under scrutiny for alleged poor living conditions and a lack of proper healthcare to foreigners who were held there before being repatriated by train. Most of them were black Africans.

This, Ndude said, came as a shock to the Dyambu shareholders because of the ANC's historical ties with African countries – the ANCWL couldn't be seen as running an inhumane, unhealthy facility where African women and children were being detained and maltreated. 'The ANC was asking the ladies about this company. We felt that we wanted nothing to do with it. Our company was about catering to miners, not running a deportation centre.' She told Watson to leave them out of the Lindela controversy, but he continued to reference the ANCWL and refer journalists to her, she said.[13]

Fellow Dyambu shareholder Nozuko Pikoli also recalled that the ANC women wanted out of the controversial home affairs Lindela contract. 'In our board meeting we all spoke with one voice, that we did not want to be associated with this new venture at all, and that our company name must be removed from anything to do with the home affairs contract.' The women didn't expect proceeds from the Lindela contract and viewed it as 'Watson's initiative'.[14]

'We exited Dyambu Operations because we didn't want to be involved in things involving government tenders,' said Myakayaka-Manzini.[15] She said that although the women had initially been interested in operating places of safety for children in conflict with the law through Dyambu, to separate them from the adults, they realised that this could lead to conflicts of interest because some of them may be in positions in government that awarded these tenders to providers of safe havens.

The Lindela controversy contributed to Watson removing the women from Dyambu Operations as shareholders.

At the same time, tensions were brewing between Ndude and her fellow Dyambu shareholders. 'The ladies were getting frustrated because Gavin would speak as if he was paying dividends to me. I was just paid a salary. They were angry with me, because they thought I took the money that he told them about.'[16]

Distrust between Ndude and her colleagues – she called them friends – grew as no money was flowing from Dyambu's business to their pockets.

Ndude's former colleagues confirmed their frustration with her and the way in which she managed the company. They weren't getting reports and had no idea how the company was doing financially. 'We became deeply disappointed by the person we'd appointed to become CEO [Ndude],' said Mapisa-Nqakula.[17]

7

Betrayal

'Remember the stories of companies who appointed their gardeners or domestic workers as BEE partners? That is exactly what Gavin Watson did to us. He signed us as domestic workers. We signed something that we were not aware of, only to find out he [was] the one who [was] going to be making millions.'[1]

Hilda Ndude was angry and emotional talking about her former business partner. 'Gavin realised that he can turn this thing around and make money because from the [outset] we were at a distance. Gavin came in as the person who was going to run the thing; not a shareholder, not the owner, but as a person to assist us to run the business. ... We said we didn't know anything about business. Maybe he took advantage of that.'[2]

Angelo Agrizzi's recollection of Ndude was Watson complaining about her that she was 'demanding' and that he had to take her shopping. 'Gavin realised the women will be very demanding and that there will be [no money] left for anybody. He took Hilda shopping and would have to carry her handbags ... He was actually very anti women empowerment.'[3]

Ndude was kept away from the operations of the company in Krugersdorp and worked from her office in Sandton. 'I was sitting there, just getting reports from Gavin on what was happening and me looking for other opportunities for the entity. For whatever reason, Gavin never wanted me to sit in Krugersdorp and to be involved in the day-to-day running of Dyambu Operations. At the time, I didn't realise [that] maybe he already had an agenda.'

Ndude says she was shocked when Watson told them he wanted to buy out their shareholding in Dyambu Operations. 'In hindsight, I realise how stupid we were. Gavin took us for a ride. Because it was our company, 100%. He used our names; Gavin's name was never anywhere.'[4]

Agrizzi told the Zondo Commission that whenever Watson was questioned on the BEE status of the company, 'he would rattle off names like Girly Pikoli and Nosiviwe Mapisa-Nqakula'.[5]

'Gavin was so clever,' Ndude said. 'He's running Dyambu Operations; I'm running the shell that is Dyambu Holdings. I was sitting in Sandton ... [in] nice, posh offices ... running this shell that is empty. And there is Gavin, running everything.

'When there [were] queries about things [that were] going wrong, he would ... give my cellphone number to the journalists. I would tell the journalists I don't know what's happening, Gavin is running Dyambu Operations, I'm sitting here in Sandton running the holding company. That ... happened for years. I don't think I went to the Krugersdorp offices more than three times.

'I called Gavin in to say, "Gavin, please, what is happening?" And Gavin would always have an answer: don't worry, the media like to exaggerate things, and he would give you an explanation that he wants you to hear.

'That's how Gavin stole it from us. This guy saw a way of making money to revive the Watson legacy by using us as these women who [knew] nothing about business, who [were] politicians, to actually take the company from us just like that.

'We were hoping that when [there was] money, Gavin would say, "We've made so much, here is money." Maybe something was in the shareholders' agreement; those things weren't paramount in our minds. We were either stupid or fools, I don't know.'[6]

Mapisa-Nqakula agreed with Ndude that they were supposed to be the shareholders. 'Gavin started Dyambu Operations, but because he was using our name, there should have been some money for that. The one and only time we got something from Dyambu, it was something like R10 000 for all of us, around 1998.'[7]

Nozuko Pikoli, too, had no recollection of receiving any dividends.

'From the start our understanding was that we were setting up something [from which] we [could] only anticipate proceeds around ten to fifteen years onwards.'[8]

Myakayaka-Manzini confirmed that she didn't receive a cent from Watson's purchase of their shareholding in Dyambu Operations, either – and that they actually had to each contribute R20 000 to Dyambu Holdings to capitalise the company 'while we were earning R2 000 per month from the ANC'.[9]

Baleka Mbete said she didn't recall owning shares, but 'we were unashamed novices in business. I remember getting R10 000. I can't confirm that it came from shares ...' She didn't know how Gavin got involved, she said. 'He was introduced to us at some point. I never personally developed a relationship with [him] and so never had any contact with him.'[10]

Ndude wasn't aware that they only ever owned 10% of the company that was doing the work they originally signed up for – catering and cleaning in the mining hostels. Looking back at what happened 'makes me feel stupid', she said. 'We felt that Gav was treating us with disdain.'[11]

Mapisa-Nqakula was loath to 'take out our dirty linen now', but spoke with sadness of the deterioration of the other shareholders' relationship with Ndude, who she believed should have done more to keep Dyambu alive. Noting that the other Dyambu shareholders were in Cape Town, working as parliamentarians, she said that they were very busy and not available for meetings, and left decisions to Ndude. 'The dream we had for Dyambu [was] never realised. There is anger and bitterness now about how the whole thing unfolded. We were betrayed by one of our own. She [Ndude] could have done better, taken better decisions.'[12]

But Ndude blamed Watson for the ultimate collapse of Dyambu. It was Watson, not the women, who portrayed Dyambu as an ANCWL company, she said. 'He was using us to bulldoze into the mines, to get in. Gavin is the biggest manipulator ... Gavin knows how to corrupt people because he realised black people don't know anything about money, especially the comrades, because really, we were never involved in issues of money. All that he [wanted was] people with struggle credentials.

'Gavin knows that a black person, if you just give money or buy him what he wants, he will be happy with that, he will be comfortable, because that is exactly what happened to us.

'Gavin is a big talker. I'm a political activist. I operated during the most difficult times; I know what to say and when to say it. Once a person says so many things in such a short space of time, you can read how that person is. I realised what kind of a person Gavin is, from how he talks. "I gave that one money, that one came for me, I paid for holiday for that one, I paid school fees to that one …" That was Gavin. He can be very dangerous. Those days as activists, if a person talks so much, you realised that a person can quickly sell you out to the enemy.

'I am very angry with Gavin, how he manipulated us and used our names. He is the one who got stinking rich out of our names, and we remain paupers at the bottom. I am a person who forgives, but all those things will catch up with him."[13]

8

Selling out

On 3 August 2000 Hilda Ndude was persuaded by Gavin Watson to sign an 'acquisition letter' that would 'delink' the women from the Lindela operation. The letter specified that Watson would 'acquire Dyambu Holdings (Pty) Ltd's effective 10% interest in the business of Dyambu Operations (Pty) Ltd'.[1]

Ndude had no idea that she was signing away their ownership in the company. 'Gavin used the word "delink"; he never said we were selling our shares.'[2]

The letter from Watson also made mention of 'franchise agreements' between Dyambu Holdings and Dyambu Operations, noting that they would cease to exist on signature of the document. Of this, Ndude remembered nothing.

Ndude never knew that their company, Dyambu Holdings, only ever owned 10% of Dyambu Operations. Watson was never supposed to own shares, she pointed out; 'he was never coming in as a shareholder. He came in to run the business, you can ask all those ladies.'

The letter from Watson outlined the conditions of the 'sale' of the women's 10%, which he said was worth R5.5 million: R1 million would be paid on signature of the agreement; a monthly amount of R83 333 would be paid for 48 months, minus expenses for the Sandton office, flat and vehicle rental. A further R500 000 would be paid on 31 October 2001.

Ndude swore she 'didn't receive a cent'. Her recollection of the transaction was that Watson deducted all running expenses from the R1 million they were supposed to receive, leaving nothing to pay the women.

The non-payment of the money caused friction in the group. Myakayaka-Manzini confirmed this, saying they struggled to get information out of Ndude and she didn't properly account to them.[3] It was clear that they suspected her of pocketing some of the money paid by Watson – something Ndude vehemently denied.

'Most of us, painful though it was, gave up on Dyambu Holdings,' Pikoli said. Parting from the company was 'painful and very sad'.

'As for the Bosasa/Watsons debacle, I have been watching with interest the developments. The Watsons are a family we got to know through our comrades and friends. We've never had a direct relationship with them, but one cannot say we don't know each other. I certainly am devastated by the revelations coming out through the Zondo Commission, and other revelations coming out through the media even before the Zondo Commission,' Pikoli said.

'There are many comrades and friends from our old struggle days that one had shared so much with. We lived a life almost like true sisters and brothers, almost being like family to each other. That was the nature of the life we were living in those days. These days, some have been mentioned in so many unsavoury issues pertaining to government. Today I remain saddened by what one hears daily. Many were trusted and senior members of our movement, the ANC. I am not sure why exactly some amongst these cadres of our movement lost direction and found themselves mired in such terrible and unpardonable acts against our government and its people.'[4]

A furious Ndude said that they'd been sold a dream about women empowerment and enriching former ANC activists who had nothing but their government salaries when they took over political power in 1994 – but four years after Ronnie Watson had brought them into business, they were out in the cold. Ndude had to make desperate moves to run the 'shell' that was left of Dyambu Holdings – which did not really have other business outside of Dyambu Operations except for a stake in Vela Phumelela horse racing – and eventually she ended up stealing money from Cope to keep the company afloat.

In 2019 Ndude looked a far cry from the fiery woman who'd stood behind Nelson and Winnie Mandela as they left Victor Verster prison in 1990. She carried the scars of living through apartheid as a black female activist – harassed, arrested and punished for fighting for the freedom to be human against a regime that oppressed her because of the colour of her skin.

When she finally overcame that struggle, she was plunged into a new one, this time of greed and what seems like being exploited by a fellow comrade. Then she too succumbed to the lure of money. 'I asked for forgiveness and made peace with my God. All the good that I have done in our history will be wiped out by this. I will be lumped together with those corrupt ones.'[5]

9

Old networks, new money

By the end of 2000, Gavin Watson had managed to rid Dyambu Operations of its initial shareholders and change its name to Bosasa. The Watson brother who'd been brought in to manage a cleaning and catering company for a group of women now owned the majority of that company.

Did he hijack the company from ANC leaders like Hilda Ndude, Nosiviwe Mapisa-Nqakula, Nomvula Mokonyane and Baleka Mbete? According to Ndude, certainly. But ANCWL leaders like Mokonyane remained very close to Watson and Bosasa's largesse. In fact, when Agrizzi started to blow the whistle before the Zondo Commission, Mokonyane's name was one of those that continually came up. In the queue of the alleged Bosasa blessees, Mokonyane was very close to the front.

Mapisa-Nqakula denied that, as minister of home affairs and later correctional services, she promoted and protected Bosasa but she also didn't act decisively to cancel the corrupt company's contracts. And as acting president, Mbete approved the transfer of Vernie Petersen out of the DCS when he turned up the heat on Bosasa.

Bosasa's shareholding was always opaque and deliberately complicated. Shares were owned by companies that were owned by trusts whose trustees and beneficiaries weren't always known. An employees' trust owned around 20% of the company, but, according to all former and current employees I spoke to, they never saw a cent of benefit from this so-called stake.

Tony Perry, Bosasa's company secretary who'd moved to Krugersdorp with Watson and Mansell to take over the running of the company, had a big whiteboard in his office with the shareholding mapped out on it. The board was covered by a curtain. 'Sometimes we had a glimpse of the shareholding, but it was complicated and layered,' said Frans Vorster.[1]

The only government tenders Bosasa had when Watson took over the company in 1996 were the Lindela contract with the department of home affairs and the Meritum youth centre, later known as the Mogale youth hostel, that was initially funded by the South African Police Service (SAPS), but later by the Gauteng social development department. He added a few mining hostels to the company's portfolio of clients, but, according to Agrizzi, Watson told him he wanted to get out of the mines 'because it had become too expensive having to pay bribes'.[2] Watson was looking for something much bigger to change Bosasa's fortunes.

The company's first taste of cooking for prisons came in 1999 when the Krugersdorp prison underwent refurbishments for a year and, with its kitchen closed, Bosasa took over the catering. Then Bosasa won a tender from the DCS to train prison staff on a new catering system for prisoners. 'Mark Taverner [the husband of the Watsons' sister Sharon], Mansell and Gillingham put together the deal,' said Agrizzi.[3]

By the early 2000s Frans Vorster was running Lindela for the company. Frans Hendrik Steyn Vorster, a burly Afrikaner with a moustache, looked every bit like the ooms of my youth in Witpoortjie. He worked as a policeman between 1987 and 1996. He spoke with a heavy Afrikaans accent and looked uncomfortable in a suit and tie, which he had to wear on the day he finally spilled the beans on Bosasa before Judge Raymond Zondo's commission into state capture in January 2019.

For Frans Vorster, Bosasa wasn't only his place of employment. It was more like home. Vorster's father, Oom Vossie, who died in 2001, had run the procurement department and fleet at Meritum when the company had only two government tenders: one from the SAPS to operate a juvenile detention facility, and another from home affairs to manage the Lindela repatriation facility. Oom Vossie had a relationship with DCS official Patrick Gillingham, who was then in charge of Gauteng's prisons.

According to Vorster, it was the overcrowding of prisons by juveniles and

39

immigrants that led to Gillingham and his father connecting – Meritum had the facilities to relieve the pressure on the DCS.

In 2003 Gavin Watson asked Frans Vorster to continue the relationship his father had had with Gillingham because he 'would love to tender for the catering contracts for correctional services'.[4] Vorster obliged and a year later the kitchens of South Africa's major prisons were outsourced to Bosasa Operations.

That was Bosasa's first major government tender, and the one that would become its biggest source of income for almost two decades. Former Bosasa employee Retief van der Merwe remembered how the 'money started to roll in' after the awarding of this kitchens tender. 'It was visible. Everyone bought new luxury cars. The directors started wearing special blue shirts.'[5]

The capture of the DCS had begun, courtesy of an apartheid-era prison warder, an ex-policeman, and their new paymaster, a suave silver-haired comrade from Port Elizabeth.

Trying to piece together a state capture episode isn't easy. Numerous role-players, agendas and dynamics are involved. In this case, it was the historical ties between Oom Vossie and Gillingham that had opened the door for Watson to enter the prisons-catering space. The common denominator was, of course, money.

Having approaching Patrick Gillingham and begun meeting with him regularly, Frans Vorster said, 'At a stage I was called to head office by Gavin Watson. We went to the vault, where he would hand cash to me. ... [Then] I would go to my office ... where I would stack the money into an A4 envelope so that it would look like ... documents.'[6]

Vorster would then drive to a restaurant in Centurion where Gillingham would hand him documents on the specifications of prison kitchens and menus. In return, Vorster would hand Gillingham an envelope stashed with anything between R5 000 and R20 000 in cash. 'I would then take [the documents] back to the office and hand [them] over to Danny Mansell.'[7] (Mansell would later flee South Africa.[8])

In his evidence to Zondo, Frans Vorster testified that the documents he received from Gillingham were given to Mansell, masquerading as a Bosasa consultant, to prepare a presentation in 2003 to senior DCS officials including regional correctional services commissioners Patrick Gillingham and Freddie Engelbrecht, and national correctional services commissioner Linda Mti.

In its 2009 report on Bosasa's prisons tenders, the Special Investigating Unit (SIU), one of the country's prime anti-corruption units, referred to a clandestine and highly irregular meeting between Agrizzi, Papa Leshabane, the flashy HR-practitioner-turned-spokesman for Bosasa, and senior DCS officials including Gillingham, Engelbrecht and Mti, at a cricket ground in Centurion in November 2003. This was months before the department advertised a tender to outsource the catering functions of the DCS.

Engelbrecht (who later fell out with Mti over his [Engelbrecht's] perceived anti-Bosasa stance and was subsequently sidelined in the department) told the SIU that Bosasa's presentation came like a bolt from the blue. At the time, outsourcing catering and nutrition had never been discussed inside the department. Engelbrecht raised his concerns about potential job losses in the DCS as a result of outsourcing and the effect it would have on inmates who were involved in growing and preparing food. Mti 'rudely instructed him to stop asking questions'.[9]

In 2004 Gillingham and Mansell delivered a presentation to more senior DCS officials. They argued that outsourcing the catering and nutrition services would save the department money.

The SIU revealed that Mti had appointed Gillingham, whose highest qualification was matric, as chief financial officer of the DCS in 2004, putting him in charge of a R9-billion budget.[10] This was after allegations emerged that Gillingham had submitted fraudulent subsistence and travel claims, had had an affair with his secretary and had intimidated staff. The former MK boss had the apartheid-era prison warder by the short and curlies, and together they perfected the state capture dance.

As Vorster later testified, '[T]he driver that was needed was Patrick Gillingham and he drove the process so that Mr Mti could approve the process.'[11]

As it turned out, Gillingham drove much more than the process.

Frans Vorster: I burnt the file

'I was instructed in 2005 to procure a vehicle for Mr Mti. It was a Volkswagen Touareg V8, silver in colour. I did the whole deal. I got a phone call from the dealership and they said, "Hey, the SIU is here; they are asking a lot of questions about Mr Mti's vehicle …" I collected the file. I burnt the file. I was asked by Mr Watson to go and get the file and destroy the file."

10

'Oh Lord, won't you buy me a Mercedes-Benz?'

Like many a corrupt politician or civil servant, Patrick Gillingham had a taste for expensive German sedans. And so, after he ensured Bosasa was blessed with the R239-million-a-year catering tender, it was time to be blessed back.

'After it was awarded, Gavin [Watson] came to me and instructed me to meet up with Patrick Gillingham and assist him to procure a vehicle,' Frans Vorster, Bosasa's chief car buyer, told the Zondo Commission. 'The vehicle that Patrick was looking for was a Mercedes E270. At that stage, he was driving a gold Mercedes E240 that he sold to the company. We as Bosasa bought the vehicle from him.'[2]

The value of Gillingham's gold Merc was about R85 000 but Bosasa paid him R155 000 for the car. 'The money was paid directly into his bank account,' Vorster testified.

During 2005 Bosasa scored more tenders from the DCS, and Watson phoned Vorster to tell him that Gillingham needed a car 'for his wife'. Gillingham told Vorster he 'would love to buy a VW Golf for his wife', which Vorster took to mean that Bosasa had to bankroll a VW Golf for Theresa Gillingham. Vorster negotiated the deal and the order was placed; money was paid into Gillingham's account by Jurgen Smith, and extras on the vehicle were paid from Bosasa's account.

After Mom and Dad were sorted with wheels, the Gillingham children also needed to be blessed. 'During April 2006 Gavin phoned me and said, "Frans, Patrick's son [Ryan] needs a vehicle." I went to Volkswagen

Krugersdorp and negotiated the whole deal, and Mr Mansell, through his [shelf] company, paid for that specific vehicle,' Vorster testified.³

A few months later it was the turn of Gillingham's daughter Megan to be gifted. Vorster was on leave so Watson turned to Bosasa's chief financial officer, Andries van Tonder, to execute the blessing. Van Tonder told the Zondo Commission that when he discussed the method of payment with Jurgen Smith, suggesting that he cash a cheque to buy a VW Polo, Smith advised him against it and engineered an elaborate scheme to hide the transaction from Bosasa's auditors. 'I signed a personal loan agreement with Dr Smith. Then Dr Smith transferred the money from his personal bank account into my personal bank account. I then transferred the money from my personal bank account to Volkswagen at The Glen in order to pay for the vehicle. One to two months thereafter, Bosasa transferred the money plus an amount to allow for tax and interest payable as per the loan agreement to Consilium Business Consultants.'⁴

Consilium was a front company operated by Smith from Bosasa's head office in Krugersdorp, through which some of the white employees were paid in order to keep them off Bosasa's books. This was done to improve Bosasa's BEE scorecard, a government points system that rated a company's BEE compliance. One Bosasa employee, a highly skilled staff member of Sondolo IT, the Bosasa subsidiary company that installed CCTV and access-control systems, only found out he was working for Consilium when he received his payslip. 'I didn't even know what Consilium was until I received my payslip. Consilium has no offices or branding. Nothing, nothing, nothing. In my entire time there, I never even spoke to the Consilium people. I reported to Sondolo IT.'⁵ The Department of Trade and Industry said it would investigate the matter in 2013, but nothing came of this.

(According to Agrizzi, Bosasa also bribed an employee of the respected BEE consulting and verification firm Empowerdex to sort out the group's BEE ratings. Agrizzi told the Zondo Commission that they paid the employee R40 000 per company.⁶)

In February 2007 Patrick Gillingham wanted a new Merc. 'Gavin phoned me and said, "Frans, Patrick has got problems with the car. We need to replace the vehicle." This was a Mercedes E320,' Vorster told the

'OH LORD, WON'T YOU BUY ME A MERCEDES-BENZ?'

Zondo Commission.[7] Vorster knew exactly what to do – he'd become a pro at hunting down cars for corrupt officials.

But this time there was a problem: the Tony Yengeni factor.

Yengeni, a former ANC chief whip, had pleaded guilty to fraud in 2003 for failing to declare to Parliament a massive discount he'd received on a Merc 4x4, and had spent just four months of a four-year sentence in jail before being released on parole.[8] In the wake of Yengeni's conviction, vehicle manufacturers and car dealers had sharpened their checks and balances to prevent cars being used as bribes.

Vorster initially ordered the new Merc in his name, and when the vehicle was ready for collection from Constantia Kloof Mercedes in Roodepoort, he told the dealer that Gillingham would in fact be paying for the vehicle. 'They said to me, "Sorry, Frans, it is not that easy. Procedure has been changed. If you order a car in your name and you are not taking that car, only a family member or a partner in business can take over that vehicle from you." I was basically then forced to go and buy a shelf company ... Oak Ridge Trading 114 cc. There were only two members in that cc [closed corporation], myself and Patrick Gillingham, and we used that cc as a way to show that we are partners.'[9]

Vorster and Gillingham were, of course, not partners. They had committed a blatant criminal act to try and conceal a corrupt transaction.

In order to pay the dealership the R180 000 to get Gillingham's car, Bosasa paid Agrizzi a fake bonus of R180 000, and Agrizzi then 'lent' this money to Vorster. The money was paid into the account of Bosasa's chief accountant Carlos Bonifacio, then back to Bosasa, and finally into Gillingham's account. Vorster told Zondo it was obfuscated purposefully in this zigzagging fashion to confuse investigators after Watson warned them about the SIU's ongoing investigation into Bosasa.

Next, it was agreed that a bogus disciplinary hearing would be conducted into Vorster's relationship with Gillingham, to be able to show investigators that the company dealt with allegations of impropriety when these reached them. It was a complete scam: there was no hearing but Vorster was issued with a 'final written warning' that was put on file for Bosasa to use if investigators ever discovered the payments for Gillingham's new

45

wheels. 'It was a smokescreen. It never took place. We only did the paperwork,' Vorster confessed to Zondo.[10]

In a final act to cover up the deal, Watson insisted that individual loan agreements be drawn up between Bosasa officials and Gillingham. This happened in late 2007 but was backdated to April that year.

And there was yet another dodgy set of wheels: a Volkswagen Touareg V8 bought by Bosasa for Linda Mti in 2005. Vorster testified before Judge Zondo how he was tasked by Watson to destroy the evidence: 'I negotiated the whole deal. The vehicle was purchased from Lindsay Saker Krugersdorp.'[11] However, he said that he wasn't part of the finances of that deal.

The dealership called Vorster in 2007 to say the SIU was asking questions and looking for the file of the purchase. On Watson's instructions, Vorster fetched the file from Lindsay Saker and destroyed it.

In their final report in 2009 the SIU found that Gillingham had been instrumental in blessing Bosasa with numerous DCS tenders. In return, he and his family had been blessed with motor vehicles, cash, sponsored travel, Blue Bulls rugby tickets, a house in Midstream Estate, an imported kitchen and a private email address.

'Given that the Bosasa group of companies were awarded large contracts, estimated in excess of R1.5 billion, and that Gillingham played an integral role in all of these contracts, the benefits acquired by Gillingham and his family, within the period these contracts were awarded, signifies the existence of an improper and corrupt relationship between Gillingham and the Bosasa Group of Companies,' the report concluded.[12]

The report was handed to then minister Mapisa-Nqakula (one of the original Dyambu shareholders), acting commissioner of correctional services Jenny Schreiner, the National Prosecuting Authority (NPA) and the Hawks – the Directorate for Priority Crime Investigation, established in 2008 as an independent directorate within the SAPS.

For ten years nothing happened – a delay later described by an SIU investigator as 'incomprehensible'.

Mapisa-Nqakula, who denied protecting Bosasa, didn't institute civil proceedings to reclaim the money her department had lost through corruption, and allowed the company's catering contract to continue.

Schreiner became an activist tweeter, particularly outspoken about matters of anti-corruption. When I confronted her on Twitter about her own apparent lack of action in the Bosasa matter, she blocked me.

After retiring from the DCS in 2010, Gillingham found employment in the private sector and continued to receive payments from Bosasa. Agrizzi told the Zondo Commission that Gillingham received R47 500 per month while he was still employed by the DCS, and R110 000 per month after leaving the government. When Gillingham's wife filed for divorce, it was Bosasa, on Gavin Watson's instruction, that coughed up the R2.2-million settlement fee that was paid to her through the trust account of Bosasa's long-time lawyer, Brian Biebuyck.[13] Bosasa also paid the bill of attorney Ian Small-Smith, who defended Gillingham during the SIU investigation and at his disciplinary hearing.

'If you were doing something for Watson, he would go out of his way to look after you,' Agrizzi said.[14]

11

Connecting the dots

'How big are these TVs? Can they make coffee?' I asked Carien du Plessis when she phoned me in March 2006 to tell me about a tender that had been awarded to Sondolo IT, an affiliate of Bosasa, to install 6 000 televisions in prisons at a cost of R159 million – R26 500 each. At the time, I had no clue who Bosasa or the Watson brothers were.

Dennis Bloem, then an ANC MP and chairperson of the correctional services portfolio committee, had also started asking hard questions when these tenders were brought to his attention.

Sondolo IT was also paid R1.4 million a month for four years to maintain the TVs – a total of almost R40 000 per TV. In 2006 you could buy a decent secondhand car for R40 000.

Du Plessis asked me to assist her with the investigation. She had the political sources in Cape Town, and I'd do the forensic digging in Johannesburg. Although working as a team is safer – it's much harder to take out two or three people than one – Du Plessis and I were warned to watch our backs.

The similarities between the Schabir Shaik and Gavin Watson cases were striking: a businessman from an ANC family trying to make it big by winning copious government tenders using his struggle credentials and political connections. I started drawing up spider diagrams on large pieces of paper, showing all the people and corporate entities linked to Bosasa. Although the company, through its lawyers, had initially tried to create a superficial divide between Bosasa and its affiliates like Sondolo IT, Phezulu

Fencing and Kgwerano, it became crystal clear to me that there was only one Bosasa and only one boss: Gavin Watson. All those around him were his pawns, controlled through money, religion and fear.

We quickly realised that the story was bigger than we'd initially thought. The tender for R40 000 televisions was only one of four massive contracts awarded to the Bosasa group between 2004 and 2006: the prisons department was effectively privatising and outsourcing its nutrition and security functions to Bosasa.

Prior to 2004, DCS employees were cooking food for the inmates, and at some prisons with farms, certain inmates were assisting with the growing and harvesting of food too. This largely came to a halt after the catering and nutrition tender was awarded to Bosasa Operations for R239 million a year.[1]

Watson and co made sure that from that point on, only Bosasa could win the cooking tender: in writing the tender document for the DCS, they included security elements such as CCTV cameras linked to a control room, in case (presumably) something went wrong with the boiling of eggs or a riot broke out. Bosasa's competitors in the catering business weren't security experts and couldn't compete with them because of the requirements for safety equipment: 'We weren't security operators; we were cooks,' the owner of another catering company once told me.

After clinching the nutrition tender, the prison doors to capture were wide open. The tender was supposed to be for three years, until 2007, but in fact it ran for a further 12 years, until the DCS was forced to end it after banks FNB and Absa shut down Bosasa's accounts in 2019 in the wake of Agrizzi's evidence before the Zondo Commission. By that time, despite numerous newspaper exposés, parliamentary debates, court cases and an SIU investigation that had found evidence of corruption, the catering tender had survived three presidents (Thabo Mbeki, Kgalema Motlanthe and Jacob Zuma), four ministers of correctional services (Ngconde Balfour, Nosiviwe Mapisa-Nqakula, S'bu Ndebele and Michael Masutha) and six permanent and acting national commissioners (Linda Mti, Vernie Petersen, Jenny Schreiner, Xoliswa Sibeko, Tom Moyane and Zach Modise).

It was the gift that kept on giving.

12

The smoking gun

The government's tender process basically works like this. When a government department or state institution needs to procure any service or product, whether it be a dozen eggs or a multimillion-rand building, it must advertise a tender in public, inviting relevant businesses to submit a quotation. This means that, for example, a prison in Grootvlei can't just go to the local Shoprite to buy milk and bread; it has to put out a tender for supplies throughout the year.

Interested companies then collect a tender document prescribing exactly what the service or product is that the department wants, and submit their bids.

Contrary to popular belief, tenders aren't awarded only on price. A number of factors are taken into account when government decides to whom to give the work, including BEE scores. In fact, a company's BEE make-up plays a crucial role in whether it qualifies for state work – in this way, the state uses its financial muscle to force companies to transform and empower black people who were, for decades during apartheid and before, excluded from the formal economy. Bids are adjudicated by a committee made up of senior managers and independent consultants, and a winner is chosen.

Although the intentions were noble, the tender system has been thoroughly abused to benefit a politically connected elite. This happened under apartheid and continued to happen under the ANC government post-1994, with plenty of examples of the state overpaying for substandard products and services. One of the most egregious happened in the Eastern Cape, where companies charged the provincial government R26 for a loaf of bread that should have been priced at R7,80c.[1]

Carien du Plessis and I started working through copious tender documents, company records and newspaper clippings, and we cultivated sources in the DCS, Bosasa and companies who'd lost out on these tenders. In those early years, nobody knew the extent of the rot that would later be exposed by Agrizzi and others before the Zondo Commission, but the same names kept popping up: Gavin Watson, Gibson Njenje, Linda Mti.

We needed a smoking gun – something that would definitely link Bosasa and the DCS. Innuendo is one thing, but we needed something solid to take this story to the next level. We needed facts.

Then, one afternoon, as I was trawling through the records of the registrar of companies, I found it: there, in black in white, was the name Linda Morris Mti.

13

Richman

Linda Morris Mti, known as 'Richman' by his comrades in the ANC, served in numerous of the party's underground structures and was a senior figure in MK, the party's armed wing, during the 1980s.

Starting his working life as a laboratory technician in the Eastern Cape in 1976, Mti was detained by the security police in 1977 with Steve Biko, after which he joined the ANC in exile.[1] During the ANC's struggle against apartheid, Mti lived in Lesotho and Zimbabwe, where he served the party alongside luminaries such as Chris Hani, Judson Kuzwayo and Ngoako Ramatlhodi.

In the 1990s Mti served as the chair of the ANC in the Eastern Cape, and was well connected to party leaders and comrades in that province, including the Watson brothers from Port Elizabeth.

In her biography about the Watsons,[2] Kristin Williamson interviewed ANC leaders who told her the Watsons were very close to ANC politicians like Mti and the late Makhenkesi Stofile, and that these politicians were 'incredibly loyal' to them. In the case of Mti, his loyalty to the family who'd generously assisted the party in its just struggle against apartheid extended into the years of democracy. In fact, Mti seemingly took it upon himself to literally pay back the Watsons for what they'd done for him and the ANC in the form of multiple multimillion-rand prison tenders.

In 1994, after Nelson Mandela became the first democratically elected president of South Africa, Mti was appointed as an ANC MP and served as the chair of the portfolio committee on safety and security. From 1996 to 2001 Mti, a former ANC security man, was deployed by the party in an intelligence capacity as head of the National Intelligence Coordinating Committee, playing a key role in coordinating intelligence between all government agencies with intelligence-gathering capabilities, including the National Intelligence Agency (NIA) and the police's Crime Intelligence division. This made Mti a key player in the murky world of smoke and mirrors in which the Watsons were also active.

He replaced Khulekani 'Mineshaft' Sithole in 2001 as national commissioner of correctional services, to – ironically – 'stamp out fraud and corruption' in the department.[3] Sithole had been a disastrous prisons boss, remembered primarily for running a soccer team from his office and proposing that mothballed mineshafts be transformed into high-security prisons to host the country's most dangerous criminals. His name cropped up at the Zondo Commission in 2019, when Agrizzi testified that Sithole had been paid by Bosasa to undermine Vernie Petersen's efforts to clean up the DCS between 2007 and 2008.[4]

When Mti took over the reins, hopes were high that he would transform and fix the department. Between 2001 and 2004 he kept a relatively low profile, focusing mainly on the findings of the Jali Commission into prison corruption that had found a deeply troubled and depraved department.

Then, in July 2004, Mti's DCS privatised its nutrition services and appointed Bosasa Operations at a cost of R800 million for three years to cook for thousands of prisoners.

Seven months later, Mti made a big mistake. He registered a private company called Lianorah Investment Consultancy – named after his mother – using Bosasa's company secretary, Tony Perry, and Krugersdorp-based auditor Bester Viljoen Inc.

The moment I read those names in the company documents, in the last week of March 2006, I knew I had Bosasa and Mti on the hook. Whatever they might say in response, it was just too coincidental that the head of the prisons department was in a company with the secretary and auditor of a firm that had been awarded four tenders worth almost R1 billion in the preceding four years.

On 31 March 2006 my newspaper, *Beeld*, and our Cape Town sister paper, *Die Burger*, where Carien du Plessis was employed, published a front-page story that linked Mti to Bosasa via the private company named after his mother. Our stories created havoc in the DCS, with Mti's loyal spokesperson Manelisi Wolela steadfastly defending his boss, labelling our reportage 'irresponsible' and threatening to sue us for defamation, which never happened. And I was inundated with calls from anonymous prison officials about the preferential treatment Bosasa had received from the department – clearly, it had long been suspected that the prisons top dog was in cahoots with the rogues from Krugersdorp. One of these inside sources told us that Ngconde Balfour, the then minister of prisons, had called senior DCS officials into a meeting, not to ask them whether our articles were correct but to find out who was leaking information to us, after which a serious witch-hunt was initiated.[5]

This marked the beginning of a 13-year journey for me into the heart of Bosasa.

At the time, of course, Mti denied all allegations of impropriety, insisting he was the sole shareholder and director of the company. He downplayed Perry's role, calling him a 'retired chartered accountant' who merely assisted 'emerging black businesses' to set up shop. Mti denied any knowledge of Bosasa's auditor, Bester Viljoen Inc, and said there was no conflict of interest between his business dealings and Bosasa's tenders.[6]

It became clear to me later that he was lying through his teeth. At the time, Mti was already deep in Bosasa's pocket, living in a fancy house built for him by Bosasa and driving a silver Volkswagen Touareg V8 for which the company had paid.

However, I had no idea at the time of the extent and depth of Mti's involvement in Bosasa's scheme.

14

Smoke and mirrors

Looking back now at our March 2006 stories, it's clear that Carien du Plessis and I had barely scratched the surface of what we now call state capture. We may have managed to find a link between Mti and Bosasa, but we had no idea of the depth of the blessings that had already been bestowed by Gavin Watson and his mafia on Mti, Gillingham and other prison officials.

But I suspected that there was much more that we hadn't uncovered, so we just kept chipping away, trying to convince more and more people to share their secrets with us. It's often only through court proceedings or commissions of inquiry – as has been the case with the Zondo Commission – that colluders find the courage or feel the urge to come clean. But back then there were no Angelo Agrizzis, Frans Vorsters or Andries van Tonders spilling the beans; they were all still feasting on the fat of Bosasa's tender successes and closing ranks to protect their criminal racket from being exposed.

Finding inside sources to talk in those early days was incredibly hard, and I realised early on that I was dealing with something more than a 'normal' corrupt organisation. Bosasa operated more like a cult than a company. At the heart of it was Gavin Watson and his abuse of the Christian religion to rule through fear. As a source once told me, 'We started the morning with a prayer session and then went into the room next door to cook up tenders.'

Meetings with Bosasa insiders took me back to the places of my youth: Westgate Mall in Roodepoort; Key West Mall in Paardekraal Drive,

Krugersdorp, where the Spur was a favourite meeting spot for sources; various attorneys' offices and obscure little coffee shops in and around the West Rand; and even a construction site. My sources – many of them still on Bosasa's payroll – were extremely afraid for their lives and livelihoods. They'd heard stories of people disappearing, being summarily dismissed and even shot at, and I had to respect the absolute confidentiality of our meetings and the information they gave me.

Du Plessis and I also put in place extraordinary measures to protect our communication with our sources; they had heard about the Watsons' intelligence links and were convinced that Bosasa had spies doing surveillance on me and any potential 'traitors'. I was told that copies of my itemised cellphone bills and bank statements were doing the rounds in Bosasa, and I began to use different phones when speaking to my sources or setting up meetings with them. As to my bank statements, I told my wife, 'At least now they know how little journalists are paid.'

The fears of whistleblowers that Bosasa was shrouded in the cloak-and-dagger world of intelligence weren't unfounded. At the time, Gibson Njenje was the chair of Bosasa. Njenje, a former member of Mbokodo, the ANC's security department, had worked closely with Ronnie Watson in exile, according to Charles Nqakula.[1] Before joining the NIA, Njenje had served as chairperson and a director of Bosasa. His brother, Collin Njenje, was also employed by Bosasa, as a technician for Sondolo IT; he died in a motor-vehicle accident.

Gibson Njenje's stints as a Bosasa director and chairperson were intertwined with his different deployments to the NIA. He first resigned as a Bosasa director after joining government in 2003 as head of operations at the NIA. After a fallout with then intelligence minister Ronnie Kasrils over a botched surveillance operation, Njenje left the NIA and rejoined Bosasa as a director.[2] In 2009 Jacob Zuma appointed Njenje as head of the newly formed domestic branch of the State Security Agency (SSA), previously known as the NIA, and once again Njenje resigned from Bosasa.

It didn't take long for Njenje and Moe Shaik, his peer at the SSA heading up the foreign branch, to butt heads with Zuma over the president's ties to the Gupta family. Njenje and Shaik had been tipped off about the Guptas' investment in uranium mines by the United States's Central Intelligence Agency (CIA), and wanted to investigate the family, but Zuma, through then intelligence minister Siyabonga Cwele, blocked the probe. Njenje, Shaik and Jeff Maqetuka, the director-general of the SSA, were fired. The three claimed they were being punished for going after the Guptas, but Cwele insisted they were running an irregular investigation, using state resources to fight private business interests.³

After leaving the SSA, Njenje, Shaik and Maqetuka set up a private corporate intelligence firm called Foresight Advisory Services, with Niel Barnard and George Fivaz, the last apartheid-era spy boss and police chief, respectively.⁴

Another alleged spook who worked at Bosasa was the mysterious political fixer Sesinyi Seopela, nicknamed 'Commander' by Watson. According to Agrizzi's evidence before the Zondo Commission, Seopela was instrumental in connecting Watson with ANC leaders, and gave him inside info on tenders emanating from the criminal-justice cluster. Seopela allegedly also pre-warned Watson when the SIU was about to raid Bosasa's offices. Staff suspected him of being an intelligence agent.

Denise Bjorkman, who ran Bosasa's wellness centre, told me that she picked up Seopela's wallet at the Bosasa head office one day. 'I opened it and saw an NIA personnel card inside. I asked Angelo who this person was. He told me he works on our premises.'⁵

15

Red flags

In April 2006 I started to forensically unpack the tender documents of the four major contracts awarded by the DCS to Bosasa-owned companies between 2004 and 2006. These were for catering services (Bosasa Operations), access-control systems and CCTV (Sondolo IT), television monitors (Sondolo IT) and fencing (Phezulu Fencing). The value of these contracts added up to almost R2 billion.

The more I studied the tender documents, the more I realised that the business connection between Mti and Bosasa was more than a coincidence. Bosasa was in bed with the DCS. It also clarified why the DCS had reacted so angrily to Du Plessis' and my reportage on Mti – we were onto something.

There were numerous red flags in the adjudication process and criteria of the tenders, and it was clear to me that Bosasa had had inside help. One example of this was that Sondolo IT had been officially registered as a company in February 2005, just seven days before bids closed for the tender to install CCTV at 66 prisons; three months later, the company won the tender for a cool R237 million, against experienced competitors. Sondolo IT had zero experience when the company won the bid, while the tender document called for companies with at least five years' experience to apply for the contract.

And in the case of the fencing tender, the DCS paid Bosasa/Phezulu Fencing millions of rands before a single pole had been planted or fence erected – the contract stipulated that 90% of the contract fee of almost

R500 million was payable on delivery of the raw materials to the construction sites. Industry insiders were aghast and told me they'd never seen anything like this before. Carien and I highlighted these aspects in a series of articles we published over the next six months.

And there was another issue: the tenders were apparently written in a way that only one company could win. I heard this theory over and over again.

In the meantime parliamentarians were growing increasingly impatient with Ngconde Balfour, the then minister of correctional services, who'd told the portfolio committee that the construction of four new prisons had to be postponed due to a lack of finances. After we broke the Bosasa scandal, Balfour's excuse of a lack of funding no longer held water: 'So you don't have money to build prisons to ease overcrowding, but you have millions of rands to spend on security equipment and fencing?' irate MPs asked the minister. But Balfour steadfastly defended Mti and the Bosasa tenders.[1]

Parliament's oversight role had been severely diminished during the period of state capture, with most MPs simply not willing to identify, interrogate and penalise the grand corruption that was taking place at multiple levels of the executive. Some of them, like Vincent Smith, who succeeded Bloem as chair of the DCS portfolio committee, were themselves implicated in eating from Bosasa's dirty hands.[2] (Smith admitted receiving benefits from Bosasa, but denied they were bribes.)

MPs Dennis Bloem (representing the ANC at the time) and James Selfe (for the DA), despite being political opponents, were absolutely crucial in ensuring Bosasa remained on the agenda, and that Balfour and Mti couldn't treat the DCS's budget as their private piggybank. The two MPs were rock solid in exercising their oversight role and they, together with the late Vernie Petersen, never gave up trying to stop the rot.

Thirteen years later, Bloem, now an MP for Cope, made an impassioned plea to the Zondo Commission, asking the judge to ensure that justice be done in his lifetime.

16

Gambling with state money

In 2005, after Bosasa had successfully won tenders to provide catering through Bosasa Operations and security equipment and surveillance through Sondolo IT to South Africa's major prisons, Gavin Watson started talking about high-security fencing with Angelo Agrizzi.

'We were both under no illusion that Bosasa did not have the internal capacity to venture into this opportunity,' Agrizzi told the Zondo Commission.[1] But the fact that Bosasa couldn't do fencing didn't deter Watson from bidding for – and winning – the R486-million contract to put up fences around 53 prison sites. His recipe was tried and tested: get your guys to write the tender for the DCS through your contacts with Patrick Gillingham and Linda Mti in a way that only Bosasa could win, for example, containing specifications of products that only Bosasa could import or security requirements – like CCTV and control rooms – which other 'normal' catering companies didn't specialise in; then subcontract companies that could actually do the work, add a hefty profit margin, and voilà!

According to Agrizzi, Watson wanted to disguise the fencing tender in order to 'hide the fact that the Bosasa group would be awarded another DCS tender', and purchased a tiny fencing company from Cape Town called Phezulu Fencing for this purpose. Danny Mansell consulted the DCS on the tender specifications, and in November 2005 Phezulu Fencing was awarded the tender.

As part of the transaction, Bosasa acquired a 26% stake in Betafence, which supplied the fences. According to Agrizzi's affidavit, the shares in

Betafence were transferred to two trusts under Watson's control.

Early in 2006, Carien du Plessis and I started receiving reports from the prisons that poles and fences were being dumped at numerous prison sites but that the fencing wasn't going up. At the same time, we got our hands on the tender documents of the Phezulu Fencing contract and found that it contained the bizarre condition that the DCS would pay the contractor 90% of the contract fee on delivery of raw materials at prison sites.

On 21 July 2006 Simmer & Jack Mines, which owned gold mines on the West Rand, announced to the Johannesburg Stock Exchange, where it was listed, that the majority of shareholders had agreed to issue additional shares for cash.[2] At the time, Simmers' BEE partner was a company called Jaganda, which in turn was owned 51% by another company, Vulisango. The main shareholders and directors of Vulisango included Gavin Watson's brother Valence; Archie Mkele, who'd been implicated in the arson attack on the Watsons' family house in 1985, and later became a major Bosasa shareholder; a long-time Watson family friend, Kevin Wakeford, who was paid a consultancy fee by Bosasa; Bulelwa Njenje, the former wife of spy boss Gibson Njenje, who'd served as chair of Bosasa and himself owned shares in Vulisango; and Nozuko 'Girly' Pikoli, the wife of former NPA boss Vusi Pikoli. Most of Vulisango's beneficiaries were ANC members from the Eastern Cape.

My eye caught something odd in the Stock Exchange News Service announcement: the last purchaser of Simmer & Jack shares was Phezulu Fencing (Pty) Ltd, which had bought 29.5 million shares at a cost of R1.50 per share, a total of R44.3 million. With the DCS fencing tender being the small company's only major contract, this sum was almost certainly made up of funds from the prepayment by the DCS. So while some prisons had only had poles and fences delivered, not constructed, Watson was already spending profit from the corrupt tender on bulking up the value of a mining house that was partly owned by his brother and other Bosasa shareholders.

Andries van Tonder confirmed that the company had experienced cash-flow problems in the fencing project after a chunk of the payment they'd received from the DCS was used to purchase the Simmer & Jack shares.[3]

But the Simmer & Jack shares story didn't end there. After Phezulu's shares in Simmers had substantially increased in value, the Watson brothers decided to gamble with a derivatives broker called Dealstream.[4] Started by businessman Russell Leigh, Dealstream traded in single stock futures and promised its clients phenomenal returns for entrusting them with their shares.[5]

Bosasa insiders like chief financial officer Andries van Tonder and company secretary Tony Perry were very concerned about the company's exposure to the scheme, but were allegedly convinced by Valence Watson that it was a great opportunity. In fact, almost the entire Watson clan fell for Leigh's scheme, with those who invested including Ronnie, Valence and his wife Eileen, Valence's sons Jared and Nkosinathi, Daniel and his wife Tracey, their son Luke, and family friends Archie Mkele, Kevin Wakeford and Bulelwa Njenje. While the others invested amounts between R350 000 and R12 million, Phezulu Fencing was by far the largest victim of the Dealstream scam, with an investment of R128 million.

Dealstream went bust in 2008, and Leigh fled to Israel. In his February 2009 report, the curator of Dealstream appointed by the Financial Services Board found that Andries van Tonder on behalf of Phezulu Fencing had instructed a brokering firm to transfer 29 million Simmer & Jack shares to Investec Securities at a price of zero rand. Ownership of the shares was transferred to Investec for an amount of R127 890 000. The proceeds of the R127 890 000 were banked in the Phezulu trust account on 16 August 2007.[6] The next day, Leigh transferred the full amount to the Dealstream composite account and used most of the Phezulu money to cover his own debts, including money owed to Rand Merchant Bank.

Bosasa insiders believe that the company lost between R60 million and R120 million in the ill-fated Dealstream transaction. This was taxpayers' money, supposed to be used to put up fences around prisons, that Watson effectively gambled with.

It's unclear how much money the Watson family itself saw go down the drain.

17

Mti resigns

Shortly after we first revealed the link between Linda Mti and Bosasa in March 2006, the commissioner called his senior staff to a meeting and started to cry. He told them he wanted out.[1]

Minister Balfour refused to accept his resignation, however, and orchestrated the fight-back against our reporting. He called us irresponsible and misleading, and insisted that Mti didn't award tenders.

It was relatively easy to dismiss the reportage of two white Afrikaans-speaking journalists. Our stories weren't always picked up by the English media, and Balfour and Mti probably hoped that the scandal would eventually disappear. At the same time, Gavin Watson told his staff at Bosasa that Du Plessis and I were driven by a racist, anti-black agenda.

I was disappointed that the Directorate of Special Operations, commonly known as the Scorpions, South Africa's first focused anti-corruption unit, connected to the NPA, didn't take up the Bosasa matter, but at the time the unit was under increasing pressure from the ANC for its investigations into Jacob Zuma and Jackie Selebi, and there was a popular view gathering support that the unit was being abused to settle political scores. And as it turned out, the unit didn't have a long future after the ANC's Polokwane conference in December 2007 at which Zuma, as was widely expected, took over the presidency of the governing party. At the same conference the ANC adopted a resolution that the Scorpions should be shut down.

But eventually state institutions took note of our reportage and slowly started to act. First up was the Public Service Commission (PSC), the watchdog body for public servants and their conduct, which announced in May 2006 that it would investigate Mti's links to Bosasa. This was followed by similar announcements by the SIU and the Auditor-General.

The pressure was growing, but not enough to deter the department from further blessing Bosasa. Their biggest up-yours to us came in September 2006, when the DCS awarded Bosasa another R123-million tender to provide catering services to seven prisons in KwaZulu-Natal. The bond between Bosasa and the DCS was clearly much stronger than we'd thought, and they seemed intent on riding out the storm.

In October 2006 Willie Hofmeyr, then head of the SIU, announced that the unit would forensically probe all major tenders awarded by the DCS. Although he didn't use the name Bosasa, it was clear he was referring to the contracts highlighted by our reportage.

The SIU is technically the state's forensic-audit firm. It employs investigators, auditors, analysts and lawyers, and although it doesn't have the powers to criminally prosecute matters in court, it can institute civil action against individuals and companies and recover wasted money. It can also recommend criminal prosecution to the NPA and the SAPS.

The SIU probe touched a nerve, and Watson was justifiably terrified about what Hofmeyr and his team would uncover. And he realised that Hofmeyr was incorruptible and this infuriated him. The thought of an independent probe into his wheeling and dealing over which he had absolutely no control drove Watson, whom his colleagues described as 'autocratic', 'narcissistic' and 'dictatorial', insane.

At one of the regular staff prayer meetings, Watson told his colleagues that he had photos of Hofmeyr and me, and that he'd blessed our pictures and prayed for us to stop besmirching the name of his company.[2] And it went further: in his garden at home Watson planted a white cross, like the ones grieving families place on the side of the road after a loved one dies in a car accident, with a picture of Hofmeyr on it. 'He hated Willie. He called him pencil-neck,' Agrizzi told me.[3]

Two major things happened in November 2006: Mti resigned; and I was leaked a 29-page document of the technical specifications for the CCTV tender, which had been drawn up on a Bosasa computer months before it was formally advertised by the DCS.

Mti's resignation was orchestrated to make it look like a seamless transition into his new job as head of security for the 2010 Soccer World Cup. He'd been removed as head of prisons to look after security for the biggest tournament ever hosted in the history of South Africa. And this didn't take place on Jacob Zuma's watch: Mti was very much part of the ANC's Eastern Cape elite that had delivered Thabo Mbeki as president.

This is how the ANC works: deployment to a government job is almost viewed as a reward for services rendered during the struggle against apartheid, and comrades, even those implicated in major allegations of wrongdoing, are given a soft landing elsewhere in government if the heat becomes too much in their incumbent jobs. There's seldom punishment for wrongdoing. The ANC's system of deployment doesn't discriminate against comrades who've stolen money, received bribes or slowed down service delivery to the poor and vulnerable due to mismanagement.

Of course, there are many examples of good ANC deployments, but Mti's wasn't one of them. It was further proof that the ANC wasn't willing to walk the talk on corruption when it came to one of their own. It was easy to suspend, discipline and dismiss prison warders for smuggling dagga or stealing tuckshop money, but when it came to the really big cases of corruption and state capture, the party turned a blind eye.

Indeed, in a statement, Balfour praised the local organising committee of the Soccer World Cup for appointing Mti, thereby 'giving due acknowledgement to a cadre that has given nearly 30 years of productive adult life to the cause of liberating, defending and developing the people of his country.'[4]

And the DCS lauded Mti as an anti-corruption champion and ignored our reportage as if it had never happened. 'Of the many achievements of Mr Mti's tenure at the helm of the department, the creation of a machinery for fighting fraud and corruption, the white paper that maps out our nation's approach to the development of a proudly South African correctional system, an improved approach to security management within correctional centres and an interdepartmental system of addressing overcrowding are those that stand out from the rest,' said chief deputy commissioner Jenny Schreiner, a dyed-in-the-wool comrade and member of the SACP.[5]

Schreiner, who would later become the acting national commissioner, received the SIU's report on Bosasa's corruption in 2009. She didn't take firm action and Bosasa continued to flourish under her and her successors in the DCS.

18

The smoking bazooka

It was late at night when my source finally gave me the 29-page digital document, 'Technical specifications misc complete.doc', that proved that Bosasa had written the specifications for a R237-million tender to install CCTV and access-control systems at 66 prisons.

The tender had been advertised in February 2005. Right-clicking on the document's properties, I saw that it had been created on 17 December 2004 at 16:26 by user 'Corrie'. It was later saved by user 'Johan'. Corrie Botes was Bosasa's compliance officer and Johan Helmand was the company's head of technology.

An independent forensic expert later examined the computer file and confirmed that the document had indeed been created and written by Bosasa employees in December 2004 on the company's computers. Basie von Solms, head of information technology at the University of Johannesburg, also examined the leaked digitial document, as well as the official DCS tender document, and found that about 33% of the tender document had been copied word for word from the Bosasa document, and that there were further similarities between the two.

On 16 November 2006, seven days after Mti resigned, *Beeld* published a front-page splash titled 'Skryf self tender – en kry kontrak!' ('Write the tender – and win the contract!').[1]

Back then I wasn't aware of the term 'state capture', but now I know that this is exactly what had happened there: the tentacles of a private company had stretched so deep into a government entity that it had taken over complete control of key government functions. In the case of Bosasa, the commissioner and chief financial officer of correctional services had been bribed, budgets had been shifted from other projects to fund these tenders, and Bosasa had written the tender specifications themselves. Essentially, Bosasa was running the DCS.

But Carien du Plessis and I realised that our work was still far from over. There was so much we didn't know about Bosasa and its government networks. It was highly unlikely that its connections were limited to the DCS.

What we didn't expect was that Bosasa's tentacles would reach right into the office of the presidency.

Vusi Pikoli: I felt betrayed

'I felt a sense of a betrayal of our values as a liberation movement because Linda Mti was and still is a senior and respected member of the ANC. We have been very close and our children regarded themselves as siblings. ... It has been very traumatic to all of us who have been close to Mr Mti and his family.'[1]

19

The Mbeki links

In 2006 Thabo Mbeki was generally viewed as an anti-corruption president, particularly after his sacking of Jacob Zuma as deputy president in mid-2005 following the conviction of Schabir Shaik. Shaik, Zuma's financial advisor, had been convicted of corruption, including a finding by Judge Hilary Squires that he'd bribed Zuma to promote his business. Mbeki was a big supporter of the Scorpions, and regularly signed proclamations for the SIU to investigate allegations of government fraud and corruption.

At the time the Bosasa scandal broke, the Scorpions were preoccupied with the Shaik and Zuma matters. In 2005, after mining boss Brett Kebble was shot down, the unit shifted a large part of its focus to the Project Bad Guys investigation, probing links between the criminal underworld and the highest police office in the land. This investigation ultimately led to the conviction of the then police chief, Jackie Selebi.

In late 2006 I started to probe the shareholders of Bosasa and its subsidiaries. It was clear that Gavin Watson was the main honcho, but I wanted to know who the other beneficiaries were of the multimillion-rand tenders that the group had won from the DCS. The shareholding structures of the Bosasa companies were complicated. Trusts owned shares in companies that owned shares in other companies.

I started drawing pictures and did company searches to trace the people behind these corporate structures. The results were interesting: Mbeki's political advisor, Titus Mafolo, was a shareholder of Sondolo IT through his

THE MBEKI LINKS

shareholding in a company called Bancar Investment Holdings. Mafolo's family trust indirectly owned 7.5% of Sondolo IT.[2]

A further link to Mbeki's office was through Seth Phalatse, former chair of the Strategic Fuel Fund, who owned 1.25% of Sondolo IT through his shareholding in a company called Kgwerano Financial Services, run by entrepreneurs Brian Gwebu and Itumeleng Moraba, who'd convinced Gavin Watson to buy into their company. Phalatse's wife Lorato headed up Mbeki's private office.

Ronnie Mamoepa, the then government spokesperson and ANC leader, held 0.5% of Sondolo IT through Bancar. After our story revealing the shareholding, Mamoepa said he no longer wanted to be associated with Bosasa through Sondolo IT and relinquished his shares.[3]

A further Mbeki link to Bosasa was through Mamisa Chabula, a medical doctor and former head of the Eastern Cape health department, who'd cared for Mbeki's father, Govan, from the time of his release from Robben Island in 1987 until his death in 2001. Chabula, who I was told was close to the Mbeki family, served as a director of several Bosasa companies for a number of years, and was quoted in 2005 as Lindela's head of medical services, after 21 detainees died in eight months.[4]

In November 2007 Mbeki signed a proclamation that authorised the SIU to investigate the tenders awarded by DCS to Bosasa. If Mbeki wasn't aware of the scandal, he would've been made aware in a desperate briefing by the late Vernie Petersen, then prisons boss, who warned Mbeki and Frank Chikane, his director-general, in 2008 of Bosasa's influence and corruption.

Another person who was well acquainted with many of the role players in the Bosasa scandal was Vusi Pikoli, NDPP between 2005 and 2007, who lost his job for pushing ahead with corruption charges against former police chief Jackie Selebi. Also hailing from the Eastern Cape, and having been involved in the ANC's underground struggle and non-racial rugby, Pikoli was aware of the Watsons and their background. Pikoli was also a friend of Mti, and his wife, Nozuko 'Girly' Pikoli, was one of the original shareholders in Dyambu Holdings.

Of his connecton to Mti, Pikoli said, 'We belong to the same political party, the ANC. He is my comrade. The comradeship developed into a family friendship which included our children growing up together. We are all from Port Elizabeth. I have worked with him closely on ANC and national security and intelligence matters since 1980.'[5]

Of the Watson brothers, Pikoli said he didn't have a family relationship with them, but got to know them through rugby.

As for Gibson Njenje, a former Bosasa chairperson and head of domestic intelligence in South Africa, he was another of Pikoli's comrades; the two had been friends in exile. It was Njenje who'd invited Pikoli's wife, Nozuko, to take a shareholding in Vulisango, a BEE mining company headed by Gavin Watson's brother Valence, which owned shares in Brett Kebble's Simmer & Jack gold mine. (At the start of Selebi's corruption trial in 2009, the then police chief accused Vusi Pikoli of having had an ulterior motive for prosecuting him because the police had discovered that the Pikolis had unduly benefited from Kebble's mining activities.[6] The Pikolis denied receiving any gratification from Kebble.[7])

'Mr Njenje and Mr Mti worked with [the Watsons] as ANC operatives,' Pikoli explained. 'This relationship continued after the unbanning of the ANC and post 1994. With Mr Njenje it developed into a business relationship because the Watsons had always been in business since the apartheid days.'[8]

Pikoli said he'd been traumatised by the revelations about his former comrades that came tumbling out at the Zondo Commission. 'The allegations against Mr Mti ... came as a great shock and disappointment. ... The revelations by Mr Agrizzi and the particularity of detail have come as a shock to me at a personal level. I hope the pending criminal trial will bring finality to this matter once and for all. ... The law must be allowed to run its course.'[9]

After Mti resigned as national commissioner of correctional services, his personal assistant, Jackie Lepinka, started looking for other work. She found a job as executive personal assistant in the office of the NDPP, who was then Pikoli. 'It wasn't an automatic transfer; it followed due process of adverts and interviews,' explained Pikoli, who denied having been asked by Mti, his comrade, to give Lepinka a job. 'It was a transfer in that she did not have to resign from the public service when joining the NPA.'¹⁰

The Bosasa docket finally reached the NPA in 2009, almost two years after Pikoli had been suspended and left the institution.

Agrizzi shocked the Zondo Commission by claiming that Bosasa had been fed confidential NPA documentation from inside the institution, courtesy of Mti. Agrizzi described Mti as Bosasa's fixer in the NPA and testified that bribes had been paid to Lepinka and former NPA bigwigs Nomgcobo Jiba and Lawrence Mrwebi to keep Bosasa out of court. Lepinka was ideally placed in the office of the NDPP to gain access to secret prosecution files. All three denied the allegation of bribery, and Jiba applied to the Zondo Commission to cross-examine Agrizzi.

Pikoli, who once said he would prosecute his mother if she did something wrong, told me that although the Scorpions had the power to initiate a preliminary investigation without his approval, he would've had no issue signing off on an investigation into Bosasa if it had been brought to him at the time. 'The first time I heard of Mr Mti's "involvement" with Bosasa was when Professor Stan Sangweni, the then chairperson of the PSC, informed me about certain allegations against Mr Mti involving Bosasa. Professor Sangweni informed me that the PSC had investigated the matter and handed the report to the SIU for further investigation of any acts of maladministration. Neither Advocate [Leonard] McCarthy [former head of the Scorpions] nor Advocate [Thanda] Mngwengwe [former investigating director of the Scorpions] informed me of the Scorpions investigating Bosasa. ... Anyway, with the SIU already investigating the matter, the SIU would have referred the matter to the Scorpions for a criminal investigation and possible prosecution. By the time I was suspended on 23 September 2007, the SIU had not referred the Bosasa matter to the NPA for a criminal investigation and probable prosecution.'¹¹¹

20

Crash and burn

In February 2009 I published several articles in the *Mail & Guardian* based on travel records that were part of the leaked documents I'd received from my sources. The records showed that Bosasa had paid for the flights and accommodation of people like Linda Mti and Gibson Njenje.

In his statement to the Zondo Commission, Angelo Agrizzi recalled in vivid detail what the consequences of my reporting had been and how important evidence had ended up literally in the toilet.

'A media report was published which indicated that a journalist had copies of documents from Blake's Travel, which apparently showed that Bosasa used Blake's Travel to facilitate travel arrangements of, amongst others, government officials. Flights, travel, accommodation and on occasion car hire would also be booked by me on the Bosasa VIP account at Blake's Travel for Linda Mti and his wife. I have supporting documentation,' Agrizzi said.

'Gavin Watson instructed Andries van Tonder and me to attend to Blake's Travel and collect all documents and computers and to destroy them. We then met with Brian Blake at Blake's Travel and informed him of what was to be done. He obliged and handed to us documents and computers.'

Agrizzi testified that he and Van Tonder then drove to Luipaardsvlei hostel, a property that belonged to Bosasa and at that stage was being revamped and was a construction site, and threw all the items into a hole. With the help of Bosasa employees Ryno Roode and Gerhard van der

Bank, the men poured petrol over the items and set them alight, then, once the fire had burnt out, filled in the hole using a front-end loader.

'An employee at Bosasa was instructed by Gavin Watson to rewrite the travel orders using fictitious names. This was done,' Agrizzi continued. 'Thereafter, on instruction of Gavin Watson, all travel arrangements for VIP clients of Bosasa would be booked under the account Venter, my father-in-law. I opened a bank account in the name of Venter and paid Blake's Travel out of this account. Dr Jurgen Smith, via Consilium Business Consultants (Pty) Ltd, would reimburse me as cash drawings. A few of my personal trips were also arranged and paid for in this manner.'

Around this time Brian Blake was subpoenaed to testify in a matter instituted by the SIU in the Pretoria High Court, and Gavin Watson instructed attorney Brian Biebuyck to ensure that Blake wouldn't implicate Bosasa in his evidence. 'I was instructed to attend this meeting. The meeting took place, but I was not convinced that we were successful in our endeavour. I do not know whether Blake ever testified,' Agrizzi said.

Early in 2009, Watson had instructed an IT specialist to fake a server crash to get rid of files that could implicate the company before the SIU investigators could gather evidence, Agrizzi said, adding that copies were made of the hard drives before they were destroyed.

Some time later, on a weekend when Agrizzi was away at a game reserve in the North West province, he got a phonecall from Watson to say that 'Sesinyi Seopela [had] informed him that he had received information that the Bosasa offices were going to be raided the following Monday morning. He also told Gavin Watson that they were looking for specific documents and transactions,' Agrizzi said.

Agrizzi immediately went to the Bosasa offices, where he met Watson and Andries van Tonder. 'We were instructed to go through all the offices and look for possible incriminating evidence. The information Gavin Watson [had] received from Seopela included reference to documents regarding the sale-of-shares agreement in respect of Phezulu Fencing (Pty) Ltd, as well as the agreement between Gavin Watson and Mti for the payment of money in return for an undertaking from him that he would ensure that Bosasa would be given preference in the awarding of tenders. I knew the latter document actually existed as I had seen it. We were instructed to specifically look for those documents. We removed the documents that we found.'

Later, in 2010, when I published details of the SIU investigation in *City Press*, Watson asked Agrizzi and Van Tonder to destroy the documents. 'Save for the agreement between Gavin Watson and Mti, the documents were then burnt,' Agrizzi testified. 'I later handed the [Mti] agreement to Gavin Watson at his house. He was visibly relieved. He took the document, shredded it, put it in a plastic bag, filled it with water and then proceeded to flush the contents down the lavatory.'¹

21

Enter the Cobras

Located just off the N4 out of Pretoria on the road to Emalahleni, the Rentmeester building in Watermeyer Park is vanilla: there's nothing exciting or modern about the structure that hosts the head office of the SIU, also known as the Cobras. The SIU's work is much more enthralling than its premises.

It was in 2007, at these SIU headquarters, that I first met Advocate Suad Jacobs and investigator Clinton Oellermann, the duo who led the SIU's investigation into the multimillion-rand tenders awarded by the DCS to Bosasa over a number of years. Although Willie Hofmeyr was the face of the SIU, Jacobs and Oellermann headed up the DCS investigation that included the four Bosasa tenders for kitchens and catering, access control, fencing, and those expensive television sets.

The SIU launched its first investigation into the DCS in 2004, in the wake of the Jali Commission's findings of fraud and corruption in the prisons system. But it was only in late 2007 that Thabo Mbeki signed a second proclamation, authorising the SIU to probe high-value tenders in the department – a direct result of Carien du Plessis' and my reporting on Bosasa. In its final report, the SIU credited the media for alerting them to the Bosasa case.

Jacobs, who would later become head of forensics at the law firm ENSafrica, is a tough-as-nails former prosecutor who cut her anti-corruption teeth in the Scorpions. At our first meeting at Watermeyer Park, she made it clear that this was going to be a one-way relationship: I could provide them with information and documents, but they wouldn't reciprocate. And, indeed, I never received so much as a tip from them during the investigation.

Journalists don't normally provide information to law-enforcement agencies or prosecutors; our primary duty is not to see to it that the crooked and corrupt end up in jail. The most we can do is to place information on the record and make sure that everybody knows about it. If someone who's committed criminal acts is arrested, fired or jailed as a result of a story, the journalist counts himself lucky and moves on. Nonetheless, it was comforting to know that a state institution was looking into the Bosasa matter and dedicating serious resources to it: Du Plessis and I weren't alone, and I made sure that the SIU was aware of the stories we published.

The 2004 proclamation didn't cover the Bosasa tenders, and the SIU only started its investigation into the multimillion-rand contracts at the end of 2007. The unit handed its report to then correctional services minister Nosiviwe Mapisa-Nqakula and acting commissioner Jenny Schreiner at the end of 2009, and a copy of the report (as required by law) to the NPA.

Patrick Gillingham was the department's fall guy: Mapisa-Nqakula and Schreiner pursued disciplinary charges against him until he finally resigned from the DCS in 2010. But even with Gillingham out of the game, Bosasa kept on scoring and continued to cater for thousands of South Africa's prisoners, courtesy of the DCS, and over the next decade made millions from the catering contract.

Explaining why she took no action, Mapisa-Nqakula said she was just following legal advice. 'When the SIU brings you a report for your information, it is to deal with matters internally. Otherwise they tell you they took the report to the NPA. I received the report, read it and said because you [the SIU] are taking it to the NPA, take my copy back. It was not like there was inaction.'[21] From her perspective, the matter was being dealt with by the criminal-justice system and all she had to do was to discipline Patrick Gillingham.

When I put it to Mapisa-Nqakula that one of the aims of SIU investigations was for departments to recoup money lost through corrupt tenders by way of civil litigation, she pleaded ignorance.

ENTER THE COBRAS

In a very cynical move, the DCS's legal department provided Gillingham with a copy of the entire SIU report ahead of his disciplinary hearing. This triggered an angry letter to Mapisa-Nqakula from Brian Biebuyck, Bosasa's lawyer, something that she referred to to underline that she had no personal links with Gavin Watson. 'It was a very arrogant letter, prescribing to me what I should and should not do. I was really pissed off. If the owner of Bosasa [Watson] was a friend, he wouldn't have asked his lawyer to phone me [he would have called her himself]. There were no calls [from Watson], nothing of the sort.'[2]

In her response to Biebuyck's letter, Mapisa-Nqakula wrote to Bosasa's directors, 'Why Mr Gillingham took it upon himself to give you the report I don't know ... I have not taken kindly to the threatening and demanding letter you sent to me via your legal representative, wherein you attempt to instruct me in this matter ... you are completely out of line by pre-empting my actions and instructing me.'[3]

Clinton Oellermann gave evidence to the Zondo Commission describing how, during the Bosasa investigation, the ten-man investigating team was sealed off from the rest of the SIU in a separate part of the building in an attempt to prevent leaks. 'We were given a specific area where all our documents and information were kept. In fact, we weren't even on the SIU servers; we were given a dedicated server outside of the SIU environment,' he said. 'We were not allowed to discuss the matter with any of our colleagues. ... We reported directly to our principals, the deputy head [Faiek Davids] and head [Hofmeyr] of the unit, and the sharing of information was very restricted. Even documents that were printed – we knew how many copies were printed, how many versions there were, [and] they were disseminated in a particular order and only to those who needed to have copies of the report,' he said.[4]

And yet Bosasa seemed to always be a step ahead of the SIU. For example, in 2007 Bosasa called the SIU to tell them that they knew the unit was planning a search-and-seizure operation at the company's head office, and asked if they could first meet at their lawyers' premises to discuss the operation. This was Watson flexing his muscles, telling the SIU that he knew what they were up to and that he could direct their probe.

Bosasa went to court to stop the probe from going ahead. Ultimately, the SIU bosses agreed not to interview key witnesses like Watson in exchange for the investigation going ahead while a final court battle was pending. That's why Watson wasn't directly implicated in the SIU report, Oellermann told Zondo. And not only could the SIU not interview him, he hardly signed any documents and barely touched his work computer. The CEO of a company that won multimillion-rand IT tenders from government seldom used his work email.

Agrizzi confirmed this during his testimony when he gave evidence about the absence of Watson's signature on key documents. They, his henchmen, had to do the dirty work for 'Nkokheli' (leader), as Watson was known on the Bosasa campus.

'The [SIU] report that was given to the DCS was a hard-copy report. We did not give them an electronic copy,' Oellermann told Zondo.[5]

But two days after the SIU gave Mapisa-Nqakula and Schreiner the report, I got a phone call from within Bosasa. 'Watson has the report,' I was told.

I called Oellermann to let him know that the report had leaked. He was flabbergasted – as far as he knew, the only people with copies were him, his bosses, and the minister and acting commissioner.

Mapisa-Nqakula was convinced the report had been leaked to Bosasa by Gillingham. 'I did not leak the report. Jenny Schreiner did not leak the report. The SIU did not leak the report and the NPA would not have leaked the report,' she said.[6]

The SIU report was deadly. The unit had managed to connect many more dots, and had obtained bank statements and internal documents that helped it to prove criminality. The report detailed how Mti and Gillingham had been bribed by Bosasa with houses, cars, home renovations, overseas trips and even rugby tickets; Bosasa business cards in Gillingham's name were found at his house during a search-and-seizure operation.

The SIU confirmed Du Plessis' and my earlier findings that Bosasa staff were involved in drafting the tender documents for the contracts they'd won. The unit also discovered that Mti and Gillingham had shifted funds from the DCS compensation fund, from which overtime to warders was paid, to pay for the Bosasa tenders – in effect, prison warders and DCS staff had been paid less because of the money diverted to Watson, Agrizzi and co.

On 7 December 2009, in response to media queries, then NPA spokesperson Mthunzi Mhaga released a media statement acknowledging the NPA's receipt of the report 'on the alleged corruption and fraud at the Department of Correctional Services relating to the Bosasa group on 30 September 2009. The information contained in the report has been forwarded to the Serious Economic Offences Unit of the South African Police Service (SAPS) for further investigation. When the police investigation is finalised, they will submit the case docket to the NPA for a decision whether to prosecute or not.'[7]

For ten years, nothing happened. The matter completely stalled at the SAPS while a focused project got underway to subvert the NPA and keep the matter out of court.

These details would only emerge during Agrizzi's bombshell evidence in February 2019.

A few days after having given his evidence, Agrizzi, Mti, Gillingham and other former Bosasa employees were arrested by the Hawks and appeared in court on charges of corruption, fraud and money laundering. The charge sheet contained information almost identical to that in the SIU report by Jacobs and Oellermann given to the NPA a decade before.

22

#BosasaLeaks

At the beginning of 2009, at a coffee shop on the West Rand, I was given four USB flash drives. The sticks had on them the inboxes of several Bosasa employees, including that of Angelo Agrizzi, the chief operating officer and Gavin Watson's henchman-in-chief.

I immediately set up an old computer in my study at home that wasn't connected to the internet, and worked day and night looking for evidence of corruption and wrongdoing in those inboxes. What I discovered was that the rot was much deeper than I'd thought.

Not only did I find proof that Bosasa had influenced each of the four major tenders it had won from the DCS between 2004 and 2008, but the ease with which Angelo Agrizzi and Patrick Gillingham were communicating over email made it clear that corruption had been normalised at the DCS. Here was a chief financial officer of a government department discussing with a service provider details about contracts and tenders that were yet to be published.

It was a brazen circumvention of every piece of legislation regarding public finances and good governance.

In early January 2009 I published an article in the *Mail & Guardian* reporting that the DCS had extended Bosasa's catering contract in prisons for another three years, despite the investigation by the SIU into tender irregularities and corruption, and over the objections of prisons boss Vernie Petersen. (Peterson had been unceremoniously removed from his job in November 2008.)

I also mentioned in my article that Minister Ngconde Balfour had been present at the opening of the tender box in September 2008, a highly unusual set of circumstances for a political head who wasn't supposed to be involved in operational matters.

The article irked Balfour, and the DCS took out full-page advertisements in three Sunday newspapers the following week, urging South Africans with proof of wrongdoing to report the matter to the police. So I gave Balfour what he'd asked for. In a two-page spread in the *Mail & Guardian*, under the headline 'Prisons graft: Here's the proof, minister', I laid out the details of the leaked emails, showing the extent of the corrupt relationship between Bosasa and the DCS. Using a detailed timeline, I showed how Agrizzi, Bosasa co-founder Danny Mansell and Gillingham had conspired to give the company an edge over the competition. In the case of the kitchens tender, we could prove that Bosasa had been in possession of more than 90% of the tender document at least three weeks before the contract had been advertised.[1]

This pattern was repeated for the other three big tenders. In the case of the fencing tender, Bosasa had left parts of the writing of the tender specifications to third parties who would later benefit from being subcontracted to Bosasa-owned Phezulu Fencing. I found an email Agrizzi had sent to Michael Rodenburg, the former chief executive of fencing company Guardiar (then called Bekaert Bastion or Betafence), and Geoff Greyling, chief executive of SA Fence & Gate, containing the full bid conditions and specifications, days before the tender was officially advertised, and giving these companies an enormous advantage over their competitors.[2]

Another gem in among all the leaked emails was a private-intelligence report that detailed how Bosasa had illegally spied on senior DCS officials at a workshop in the Drakensberg in June 2006. The report, sent by Agrizzi to Gillingham, detailed the movements of senior DCS commissioners Willem Damons and Tonie Venter at a bosberaad to discuss security at South African prisons. During his testimony at the Zondo Commission, Agrizzi said Watson wanted him to spy on anyone who was 'negative or problematic'.

Also included in the leaked material were Bosasa's travel records showing how the company paid for prisons boss Linda Mti and his family to fly to and stay in the Eastern Cape while his department was showering Bosasa with government tenders.[3] It was, in fact, this article that led to Watson instructing Agrizzi to physically destroy the computers of the company's travel agent.

As a result of my own #BosasaLeaks I could finally prove what I'd suspected for many years – that Bosasa and its friends in the DCS were corrupt to the core.

Angelo Agrizzi: I was told to bribe you

'Gavin said to me, "Why don't you go and speak to Adriaan [Basson], all right, and just take him a package of a million bucks and say to him, 'Don't worry, there's more where that came from.'?" I refused to; I just said I wouldn't.

'Itu [Moraba] and Joe Gumede bought 30 or 40 burner phones with your number programmed in on [them], and Carien [du Plessis'] number, and they said those were the only two numbers they could phone. They blocked the phones [to phone other numbers]. They were issued out [to Bosasa employees]. "Phone the guys, all hours of the night and day, and threaten them. Or just phone them and constantly harass them."'[1]

23

Burner phones and death threats

'Stop writing shit about us.'

The man at the other end of the line sounded aggressive and uncompromising. He didn't introduce himself but said he worked for Bosasa and that I was going to cost him his job. He wasn't interested in listening to my explanation of why investigating Bosasa was in the public interest. His call had only one purpose: to scare and intimidate me.

By 2009 I'd been investigating and writing about Bosasa for three years, and up to that point the only bullying I'd encountered had been through attorney Brian Biebuyck, who'd tried to scare off Carien du Plessis and me with heavy-handed letters. This hadn't worked, and now Bosasa had apparently turned to its employees, who were told that our reporting on the company would lead to job losses. At the time, I was told by a source that Bosasa directors had distributed my cellphone number to their employees and told them to threaten us. Du Plessis received similar calls.

The threats came thick and fast after I started publishing details from the leaked emails in the *Mail & Guardian* in early 2009. The calls came at all hours of the day and night, and the message was always the same: 'Why are you writing shit about us? You will cost us our jobs. You're a racist. Stop writing shit.'

At the same time, I received a call from an Afrikaans man, supposedly warning me that the NIA had compiled reports 'because of [my] negative attitude towards BEE companies' [like Bosasa] and was discussing options to 'silence [me] permanently'. There were supposedly two methods of eliminating me being considered – either in a way that would look like an accident, or by abducting me and taking me to a 'hellhole prison' in Zimbabwe or Zambia. I realised the man's aim was to intimidate me and never heard from him again.

Inside sources told me that Watson had convinced his fellow directors that the 'media war' on Bosasa was somehow being directed by the so-called Stellenbosch Mafia or Afrikaner Broederbond (which no longer existed), of which Du Plessis and I were supposedly the mouthpieces, driven by racism and outrage that business was being taken away from so-called Afrikaner companies.

On the face of it, it was a credible cover story: both Du Plessis and I had started our careers at Afrikaans newspapers, and we'd broken the Bosasa scandal in *Beeld* and *Die Burger*, both newspapers owned by Naspers subsidiary Media24. Naspers's history was intimately interwoven with that of the NP and apartheid and segregation in South Africa – the company had been founded by a group of Afrikaner entrepreneurs in 1915 with the aim of promoting Afrikaner nationalism in the aftermath of the Anglo-Boer War. Its newspapers, particularly *Die Burger*, whose founding editor was DF Malan, had become the mouthpiece of the NP.

But things had changed. In 1997 a group of brave Naspers journalists had made a submission to the Truth and Reconciliation Commission (TRC), apologising for the company's role in supporting and promoting apartheid. In 2005 then Media24 CEO Esmaré Weideman had also formally apologised for Naspers's complicity in maintaining apartheid.

Irrespective of this, and being steeped in the ANC's culture of suspicion and conspiracy, Watson realised the power of calling someone a racist and anti-transformation in a country battered by racism and inequality. Long before the Guptas and Zuma, in cahoots with Bell Pottinger, invented the 'white monopoly capital' campaign to discredit their critics,[2] Watson and co had begun to smear my reporting on the basis that I was white and had worked for 'the enemy'.

After I blocked several telephone numbers, the calls subsided, and I continued my reporting on Bosasa. The company evidently then realised that it had to take its campaign against me to the next level. In February

2009, shortly after publishing a number of Bosasa stories in the *Mail & Guardian*, I received a call from a woman with a raspy voice. The caller's number showed up on my cellphone's screen, which is why I took the call. The woman told me that she was a colleague in the media and that she wanted to warn me about 'the dangers' of reporting on Bosasa. Saying that she would 'kill' me if I told anyone about our conversation, she proceeded to read from a report that she said Bosasa had commissioned a private investigator to do on me. Claiming to 'want to be sure' she was talking to the right person, she rattled off the details of where I was born, my ID number, where I'd lived, where and what I'd studied, who my friends and family were, and what their occupations were.

I googled the cellphone number, and it came up as the contact detail for journalist-turned-PR-strategist Benedicta Dube. A former respected journalist, Dube had worked for the SABC, the *Financial Mail* and e.tv.

I told Ferial Haffajee, my editor at the *Mail & Guardian* at the time, what had happened, and we asked our lawyers to write letters to Bosasa and Dube, demanding the return of my private information. Bosasa denied acting unlawfully and said the information in Dube's possession fell within the public domain, which was complete nonsense – some of the information could only have come from home affairs.

Dube claimed not to recall our conversation and accused me of 'blackmail journalism'. A source later told me that she was on Bosasa's payroll, which Agrizzi confirmed at the Zondo Commission in 2019. He said that Bosasa had employed two 'media consultants' to 'get rid of negative publicity and also to discredit the journalists who were writing those articles'. One was Dube, and Agrizzi claimed that she received more than R1 million for her services.[3]

The other Bosasa 'media consultant' was a KGB-spy-turned-journalist-turned-spin-doctor named Stephen Laufer. A South African with a German accent who traded in charm and his credit card, Laufer had in the mid-2000s landed a job wining and dining journalists on behalf of European arms companies implicated in the arms deal.

After he was named by Agrizzi at the Zondo Commission, Laufer issued a statement claiming that he'd fired Bosasa as a client after being asked to conduct 'unethical activities'. I asked Carien du Plessis, who was then working for the Independent Newspapers group, if Laufer had ever tried to pressurise her into dropping the Bosasa story, and she replied that he'd taken her to a fancy lunch and tried to convince her not to be hard on Bosasa because it was a BEE company. 'He tried to appeal to my sense of patriotism by explaining to me that Bosasa was a black empowerment company and, for that reason, we should not report so negatively about it,' she told *News24*. 'I asked him if the end, however noble, justified the means.'[4]

Du Plessis and I were up against not only corrupt businessmen and their political blessees, but also colleagues who'd traded their journalistic compasses for thirty pieces of silver.

The Zondo Commission's chief investigator Frank Dutton called me shortly after Agrizzi's testimony to ask if I'd be willing to give evidence on the intimidation and harassment I'd suffered at the hands of Bosasa. Journalists don't normally divulge information to law-enforcement agencies or commissions – we publish what we know – but in this instance I felt that my story could contribute to Judge Zondo's mammoth task of piecing together the elaborate tapestry of state capture.

Testifying about his little black books, which contained the names of Bosasa's blessees who'd received monthly cash bribes from the company, Angelo Agrizzi said Papa Leshabane, Bosasa's flashy spokesperson, was given R30 000 a month to pay off journalists for providing tips or writing positive stories.

One of the names I truly hadn't expected to come across during this part of my investigation of Bosasa was that of investigative journalist Barry Sergeant, who died in 2017. Sergeant had written a positive portrayal of the Watsons in his book *The Assault on the Rand*, which detailed businessman Kevin Wakeford's role in the Commission of Inquiry into the rapid depreciation of the exchange rate of the rand in 2002. I'd picked up Wakeford's name in Bosasa's leaked travel records in 2009.

Wakeford, an old friend of the Watsons from their school days at

Graeme College in what was then Grahamstown (now Makhanda), had become one of Gavin Watson's confidants at Bosasa. According to Agrizzi, Wakeford had received monthly payments from the company of up to R100 000, something Wakeford would later deny, threatening legal action against Agrizzi and the Zondo Commission.[5] Agrizzi testified that Wakeford had assisted Watson with Bosasa's tax problems and advised him on 'media attacks'. (After Agrizzi's evidence, Wakeford, who'd become CEO of Armscor in May 2015, resigned his position.)

In *The Assault on the Rand*, published in 2013, seven years after the first allegations of corruption against Bosasa had appeared in the media, Barry Sergeant wrote warmly about the family who 'give white South Africans genuine credibility, a sense of redemption.'[6] Many whites remained 'deceived as to who the family really are and what they truly stand for', according to Sergeant. 'The propaganda against the family has been sustained to this day, possibly as a reminder to most whites of what living non-racialism is truly about.'[7]

I was perplexed. What was the 'propaganda' Sergeant wrote of against the Watsons? My and others' stories about Bosasa's capture of the ANC and the DCS?

But it got worse: later in the book, Sergeant quoted Wakeford on the 'pathetic and facile attack against Gavin and [his] companies where he is the CEO [Bosasa] by the right wing in the press and the criminal justice system'. Wakeford told Sergeant, 'They are obsessed with destroying a good man because he and his brothers had the guts to stand up against apartheid ... Gavin will prevail and those second-guessing his integrity will be left wanting.'[8]

Denise Bjorkman, Bosasa's resident counsellor who also edited the company magazine *Bosele*, told me about a meeting between Watson, Wakeford and Sergeant that she was called into in 2011. 'Barry looked very unhappy. Gavin in his very domineering voice told him that he was now going to do this, he was not asking him nicely, and he will be doing the right thing, and he is going to write nice things about Bosasa and he is going to change the way the public sees Bosasa. He was going to be paid handsomely. Barry just sat and listened, but his face was a picture. His eyes were getting bigger and bigger.'[9]

BURNER PHONES AND DEATH THREATS

Bosasa's former head of marketing, Jason Stoltz, confirmed to me that Sergeant had indeed been briefed on writing profiles of the company's directors, but that he'd never delivered. Stoltz didn't know if Sergeant had ever been paid.[10]

Sergeant was described to me as 'incorruptible' by Alec Hogg, editor of the online publication *Biznews*. Hogg had been involved in introducing Sergeant to the Watsons, and when I asked him about his role in this, Hogg told me that he'd had to act as 'peacemaker' in a heated meeting between Sergeant and Watson brothers Ronnie and Valence, about their shareholding in mining company Simmer & Jack through BEE outfit Vulisango.[11]

Then things took a strange turn. Following our conversation, in August 2019, Hogg published a puff-piece interview with Valence Watson on *Biznews* in which he trashed Agrizzi's evidence at the Zondo Commission, but without providing proof, facts or context. Hogg started the interview by saying that if Barry Sergeant were still alive, he would have written the 'other side' of the Bosasa story – as if those of us who'd been investigating the company for much longer than he had, had based our stories solely on allegations and hearsay.

'For me, after listening to Valence Watson over much of the past two days, checking documentation and timelines and using a bit of common sense, much that was confusing in the Bosasa saga is finally starting to make sense,' Hogg wrote in introducing the interview.[12] Then, for almost 30 minutes, Valence Watson rambled on about how Agrizzi was alleged to have stolen from the company without his brother's knowledge, despite reams of evidence and documentation over 13 years showing how the Bosasa racket had operated, which Hogg had chosen to ignore.

By September 2019 Hogg was actively participating with the Watsons to whitewash Gavin's legacy by portraying Agrizzi as prime evil and Watson as a naive, innocent victim.[13]

In September 2018, as the publication I edit, *News24*, was revealing more details about payments by Bosasa to ANC politicians, Leshabane and Bosasa chairperson Joe Gumede submitted a 'dossier' to my bosses at

Media24, detailing my international flights over the previous two years and making spurious claims about my finances and the funding of a holiday to Italy I took with my wife. It was an amateurish attempt at disinformation, and I had no difficulty debunking all the allegations with facts, but it illustrated to me the desperation of those involved to find any so-called mud that might stick to their critics.

Was I scared at any point during my investigation into Bosasa? Yes, I was. I'd heard about Bosasa staff being followed, shot at or confronted in public. I'd heard about threats against journalists, but the first time it happened to me, it still came as a shock. I was warned to watch my back. 'Take different routes to work. Look around you when you drive. Don't fall into a routine,' I was advised by a security-industry operator who'd had a fallout with Bosasa.

I started to contemplate the meaning of life and my career choices: was it really worth messing with dangerous crooks with money and access to thousands of prisoners, guns and mine dumps? Unfortunately (or fortunately) for me, I couldn't objectively answer that question. I deeply believe in the power of the media to change society for the good, and simply didn't have the mental or physical ability to walk away from a story like this.

I have no regrets for sticking it out for over a decade on the Bosasa scandal, until the enormity of it finally dawned on the South African population at large.

Judge Moroa Tsoka: Protect your sources

'It is apparent that journalists, subject to certain limitations, are not expected to reveal the identity of their sources. If indeed freedom of the press is fundamental and sine qua non [an essential condition] for democracy, it is essential that in carrying out this public duty for the public good, the identity of their sources should not be revealed, particularly when the information so revealed would not have been publicly known. This essential and critical role of the media, which is more pronounced in our nascent democracy, founded on openness, where corruption has become cancerous, needs to be fostered rather than denuded.'[1]

24

Protecting my sources

In July 2009 Bosasa filed a R500 000 lawsuit against me and the *Mail & Guardian*. The sheriff of Johannesburg served the papers on us after I'd reported on Benedicta Dube's phone call. Bosasa was suing us for calling them 'corrupt' in the article.

My editor, Nic Dawes, agreed to defend the case and we started putting together our defence. During this period, Bosasa insisted that I hand over my notebooks and the recordings of interviews with my sources, source documentation, unpublished drafts of my stories, internal emails between myself, Dawes and other colleagues, and basically every piece of paper I had that referred to the company, its staff or directors. I refused.

For me, the first rule of journalism has always been, 'you shall protect your sources'. If you aren't prepared to go to prison for your sources, you shouldn't be in journalism. There was just no way that I would endanger the lives of the people who'd helped me to unravel the Bosasa scandal by handing over my notebooks to Watson and co, although the thought of eating Bosasa's prison food was almost too ghastly to contemplate!

Dawes agreed. Because of Bosasa's insistence that journalists shouldn't receive 'exceptional' protection to protect the identities of sources, a separate case was heard in February 2012 by Judge Moroa Tsoka on the matter of source protection. The *Mail & Guardian* briefed advocates Wim Trengove SC and Steve Budlender, while Bosasa brought in Jeremy Gauntlett SC from Cape Town. The South African National Editors' Forum (Sanef) supported our case as friends of the court through Advocate Kate Hofmeyr.

The hearing was brutal, with four of the country's legal heavyweights battling it out over my right to keep my sources secret. Angelo Agrizzi, Papa Leshabane and their colleagues were out in full force in the public gallery, dressed in their blue Bosasa shirts and ties.

Gauntlett hammered home his point that the press couldn't claim exceptional protection of its sources' identities simply by flashing a media card.

Trengove hit back by arguing that a ruling against me would have a chilling effect on uncovering corruption because journalists regarded the protection of their sources' identities as sacrosanct. 'Valuable resources of information that come from high places would be very significantly diminished if journalists were not able to give sources the same assurances that policemen and detectives give their informants, that their identity will be protected,' he argued.[2]

Judge Tsoka ruled in our favour in April 2012, saying we had a 'valid objection' to revealing our sources. 'Had it not been [for] the defendants' sources, the public's right to know whether the plaintiff won the tender fairly would never have been known. The public would be poorer for it. The public interest will, in my view, be served by not revealing the identity of the defendants' sources at this stage.' He rejected Gauntlett's arguments on 'press exceptionalism' and said that Bosasa should deal with the correctness of my reportage on their corruption rather than try to uncover the identities of my sources.[3]

The ruling set a legal precedent for future generations of journalists that will safeguard the protection of their sources' identities. Sanef called it a 'ground-breaking decision for media freedom'.[4]

Bosasa failed in its attempts to appeal, with the Constitutional Court ruling that it was 'not in the interest of justice' for Judge Tsoka's judgment to be challenged.[5] And the company never reinstituted the defamation suit.

Gavin Watson and his friends had spent millions trying to find out who my sources were. They clearly had plenty to hide.

PART TWO

Depravity

Denise Bjorkman: The bride of Christ

'She was always telling us that at 02:00 in the morning she had visitations from Christ, who spoke to her and gave her instructions for the day. And Gavin believed her. Gavin believes every single word Lindie Gouws says.'[1]

25

The 'affair'

For two decades, Gavin Watson presented Bosasa as a Christian company to staff and the public, while at the same time bribing politicians and civil servants; he presented the company as a BEE flagship while he was paying his white employees higher salaries from a shelf company.

He allegedly also contravened another of the Ten Commandments: 'Thou shalt not commit adultery'.[2]

Lindie Gouws, who grew up in Randfontein on the far West Rand, was a rag queen and a leader of her hostel at university. Initially employed by Meritum in the late 1990s as a personal assistant for Fanie van Zijl, she later became Watson's assistant, advisor and strategist. Gouws said she met Watson in 1996, on the day her father died, and he told her to go to the hospital and pray for her father. 'He [Watson] was like a father to me; he was phenomenal,' she said.[3]

Gouws later started a Christian ministry with Bosasa's assistance and published a (short-lived) Christian magazine called *My World* with Bosasa's money – R20 million, according to Angelo Agrizzi.[4] She disputes the amount.

A self-professed 'bride of Christ' (a title she says was used as a 'parable' to illustrate the 'relationship between us and Christ')[5] and evangelist, Gouws was a dark-haired, brown-eyed enigma. Some called her Jezebel after the 'morally unrestrained' queen in the Bible. Others referred to her as 'Mrs Watson'. A few of my interviewees described her as the most powerful

99

person at Bosasa. She was the company's spiritual leader, and decorated the office park with brass plaques engraved with Bible verses.

According to numerous former Bosasa employees, she was also Gavin Watson's mistress.

Watson's wife, Leigh-Ann, had stayed behind in Port Elizabeth when he'd moved to Johannesburg in 1996 to run Bosasa. It hadn't taken long for employees to start speculating about Watson's involvement with Gouws, who was many years his junior; and the rumours seemed substantiated after company cleaners started reporting back on what they'd seen in Watson's house in Constantia Kloof.

The stories started spreading: Gouws's underwear was seen hanging on Watson's washing-line at his house, they were seen shopping together at Dis-Chem, putting their purchases into one basket, and they were seen arriving together at a restaurant. Staff also saw interactions between them that seemed to represent a much closer relationship than Watson had with anyone else at Bosasa: Gouws shouted at the much-feared Watson in the office and spoke to him like no other employee.

Finance head Andries van Tonder remembered that he once had to finish a business plan for Watson at short notice. It was after hours when he was done. He called Watson, and 'Gavin said I can just give it to the driver to bring to his house, but I wanted to make 100% sure he [got] the document on time. So I drove to his house. The guards at the gate [to the complex where Watson stayed] normally let me in, but that night they called Gavin first. After a while, they opened the gate.

'I drove in and saw Lindie's car [at Watson's house]. I immediately realised what was going on.

'He opened the door wearing only a pair of boxer shorts. I gave him the business plan. He leaned on Lindie's BMW, just quickly paged through it, and abruptly said it was fine and he had to go.'[6]

Gouws strongly denied she had a romantic affair with Watson and said that those who implied a sexual relationship between them had made this up. 'The rumour was purposefully spread on the [Bosasa] campus that we had an affair. People have a perverted image [of our relationship].'[7]

Gavin Watson was certainly not the first CEO to allegedly have had an

THE 'AFFAIR'

affair with a female colleague, nor would he be the last, but the story is worth telling because, if true, it illustrates the depravity at the heart of a company that portrayed itself as a wholesome Christian-based haven for the most vulnerable people in society. 'The only way you can make a difference is that God must be at the centre of whatever you do,' Watson was recorded telling a men's conference at the Moreleta Park Dutch Reformed Church in 2009. 'Once he is at the centre, then you start blessing everyone around you ...'[8]

There was an urban legend on the Bosasa campus that attempted to explain Gouws's powerful status in the company. Gouws, the story went, had saved Watson's life during an armed robbery in the late 1990s, shortly after he took over management of what was then still Dyambu Operations; she'd somehow inserted herself as a human shield between Watson and a robber's bullets.

According to Angelo Agrizzi, Gouws's role in the story was exaggerated. 'There was a robbery at the Stubbs Street [Randfontein] office. They stole everybody's jewellery and made them lie down on the floor. They kicked Danny Mansell around a bit, and they wanted the safe's keys. Apparently, Gavin was on his way to the offices [and] Lindie then climbed through a window and ran and phoned [him]. She told everybody they were looking for Gavin. Truth be told, they weren't looking for Gavin. They just came to rob the business. But she convinced everybody there was an assassination attempt on Gavin's life and [that she'd] saved his life.'[9]

Gouws denied portraying herself as a 'human shield' and agreed in essence with Agrizzi's version of what had happened. Watson was 'very thankful that I had phoned him', she said.[10]

In interviews about Watson people described him as 'overpowering', 'dominating' and 'forceful' – except when it came to Gouws. 'They were like Yeats and Maud Gonne,' Denise Bjorkman said, referencing the Irish poet's turbulent affair with the actress. 'She could tell him any crap and he would believe it.'[11]

Bjorkman, a behavioural scientist, joined Bosasa in 2003 as a contractor to train the company's security guards to identify potential criminals on CCTV. She stayed on for 13 years as editor of the in-house magazine and counsellor to staff who'd experienced trauma. She was perturbed by the hold Gouws seemed to have had on Watson, and by extension on Bosasa. Bjorkman remembered witnessing Gouws throwing her car keys at Watson outside the Bosasa office once, shouting 'Where is my fucking laundry?'[12]

Bjorkman saw Watson stand up to Gouws only once. '[A]fter introducing me to the staff [as] the editor of the new magazine, Gavin said to me, "I need you to write the CEO's letter for *Bosele*," which I wrote.

'[Later,] Lindie came running into the office when I was there with Angelo [Agrizzi] and Gavin on her tail. "How dare you? Who do you think you are? Who the fuck do you think you are? How dare you write anything for Gavin? I am the only one who writes anything about Mr Watson and you have no right to do that without my permission."

'Gavin ... said, "Lindie get over yourself; I told Denise to write it."'

According to Bjorkman, Gouws's response to that was, 'Gavin, you know I know too much about you. Be careful.'[13]

But Gouws disputed Bjorkman's stories about her and said she was concerned about the impression that Watson had had to calm her down.[14]

Agrizzi recalled the CEO being 'reduced to nothing' by Gouws during a phone call while he and Watson were in Abu Dhabi to attend a Grand Prix. 'Here was this man who commanded respect with everyone else, saying sorry this and sorry that.'

Agrizzi says he stood outside Watson's hotel room until the call was over, then said to him, 'When will you stop this shit?' Agrizzi referred Watson to a Bible passage that 'you cannot expect to be blessed if you don't honour your wife'.

'And he turned around and he said, "I'm not having an affair."

'I said to him, "You are having an affair, I'm telling you now. You are the only one who doesn't know you're having an affair. Everybody fucking knows."'[15]

Agrizzi related the story of how once, when a Bosasa employee had to take Gouws to a car-repair workshop to have her BMW fixed, the owner of the garage shouted to his staff, "How far are you? It's the *grootbaas se cherrie* [big boss's girlfriend].' Gouws freaked out and insisted that the staff member be disciplined, and Bosasa never used that panelbeater again.[16]

'Everybody was scared of her and they scattered when they saw her,' Bjorkman said. Other former employees told me how Gouws would dismiss staff willy-nilly and walk around asking people if they knew who she was. Once, she fired a staff member for receiving an email with an image of a shirtless man attached. 'Lindie freaked out and the next moment the woman was chased away.'[17] (Gouws denied that she dismissed the woman for receiving a photo of a shirtless man.[18])

Both Agrizzi and Bjorkman confirmed that Gouws would tell Bosasa employees that she'd died before and had been resurrected. 'She would … tell everybody that she was brought back to life because Jesus Christ came to her and brought her back to life exactly [how] Lazarus was resurrected.'[19]

Not true, said Gouws. She was in Jerusalem during a working visit to improve relationships between South Africa and Israel when she blacked out while walking through the Old City. 'The last thing I remembered was seeing a traffic light. The next moment I woke up in the hospital.'

According to Gouws, the paramedics told her colleagues in the ambulance on the way to the hospital that they would be taking a body back to South Africa. Pressed to confirm or deny whether she believed she'd been resurrected, she said, 'I didn't leave my body, I didn't have an out-of-body experience, I just know that I came [to].' She described the stories of her so-called resurrection as 'something very precious, very intimate, that has been perverted'.[20]

Van Tonder recalled how, in his final years at Bosasa, Gouws accompanied him to KwaZulu-Natal to hand over a cheque for R1 million to *Faith Like Potatoes* preacher Angus Buchan. Gouws said she accompanied Van Tonder 'because I know uncle Angus'.[21]

Van Tonder confirmed having flown with Gouws to Buchan's farm in Greytown to deliver the cheque. 'When Gouws asked Buchan if she could speak to him alone, he refused and said I must come with.'[22] Van Tonder was under the impression that Gouws had wanted to pitch the female version of Buchan's 'Mighty Men' conferences to him.

Gouws was allowed to print her magazine, *My World*, despite the fact that the magazine made no money for Bosasa. 'It lost the company hundreds of thousands of rands per month. We joked that it was named *My*

World because she was in a world of her own,' said former employee Retief van der Merwe. 'Lindie was speaking as if she was in constant conversation with Jesus. For example, she would say that last night while she was playing the piano, the Lord said to her to speak to us about X or Z. I thought, the Lord doesn't speak to me like that. It was amazing; she had a main line to the Lord.'[23]

Bjorkman recalled, 'One day Lindie Gouws came into my office and said she was going to exorcise my office because I was married to a Jewish man. She came back a week later to say the Jews gave us Jesus and she forgives me.'[24]

Watson paid salaries to both his wife and Gouws, but according to bank statements from Consilium Business Consultants that I saw, Gouws was earning substantially more. The bank statements for November 2016 and April 2017, respectively, show Gouws earning R175 259 and R74 901 per month, while Leigh-Ann Watson was paid R46 000 for running Watson's home office in Port Elizabeth, according to Jared Watson.[25]

Gouws said the lower amount was closer to her salary, while Van Tonder remembered that she earned about R300 000 before tax per month.[26]

Auditor Peet Venter stated under oath that Gouws received a monthly salary from Consilium of R137 717 and an additional payment of R42 000 per month to cover the costs of her bond.[27] Gouws confirmed that Bosasa had paid the deposit on the purchase of her private property in an estate close to Watson's, but claimed she'd repaid the money.

Venter, who wouldn't question Watson because he would 'get upset' with him, said the payments to Gouws were 'morally disturbing' but that he couldn't complain because Watson had threatened to terminate his services.[28]

The alleged affair between Watson and Gouws became a major issue at the company's wellness centre, where Bjorkman was offering counselling. 'One of the things that came to us most often in the wellness centre was the fact that staff said this was supposed to be a Christian organisation, but why has he got the girlfriend? He [Watson] made the mistake of using the cleaners of Bosasa to clean his house. They were very smart and saw Gavin's bathroom being filled with cosmetics for him and Lindie. They would come back and ask us, "He is supposed to be a Christian, how does he justify this?"'

Gouws denied ever using or having cosmetics at Watson's house.[29]

Bjorkman said that a number of Bosasa colleagues, and especially those who attended Watson's early-morning prayer meetings, struggled to reconcile the stories of his alleged philandering ways with his religious persona. 'Some would say, "But he is a religious man; he does communion. He [can't] be a bad man." That's where faith comes in. It totally obliterates. People believed he was doing good, but he was establishing a messianic culture at the same time.'[30]

After one fallout too many with Gouws, Agrizzi told Watson 'it's me or her'. Watson roped in his trusted friend and confidant Kevin Wakeford and a pastor from Port Elizabeth to negotiate an 'exit plan' from the Bosasa campus for Gouws, who then proceeded to work from her home. But a few years later, after Agrizzi's exit from the company, Gouws was back on the Bosasa premises – this time, working from the company's guesthouse.

When I met Gouws for our interview, she showed me a R5 coin, saying that I'd got only one side of the coin and that there was 'another perspective'. For example, she said, while Watson's grownup children reportedly didn't like Gouws and gave her the cold shoulder, according to her she now enjoyed a close relationship with the Watson family.[31]

I asked her why every single person I'd spoken to who'd worked at Bosasa believed that she and Watson had had an affair. Saying that she didn't feel she had to 'give an account or make an excuse for a very good intellectual input and/or friendship [of] long standing with friends, companions and family', Gouws accused a small group of people – without naming them – of spreading this 'perverted image' of their relationship.

'Gavin was a very, very great person. I have never disclosed the impact that he has had on my life ...'[32] But 'I choose not to tell my story through you,' she said, and declared her intention to write her own book about Bosasa.

26

Let us pray

A devout Christian, Retief van der Merwe was appointed in 2004 as Bosasa security coordinator at OR Tambo International Airport in Johannesburg.

When, during his interview for the position with Gavin Watson and Angelo Agrizzi, the former highway-patrol policeman from Krugersdorp saw the bookshelf filled with Bibles, he knew Bosasa was the company for him. 'I immediately thought I could associate with these guys. We had touchpoints.'[1]

One of these was that Watson and Lindie Gouws were congregants at the church Van der Merwe himself attended, Little Falls Christian Centre. 'Angelo said he saw on my CV that I was at Little Falls Christian Centre, and said [that the company had] a prayer meeting every morning from 06:00 to 08:00 and I [was] welcome to attend. I thought that was indirectly an answer to my prayers. Angelo said Gavin Watson was there with directors of the company and they prayed together. I got the impression they wanted to see how committed you were.'[2]

Van der Merwe said that attendees at the prayer meetings included 'Gavin, Angelo and Lindie Gouws ... Andries and Leon van Tonder, Joe Gumede, Papa Leshabane, Ishmael Mncwaba, Thandi Makoko, Jackie Leyds, Ryno Roode and Danie van Tonder.'

Watson would decide who in the group would 'bring the Word' and that person was required to read a few verses from the Bible, which would then be discussed by the group. 'Sometimes Gavin would elaborate on the section and put it in context with what was happening in the world, and then everyone [got] a chance to pray.'

Van der Merwe sometimes felt that Watson's 'sermons' weren't on point, but he soon realised his CEO wasn't someone you could confront or challenge. 'If he spoke, you listened.'

And it didn't take Van der Merwe long to figure out that attendees were there to 'impress Gavin, not to have a conversation with God'. Lindie Gouws in particular would 'go on and on and pray for his wisdom and call him the pillar of the company'.

One day, Van der Merwe recalled, Gouws told the group that the Lord had told her that the three windows behind Watson symbolised the Father, the Son and the Holy Spirit. 'She said Gavin was the anointed one and that we must bless him. We had to point our hands towards him and pray for him, the Alfa and the Omega.' Van der Merwe said this was when he realised that there was was more going on than met the eye.[3]

Bjorkman mentioned that Watson would even organise communion for staff, with wafers and mock wine.[4]

Angelo Agrizzi said Bosasa's 'Christian culture' also attracted him. 'I believed it was Godsent.'[5]

As Gavin Watson's right-hand man, Agrizzi had to attend the daily prayer meetings. 'So we started every morning, and I believe, I really do, that it was sincere. So from 06:30 to 08:00 it would continue, but it became kind of a cult. They would invite prophets, not much dissimilar to what you see on TV. They would invite certain pastors from occasion to occasion. They would lead these prayer meetings and then they would have all-night prayer meetings as well, but quite simply, it was a mockery, and I had compromised [myself] by even being part of it. But, you see, Gavin Watson was a very charismatic leader and he had a lot of influence over all his employees.'[6]

Watson would sometimes use the prayer meeting to embarrass or challenge people, Van der Merwe said. '[The company's auditors Ryno Viljoen and Gerrie Bester] were put under pressure by Watson to pray. Gerrie didn't want to pray but Ryno prayed. They didn't like what Ryno was praying at all. He asked the Lord to give us wisdom and help us stay on the right path. After that, he was banned from attending the prayer meeting again ... [The financial director] Andries van Tonder was given an instruction to look for new auditors. We never saw Ryno again at the prayer meeting.'[7]

Over time, the prayer meetings became more general, with attendees discussing company matters. 'There was no longer intense praying. I just sat and read my Bible. They spoke about meetings that would happen outside of company structures. They [Watson and the other directors] would often meet at night, probably to discuss the corruption. I started realising that what they said before and behind you were not the same thing.'[8]

Leshabane, a company director and spokesperson, often reeked of alcohol during prayer meetings, said Van der Merwe. 'He started attending less and less. Papa sat next to me and I could smell him. Gavin said no booze was allowed in the company; he even removed the alcohol from Bosasa's suites at sport stadiums. I just laughed when I heard from the testimony at the Zondo Commission that they used Jumbo Liquor to launder money.'[9]

It was well known by then that one of the directors had had an extramarital affair with a staff member and they wanted Watson to address it with him. 'But it was clear to me that Gavin was compromised and couldn't speak to [the director] about this. His own sexual life was in dispute.'[10]

Watson introduced the 'Daniel fast' at Bosasa, during which those who participated had to avoid meat, alcohol and rich foods for 40 days. The company made fruit and vegetables available for those who were fasting, but not everyone complied after hours. 'Driving home, I would see Andries van Tonder stuffing his [face] with hamburgers at McDonald's.'[11]

Van der Merwe spoke about a prophet who regularly visited Bosasa to pray for the directors and staff. He was paid a monthly stipend and also given cash from Watson's walk-in safe. 'One day he arrived and told Watson in front of all of us that Bosasa was built on the wrong foundations. He told Watson to sort out the foundations of the company fast, because if he [didn't], the company would crumble. ... [The prophet] was chased away and his monthly payments stopped.'[12]

A few days later, Watson brought a family friend, the gospel singer Ken

Larkin, to Johannesburg from Port Elizabeth to 'give a prophecy to us that everything will go well with Bosasa. I saw right through their façade. This was not about the Lord, but about them,' said Van der Merwe.

Van der Merwe started asking questions in the prayer meetings after my articles about Bosasa's alleged corruption started to appear in the press. 'In my naivety, I asked Watson if any of these allegations [were] true. He exploded like a cracker. "How dare you ask this?" he shouted. I was made out as the biggest idiot.'

Denise Bjorkman remembered that staff aspired to be invited to the prayer meetings, where company secrets were shared. 'They enjoyed a Freemason type of reputation, suggesting something secret, their own religion, their own God and their own rules, contrary to mainstream religious sects. Some attendance was motivated only to get acceptance into the Watson inner circle. But information sought was doled out piecemeal like crumbs in a bird park. Watson had an acute sense of timing and the dramatic, and knew how to drop tidbits of information about what was really happening behind the scenes, and then pull back abruptly, leaving attendees gasping for more.'[13]

When she asked Watson which church's beliefs he was following, he told her, 'I am the church.' 'Membership to his church drew disproportionally from management and the board of directors. Christian Bibles were ubiquitous.'[14]

When in the late 2000s Watson tried to give money to Pastor Theuns Blom from Little Falls Christian Centre (LFCC), Blom declined, saying it was against the church's principles. 'Gavin believed you could smooth anyone with money,' said Van der Merwe. (After his death in August 2019, a memorial service was held for Watson at the LFCC.)

The ex cop, who was still a deeply religious man, told me that Watson had printed photos of me and Willie Hofmeyr, the SIU head who was pursuing the Bosasa-corruption investigation. 'He blessed you; he prayed for you,' Van der Merwe said.

And Agrizzi told me that I had my own scripture at Bosasa that Watson quoted over me – Psalm 35. I looked it up.

> 1 *Plead my cause, O Lord, with them that strive with me: fight against them that fight against me.*
> 2 *Take hold of shield and buckler, and stand up for mine help.*
> 3 *Draw out also the spear, and stop the way against them that persecute me: say unto my soul, I am thy salvation.*[15]

'You must understand that when someone prays for you and blesses you, but they are busy with other things, it can turn into a curse,' Van der Merwe told me. 'That's what is happening to Gavin today. The cult that he had, where everyone had to worship him, where he was the authority in those prayer meetings, it turned into a curse.'

Van der Merwe confessed to me that he went through a deep religious crisis after realising that Watson was using religion to hide his corruption and manipulate his staff. 'It took me a year after leaving Bosasa to figure out how you [could] reconcile Christianity and manipulation through Christianity and money. How [could] you do that? I realised the mistake [was] not with Christianity or the Bible, but with them. They made compromises. Gavin made compromises with Lindie Gouws and with money. All the guys around that prayer table made one or other compromise to manipulate the word of God to fit in with their lifestyles. To me, they became an embodiment of the devil. The devil bamboozled them with money; they suddenly had money.

'At one point in his life, all the Watson brothers lived in one flat. They had poverty. Angelo's evidence was that he came out of poverty. That poverty brought them to a point where they only had money. There is a saying, "They were so poor, they only had money." Their people relationships completely collapsed; they valued themselves higher than other people because they had money.'[16]

Watson thought he was the 'king of the place and the story', said Van der Merwe. 'He was the king of South Africa. In his brain, he was on his way to become the king of Africa. If you [were] a young Christian or a Christian just in name, you [would] fall for his nonsense. He's got a very strong personality; he [was] very persuasive.'

Bosasa's success in winning government tenders contributed to many employees believing that Watson was a 'saviour, a highly religious man, appointed by God', Bjorkman said.[17] She explained, 'Many staff had normal religious beliefs. But there were people who were religious fanatics. They would come into your office and "Hallelujah!" and start praying and put their hands on you. There were these little plaques all over the park with quotes from the Bible. Lindie Gouws put these up all over so that the entire park was blessed.'

Van der Merwe said, 'In the prayer meetings, upcoming tenders and how they must position the company were discussed. This information wasn't even in the public domain. If you are a Christian in good standing and a Christian principled company, you don't buy cars and overseas trips for senior government officials like Patrick Gillingham and Linda Mti. Bosasa's corruption was clouded in this Christian cloud and they might have thought that hiding in this cloud will cover or blind people to see the truth.

'That is where the Bosasa cult came in; all the prayers were focused to enrich a few, although it was said that a large portion of the company was going to benefit from an employees' trust. No employee ever benefited from this trust. The objective of all the prayers and Christian functions was to enrich the directors, [and] ultimately the Watsons, their close friends like Agrizzi, ministers and people who assisted to get the tenders awarded. The Bosasa way was to manipulate, corrupt and steal from companies and the government and sugarcoat it in a Christian façade.'[18]

After hearing how speakers at Watson's memorial service in August 2019 mocked the idea that Bosasa was a cult, Van der Merwe revealed to me how boxes containing tender submissions were anointed with oil before they were submitted. 'When the tender is announced in the *Government Gazette* you attend all the site visits, the tender briefings, and collect all the documentation and information. You prepare your documentation and technical and financial response, and even get somebody on the adjudication committee to come and advise and peruse your submission. However, you do this after hours [so] that your staff don't see what is happening.

'You then seal the tender boxes with your final submission, take them to the prayer meeting on the morning of the submission, anoint them with oil and pray over the submissions. All of this was part of the Bosasa cult ritual."[19]

What particularly irked Van der Merwe was how religion was manipulated to deify Watson. At his memorial service, Watson was hailed by his family and former colleagues as an exemplary Christian leader, and former minister Nomvula Mokonyane even went so far as to compare him to Jesus Christ.[20]

27

The Donald Trump of Krugersdorp

'He talks like Donald Trump. He relies on stock phrases, like "it's amazing!" or "you'll never believe it!". He's not the brightest. He lacks vocabulary,' said behavioural scientist Denise Bjorkman, who's analysed thousands of people and personalities, and who worked closely with Gavin Watson for many years.[1]

And talking, it seemed, wasn't the only thing Watson had in common with Trump. During all my interviews, the struggle-brother-turned-businessman was described to me as 'narcissistic' (he exercised obsessively and received Botox injections, according to former colleagues), a bully and, above all, a hypocrite who was preaching the gospel while bribing his way to the top.

Retief van der Merwe said, 'Gavin became a demigod. Lindie Gouws whispered [sweet nothings] in his ear and told him how good and beautiful he was, and he believed it.'[2] Witnesses at the Zondo Commission called him 'untouchable' and said he was 'intimidating' and that they feared him.

Bjorkman said that while Watson probably didn't ever consider himself a cult leader, this impression was created by 'the ingredients he put in place unwittingly, unconsciously, which fed his ego and his hubris ... together with the constant messages that were all around on the brass plaques and the behaviours that were expected' of Bosasa employees – 'the way we honoured him'. 'We would call him Gavin, but if you crossed the line, he would pull you back and you would have to call him Mr Watson. He constantly reinforced that.'[3]

'Status and dominance' were very important to him, said Bjorkman, who described how, when Watson walked from his office towards those of other staff members, 'you could hear him shouting, because he never spoke quietly; we could hear him coming from 300 metres away' and 'all of us would move into position straight away ... So it was that obeisance, that adulation, that forced respect, that pervaded and that he inculcated.'[4]

Watson was 'very, very loud', Bjorkman added. 'I have never heard Gavin speak quietly. He walks in and he shouts. He overwhelms a room.'

Watson styled himself as a 'big man' leader and ruled with fear. Bjorkman believed Watson fit the profile of Machiavelli – the Italian politician, philosopher and poet famous for saying it was better to be feared than to be loved. 'He could turn on the charm, turn on the empathy, and switch right back again.'[5]

I heard countless stories of how staff would shake in their shoes when Watson walked around the Bosasa business park and popped into different offices. 'The energy completely changed when he came walking towards your office. We were afraid of him. He demanded fear,' an ex-employee told me.[6]

'He totally disregards you in terms of who you are. There is no respect,' said Bjorkman. 'He will get straight to the point and then walk out in the middle of a conversation as if you don't exist. ... Sometimes he would greet you and sometimes he would just walk past you although you greeted him. He would ignore you.'[7]

During staff meetings, Watson would humiliate employees who dared to ask questions about the employees' trust, which supposedly owned 22% of Bosasa but never paid dividends to employees, or about bonuses.

And he would often belittle staff in other ways too. 'One day Gavin walked into our office and asked me there and then to recite the Lord's Prayer,' said the ex-employee. 'I didn't know the English version and told Watson it wasn't part of my job to recite the Lord's Prayer. He was furious and told my line manager to sort me out.'[8]

Like Donald Trump, Watson was known for making cruel and disparaging remarks about overweight employees, shaming them in front of their colleagues. 'He would walk up to an overweight lady and ask her in front of everyone, "Why are you so fat?"[9]

And the Trump comparison went further than Watson's platitudes. 'Labour laws meant little to Watson,' said Bjorkman. 'He would shout, "You're fired!" in order to embarrass select individuals who were believed to [have shown] disrespect or displays of behaviour which ran contrary to his own code of ethics …

'Staff were convinced that Watson was influenced by Donald Trump and the dictatorial role he crafted for himself in his famous *The Apprentice* TV programme. His posture and use of the ejecting words, "You're fired!" mimicked Trump's style with little deviation. Watson's summary dismissals led to a significant number of CCMA [Commission for Conciliation, Mediation and Arbitration] hearings.'[10]

Agrizzi said that Watson was 'absolutely obsessed' with his health and longevity. 'He would take in the morning, I counted, 28 vitamins. Gavin is fighting death. He believes he will live forever; he believes he is immortal. He sat with me in the car and said, "I won't die soon. I'm gonna live [to] over 100."'[11]

Bjorkman had a similar view. 'You could see when he was Botoxed. He would have the wrinkles, then he would come back a day later and he would have this Helen Zille face.'[12]

Watson was prone to paranoia, which was particularly triggered by the stories journalists such as myself were writing about Bosasa's corruption. 'Once you started publishing … there was paranoia in the park,' Bjorkman told me. 'Everyone was under suspicion. We had an idea that our offices were bugged … Everybody was paranoid, too scared to speak to anybody. When the directors came to us in our offices, they spoke quietly, in hushed terms, so the paranoia prevailed and everybody thought Armageddon was coming, and of course you [here Bjorkman was referring to me personally] were the *verraaier* [traitor]. You were the focal point of everything that was going to happen. You were the all-powerful and I remember Gavin saying once, "Find dirt on him, find dirt on Adriaan Basson." I remember him saying that.'[13]

Van der Merwe put money at the centre of Watson's personality and behaviour. 'Money became everything for him. Everything revolved around money. He would walk around at OR Tambo airport, and between his car and building, greet security guards in Xhosa, and walk with a roll of bank notes and give them each R100. I think it was an embarrassment for those guys. Everything in the company was about money.'[14]

Bjorkman concurred. 'Gavin [was] driven by money ... status, money and glory.'[15]

Van der Merwe once overheard Watson telling someone that he had no scruples about bribing traffic officers. 'He said when he was caught in a speed trap, he easily pays R200. He refuses to pay for speeding fines or traffic fines.'

Watson, who didn't have a tertiary qualification, styled himself as a self-made entrepreneur and business guru. 'He would say that even though all his brothers and his wife had degrees and he didn't, he had the Bible. Yes, there are lots of lessons in the Bible, but you can't learn from the Bible how the JSE or a balance sheet works. There is a big difference between wisdom and knowledge,' said Van der Merwe.

At the height of Watson's hubris he established the 'Watson Corporate University', Bosasa's training facility, where senior staff members taught employees for a pseudo qualification. He also launched blogs called WATSONline and TRUTHonline, on which he would share business platitudes.

Van der Merwe believed that Watson surrounded himself with weaklings and people from poor backgrounds whom he could 'buy'. A number of Bosasa's senior executives, for example, didn't have any relevant business qualifications or the experience required for their roles, but received massive salaries and couldn't leave. Watson reminded experienced white employees that they would struggle to find other jobs in South Africa. Others had addiction problems or were personally compromised in other ways, such as for sexual indiscretions, which Watson knew of.

'He makes you feel like a million bucks,' recalled Agrizzi about the initial few meetings he had with Watson when he first joined Dyambu Operations. But after working closely with him for almost two decades, Agrizzi came to believe that Watson's management style – if it can be called that – was to create camps in the organisation and set people up against each other.

First, Agrizzi himself was brought into the company and set up against Danny Mansell, one of the original founders, to head up operations. In later years Papa Leshabane was groomed as a future CEO to take over from Watson while Agrizzi was waiting in the wings for this position. This created enormous polarisation in the organisation and ultimately contributed to Agrizzi's exit.

Van der Merwe described an incident that also illustrated this. In 2010 he went on a work trip to Germany with his colleagues Joe Gumede and Trevor Mathenjwa, who headed up Sondolo IT. While there, Van der Merwe received the news that police chief Jackie Selebi had been convicted of corruption for accepting bribes from drug dealer Glenn Agliotti. He shared the news with his colleagues. 'I said it was excellent news and that justice had prevailed.'

A few months later, on his way to the daily prayer meeting at Bosasa, Van der Merwe overheard Gumede telling Watson about how he (Van der Merwe) had supposedly jumped with joy at hearing about the Selebi conviction. 'He's out! He's out of this company!' Watson had allegedly responded. 'Gavin went off about my "apartheid thinking" and kept on saying, "He's finished! He's out!"'

And yet when Van der Merwe entered the prayer room a few minutes later, everyone continued as if nothing had happened and Watson never confronted him.[16]

28

Sex on the desk

'He was a real hustler. He was screwing every woman in the park. But he had a standard – after having sex with them, he would buy them a fridge. So you knew, anyone who got a new fridge had had a good time with him.'[1]

Bosasa's 'Christian character', exemplified in the daily prayer meetings and brass plaques plastered with Bible verses all over the Mogale Business Park, didn't prevent a culture of sexual promiscuity from flourishing at the company.

One director in particular – one who attended the prayer meetings – was named as a sexual predator who had an eye for 'young girls and virgins' at the office park. 'It was a sexual free-for-all on the campus for him. He had his hands up the girls' dresses. These little girls were fresh out of university and very virginal. He didn't give a damn; he would screw these women in the office and these girls saw what was happening.'[2]

Another senior executive was caught having sex with one of the company's accountants on the desk of a boardroom. 'It was very clear what was happening. Someone walked into the boardroom and the two of them were there. He [the executive] played the field.'[3]

More than one of my sources told me about a luxury penthouse in one of Sandton's five-star hotels where 'wild orgies' were allegedly organised for politicians and other influential people who could bless or were blessed by Bosasa. 'We thought the suite was used for meetings. Little did we know,' said one.[4]

Then there was the Mogale Lodge, situated in a leafy part of the Bosasa campus and built to accommodate the company's guests and visitors. Decorated with the type of very bright African paintings typically sold at flea markets, brown leather couches and a variety of pot plants, the lodge was also allegedly the scene of numerous trysts between employees, executives and visitors. 'The cleaners started to complain of all the semen in the lodge – on the desks, on the floor, on the beds.'[5]

Another famous Bosasa legend tells of a delegation of male software developers, visiting from India, who stayed over at the lodge during a working visit, and many of whom had intimate encounters with a certain senior female employee of the company.

These salacious stories are merely an illustration of how large-scale corruption doesn't occur in a void; the breakdown of morality and the rise of depravity doesn't just happen overnight. These anecdotes illustrate the two realities in which Bosasa operated – the world of Bible scriptures and prayer, and the parallel world of sexual predators, promiscuity and extra-marital affairs.

And all these stories came to the same conclusion: 'There was nothing Gavin could do about it because of Lindie Gouws.' Watson's own moral standing was fatally compromised by his alleged affair with the editor of Bosasa's Christian magazine.

29

The k-bomb

'And then one morning Gavin Watson dropped the k-bomb in front of me.'

Retief van der Merwe recalled the shock of hearing this – like 'a bucket of cold water'. 'Me, him and Angelo were in the room. He told Angelo, "You'd better get these k****rs in line." After that he called them "darkies".'¹

So Watson's hypocrisy wasn't restricted to having an alleged affair and bribing politicians while preaching the Lord's word, my sources told me. He – the struggle hero, model Christian and champion of BEE – was also incredibly racist.

Four other former Bosasa staffers confirmed to me that they'd heard Watson using the k-word to refer to the company's black employees. Coloured people would sometimes be referred to as 'hottentotte'.

Using this kind of extreme derogatory language isn't only morally reprehensible; it's illegal. In November 2017 Johannesburg estate agent Vicki Momberg was convicted on four counts of criminal crimen injuria for using the k-word towards a black police officer after a smash-and-grab incident. She was sentenced to two years in prison.²

Bjorkman said that Watson once told her and Agrizzi, 'Why do you think I employ these k****rs? Because they're stupid. They've got nothing between the ears. They're thick and I can control them. I can do whatever I want with them; they need the money.'³

(In June 2019 Gavin Watson was ordered by the Gauteng High Court to pay back millions in BEE mining shares in Ntsimbintle, a company that owns the majority of a manganese mine in the Northern Cape, after he effectively stole from black investors by pretending they would benefit black entities. In reality, Watson and his family had pocketed the money.[4])

In September 2018 the racism at Bosasa burst into the open when a secret recording of a meeting between Agrizzi and Watson's children, Roth and Lindsay, and nephew, Jared, was leaked to *City Press*. In the recording, Agrizzi goes on a racist tirade against Bosasa's black directors, particularly Papa Leshabane and Joe Gumede, accusing them of misleading Gavin Watson. 'Those k****rs ... I'm telling you, they are k****rs alright, because they are screwing your father with information that he shouldn't listen to,' Agrizzi ranted.[5] 'Those k****rs have done nothing for your father. What is it that they are holding over his head? What is it?... That k****r just needs a good hiding.' Roth, Lindsay and Jared can be heard laughing.

Bjorkman said she was surprised to hear Agrizzi's racist tirade because she'd never heard him making racist remarks at Bosasa. 'The black staff loved Angelo. He treated them with respect. He never made racial comments in my presence,' she said.[6]

The timing and context of this meeting and the leaked recording are worth noting. A few weeks before, in mid-August 2018, Agrizzi had released a media statement saying that he was ready to blow the whistle on 'racketeering, corruption and money laundering' that he'd been aware of 'over the last 18 years' at Bosasa.[7] I knew this was big: Agrizzi was at the heart of the company's capture of state institutions, politicians and civil servants. Jason Stoltz, Bosasa's former head of marketing, described Watson and Agrizzi, respectively, as 'the king and the general'.[8]

It wasn't long after this that Roth, Lindsay and Jared Watson had the meeting with Agrizzi at his palatial Dainfern house, which one or more of them recorded without Agrizzi's knowledge.

At the same time, my colleague Kyle Cowan, an investigative journalist, was working on a story that veteran ANC MP Vincent Smith had been a recipient of Bosasa's largesse during and after his tenure as chairperson of parliament's portfolio committee on correctional services, which is supposed to keep tabs on the DCS's spending patterns. Cowan had obtained proof that Smith had received at least R670 000 in cash (which Smith called a loan) and home-security equipment worth R200 000 from Bosasa.[9] This was crushingly disappointing: at the beginning of his term in 2009, Smith had been a vocal critic of Bosasa. I'd had several off-the-record telephone conversations with him at the time, during which I'd given him background on Bosasa's corrupt relationship with the DCS.

A day before we published Cowan's story on *News24*, I called my colleague Mondli Makhanya, editor of Media24's Sunday newspaper *City Press*, to offer him the Vincent Smith-Bosasa story, and Makhanya burst out laughing – they too had a Bosasa lead for the following day. The Agrizzi racist recording had been leaked to them and they'd built a lead story out of it.

It was immediately clear to me that the Watson faction in Bosasa had leaked the recording to *City Press* in an attempt to distract attention from the story *News24* was about to publish about Bosasa's payments to Vincent Smith. Makhanya and I decided to publish both stories in both titles the next day.

The following day, writing on *News24*, I quoted Professor Xolela Mangcu, who said that South Africa had two big problems: racism and corruption. 'The racists, he explained, point fingers at the corrupt to justify their hateful ways, and the corrupt point to the racists when they are caught with their hands in the cookie jar.'[10] I pointed out that both the Bosasa stories were important: 'If Watson and his cronies hope the story about large-scale corruption at Bosasa (now trading as African Global) will disappear because of the k-word, he is wrong. And if Agrizzi hopes the story about his alleged racism will disappear because of the c-word, he is mistaken.' And both should face the wrath of the law, I concluded.

On 27 June 2019 Agrizzi pleaded guilty to hate speech in a settlement reached with the South African Human Rights Commission (SAHRC) that saw him donating R200 000 to the Barney Mokgatle Foundation in Alexandra that promotes social cohesion, non-racialism and social justice; he would also participate in the foundation's activities. And he issued an unconditional apology for his racist outburst.[11]

Buang Jones, regional manager for the SAHRC, said that they would pursue the Watson children, Lindsay and Roth, and their cousin, Jared

Watson, for disseminating and publishing the racist recording.[12]

Jared admitted to secretly recording Agrizzi, but said it was done for a good reason: Agrizzi was effectively trying to blackmail them with the press statement into handing over control of Bosasa to him and his partners. 'I was just allowing him to talk. He was spilling the beans,' Jared said. 'I wasn't there as a moral agent. I significantly objected to it [the racist language] … he was getting loose-lipped, [and] I wanted to see if he would admit that what he'd said in the press statement [that he was ready to blow the whistle on racketeering, corruption and money laundering] was nonsense.'[13]

During my interviews for this book, I asked numerous former Bosasa employees about the prevalence of racism in the company and how this influenced power dynamics, bearing in mind Bosasa was presented as a model BEE company and was richly rewarded for this by the government.

'There was very much white control in the company,' said Stoltz. 'The head of IT, the head of Kgwerano, the head of HR, the head of marketing, compliance, Sondolo IT, were all white; there [were] still a lot of white decision-makers. A director called Agrizzi "Treasury" because he carried the chequebook.'[14]

In the last two to three years of Bosasa's existence there had been 'massive racial undercurrents in the group', Stoltz said, adding that this was driven largely by Watson himself. 'When he sits in front of the white guys, he would say, "These bloody [black] guys don't know what they are doing." And when he sits in front of the black directors, he would say, "The whites are defunct." He would play you.'

A former senior manager who wanted to remain anonymous said he'd personally heard Watson use the k-word. 'I've heard him use the k-word in the office, with white staff around him. I was in the car with him and he said, "These bloody oxygen thieves", referring to the black security guys. He was by no means a person who was completely transformed [but] he would always preach empowerment because he knew he had business with government and had to sing that song.'

Towards the end of Bosasa/AGO's existence, there was a big drive by some of the black directors to get hold of the payslips of white managers to expose the discrepancies in salaries. 'They didn't know … what the white guys earned; they could only see salaries to a certain threshold,' Stoltz said. 'A week after I was retrenched, they put my salary up on a screen for everyone to see. The undercurrent was that Agrizzi wielded too much power [and white employees were paid more]. I sat in a meeting where Gavin said this out of his own mouth to me and Agrizzi: "A white guy will never be a director in this business while I'm here. Whites can earn more than the blacks, but you will never be a director." Out of his mouth.'[15]

When Watson was confronted about the payment discrepancies, he would blame Agrizzi, even though he (Watson) had approved all the salaries. 'Remember, Gavin never signed anything,' said Stoltz.

In his affidavit to the Zondo Commission, Agrizzi stipulated how his annual earnings had skyrocketed from R187 000 in 1999 to an astronomical R5.1 million in 2013, excluding a bonus of R2.4 million. Parallel payments were made to his wife, Debbie, until 2004; from 2005 Agrizzi received two salaries – one paid by Bosasa, and the other from Consilium, the Bosasa front company that paid white employees to keep their salaries off Bosasa's books for BEE purposes.

Leaked bank statements from Consilium prove that mostly white employees and managers, Watson family members and Lindie Gouws were paid from this company's account. But in November 2016 Leshabane and Ishmael Dikani, two black directors, were paid R100 each from the Consilium account. Why? 'Just so that they could say it is not true that only whites were paid from Consilium,' said a source.[16]

Bjorkman told me about a conversation she had with Jurgen Smith, who operated Consilium for Watson, shortly before his death. 'He was very ill and came to my office. … [Colleague] Thembi [Modungwa] and I were sitting there and he bends down and pats us both on the shoulders and he said, "I just want you to know, I want a clean slate. I did what I had to do because Gavin told me to. I don't want to die with this as a blemish on my character." And that was that. We never saw him again.'[17]

30

Rape and death

Bosasa had tenders with the provincial social development departments in Gauteng, North West, the Western Cape, Limpopo, the Northern Cape and the Eastern Cape to manage facilities where 'child inmates' between the ages of 14 and 17 were kept. And, aside from counselling Bosasa employees on being bullied by their bosses, sexually harassed by their colleagues or experiencing internal moral conflict about lived hypocrisy, Denise Bjorkman and her staff at the wellness centre had to treat caregivers and educators who had been raped by young inmates at these youth development centres.

'The caregivers were reportedly raped by the youth. They were strong, violent, and a number of times rapes, muggings and assaults were reported to us,' Bjorkman said.[1] 'Maybe five a year that we knew of who were assaulted, raped or told to bring in drugs or their lives would depend on it.' But 'the physical attacks on these women were fairly common', Bjorkman added, and stressed that 'one rape is too much'. 'My understanding from these people was that they weren't debriefed, given compassionate leave or any special consideration.'[2]

The women, who were mainly in their 20s and 30s, 'would come to us completely traumatised, not knowing if they have Aids', said Bjorkman. 'They were just told to come back to work the next day. Some of the heads of the youth centres were cruel and vicious.'

Bjorkman said that many of the educators seemed poorly educated for the responsible task at hand. 'A lot of them couldn't read or write; they were illiterate. We had a programme to teach these people the basics, how to read and write.'

Describing the setup in the youth centres, Bjorkman said, 'You had a whole line of classes and there was a corridor, and what they did was to put the youth educators inside ... The security guards would lock the educators in the classrooms alone with these young inmates. That's where the violence took place. They would lock them in, and the security guard would sit outside, and sometimes he would disappear or be fast asleep and they [the teachers] could not exit the classroom.

'One of them was so traumatised we had to hospitalise her. She was attacked. She was locked in and she had a medical condition ... she took high-blood-pressure drugs which made her feel like she has sinusitis and the sinus medicine made her very sleepy. She became a direct target [because of her drowsiness]. She came to us and we got hold of the in-house doctor and asked him to review her medication.

'Eventually she died. I am not sure what the reason was, but these women were incredibly traumatised being locked up with these very violent youths.'[3]

The Lindela repatriation camp, which Meritum/Dyambu/Bosasa/African Global Operations had managed for the department of home affairs since 1996, was another scene of crime. (According to the National Treasury's database, by March 2019 the company had been paid R1.8 billion for this contract, making it Bosasa's second-most-lucrative contract after the DCS catering tender.)

Shortly after Watson and Mansell took over the running of Lindela in 1997, negative stories began appearing in the media about the maltreatment of foreigners at the centre – it was this that prompted the ANC women who owned shares in Dyambu to request Watson to 'delink' them from Lindela.

Lindela is essentially a privately run prison for detained foreigners who've been arrested by the police for various reasons, but often for being in South Africa illegally or not having the correct documentation. Between 1.5 and 3.5 million immigrants live in South Africa, most of them from Zimbabwe, which makes running a repatriation camp a lucrative business, particularly in a country with xenophobic tendencies where foreigners often have to seek shelter from attacks.[4]

Horror stories about human-rights abuses, assaults and deaths at Lindela abound. In 2017 Doctors Without Borders, the international humanitarian medical non-governmental organisation known for its projects in conflict zones, released a report in which it detailed how Lindela had illegally detained dozens of children and how seven immigrants had died there in suspicious circumstances in 2015.

In 2005, when home affairs had extended Bosasa's contract to operate Lindela, it took away the provision of health and medical facilities. Another service provider was supposed to be brought in to provide healthcare, but this never happened. In 2014 the SAHRC had found that Bosasa had infringed detainees' rights to health care but still home affairs extended the company's contract for a further five years. So the clinic at the facility was dysfunctional, and five of the seven people who'd died had been given headache tablets for serious injuries.[5]

Journalist Joan van Dyk closely tracked the dysfunctionality that was Lindela and published the harrowing account of a toddler's death at the hands of Lindela staff in February 2019, after Agrizzi started spilling the beans at the Zondo Commission.[6]

Four-year-old Sinoxolo Hlabanzana was with his aunt Irene Malumbu, a Congolese citizen, when she was arrested by police on the streets of Yeoville in 2004 and taken to Lindela. Although Sinoxolo was a South African citizen and his mother was at home, the police refused to let him go.

Malumbu and the little boy were kept in Lindela's women's ward for two weeks, during which time Sinoxolo's father tried in vain to get his son released. The child developed a fever and diarrhoea, and Lindela's clinic did nothing to help. He went hungry and without medicine. Eventually, he was taken to Leratong Hospital, where he died alone. He was buried at the Kagiso Cemetery, without his parents being informed.

Van Dyk reckoned that many more Lindela detainees died and were buried there without a nameplate or a cross. My sources agreed, with some being even more cynical about what really happened. 'We heard many stories of bodies being dumped down mine shafts or buried under concrete blocks. Remember, there were many camps at Lindela – the Somalis, the Nigerians, the Zimbabweans – and they would fight. People knew where to get ammunition and sometimes there was enough violence for someone to be killed [by security guards]. Bodies would just disappear.'[7]

Nobody wanted to go on the record about this, but I was told about bloodied bakkies that came back late at night and had to be hosed down; of bloodied pools of water in the morning; and of registers that had to be rewritten to remove the names of deceased immigrants.

The authorities' investigation into Bosasa's remains should go deeper than the corruption perpetrated over two decades, to bring justice to the loved ones of Sinoxolo Hlabanzana and all the other victims of human-rights abuses at the company's facilities.

PART THREE

A good comrade

June Petersen: Vernie's oath

'He said to me, "You know I've always told you that I would lay down my life for the ANC." He said, "If they need me now, I will go and I will do it."'[1]

31

The Mitchells Plain Youth Movement

Vivian 'Vernie' Patrick Petersen was born on 22 March 1958 and grew up in Constantia, the affluent and beautiful Cape Town suburb known for its rich history and wine farms. When Petersen was 3 years old his family were forcibly removed from their precious land because they were coloured and Constantia had been declared a white neighbourhood.

The Group Areas Act of 1950, introduced by the NP government of DF Malan, was one of the most brutal pieces of racist legislation used by the apartheid government to segregate races and enrich white people for generations. It handed the most valuable and pristine land to white property owners through law, and left a legacy with which the country is still grappling 70 years later. If it hadn't been for apartheid and the Act, the Petersen family would have been well-off today as the owners of some of the most prestigious suburban property in the country.

Vernie Petersen's family was moved to a flat, desolate stretch of the Western Cape called the Cape Flats, which would become a landmark of poverty and violence over the next few decades. His mother died when he was very young, and he had to compete with eight siblings for attention and pocket money. Every day he walked for almost an hour from his family home in Heideveld to attend Modderdam High School in Bonteheuwel, where he met close friends and activists Trevor Oosterwyk and Leon Scott.

Because of hardships at home, Petersen had to move to his Auntie May's in Heideveld. She taught him how to cook – 'rotis, pastries, curries and biryani'. 'He loved cooking,' said June Petersen, his widow and the mother of their two boys.²

Maybe it was the hardships of his childhood years that influenced Petersen's life choices – to become a social-justice warrior for the frail, fragile and downtrodden in society. He passed matric and won a bursary from the Garment Workers Union through one of his sisters to study for a diploma in social work from the University of the Western Cape. He finished his diploma and got a job at Child Welfare in Mitchells Plain. 'He wanted to make a difference in children's lives; he wanted to make sure they were safe,' said June.

It was in Mitchells Plain that Vernie Petersen's political activism germinated. In the 1970s he and June were part of the electricity petition committee, protesting to the city council for issuing electricity bills before the end of the month and then adding interest to the amounts unpaid because residents hadn't yet received their salaries.

'We used to be a group, and then we said okay, let's go and work,' June recalled. 'So the two of us [June and Vernie] would go down the street and you would knock on every door and you would go and speak to each and every person ... And we would do the street meetings. Then we would meet in one person's house ... and then there would be a mass meeting in the civic. So everybody in the community was on board about this, you know. And then I noticed that when I came out of the last house, Vernie would be waiting for me and that is how I suppose we started going together.'³

The young group of activists then started the Mitchells Plain Youth Movement, which had a branch in each area to mobilise around campaigns like opposing the apartheid tricameral parliament of 1984–1994, in which coloured and Indian people exercised a measure of authority but black South Africans were excluded. 'We did the Portland branch. It was Bonita Bennett, myself, Neil Cole, Zelda Holtzman, Trevor Oosterwyk and those guys.'

Michael Weeder, the dean of St George's cathedral in Cape Town, remembered Vernie Petersen as part of an 'informal group of activists' who mobilised the residents of Mitchells Plain, with a focus on the youth. 'We walked all over Mitchells Plain. We went to the house of Marcus and

Theresa Solomon [the first democratically elected mayor of Cape Town] in Woodlands where we met [activist] Johnny Issel, listened to music, read poetry and had Xhosa lessons. Johnny and Vernie had a good relationship.'[4]

In 1983 Petersen was employed by the Anglican Church's Board of Social Responsibility, where he worked alongside Syd Luckett, 'a deep thinker'.[5]

'Guess who was the other community worker at the board? Ngconde Balfour,' said June, struggling to hide her disgust for the former minister of correctional services who made her husband's life such hell as he tried to put an end to Bosasa's capture of the department. 'Syd, Vernie and Ngconde worked together. They were friends. We visited Balfour's house at the time. He had three daughters,' she said.[6]

In the early 1980s, as political and military commander for the ANC in the Cape province, Tony Yengeni established a church unit to which Petersen, Balfour, Luckett and Derrick Marco belonged. 'I was the link with Yengeni. The purpose of the unit was propaganda through the church,' Weeder said.

In the 1980s Petersen started social-justice groups in the neighbourhoods in and around Cape Town, but June isn't exactly sure how deep his political activities went at that time. 'I only remember him hinting at things during two incidents. The first was a letter we found in our letterbox at our house in Rocklands in Mitchells Plain. It was written very cryptically, saying that we had to be at this particular place if we would like our house to be used as a safe house. During that time, the Special Branch was all over and Vernie explained to me that we are not going to trust this letter. We are going to ignore this.

'Then, one day – this is what the police used to do – very early in the morning there was a knock on our door and on the window. They were asking for a certain person and Vernie didn't open the door; he just said they were at the wrong house. It was all part of the intimidation.'[7]

These incidents prepared Petersen for the threats and intimidation he later faced as national commissioner of correctional services; this time, not from the apartheid police, but from his own former comrades.

In the 1980s, during outreach programmes as part of the Urban Rural Mission to Zimbabwe, Petersen smuggled money in his shoes to the

ANC-in-exile. 'He was definitely political; he was involved and aware, and he knew the people. He also had a formal career [as social worker] and a life,' said June.

Petersen was always very aware of walking the talk. 'Before we got married, he was driving one of Child Welfare's [Volkswagen] Beetles,' June recalled. 'And then we bought a car together, a brown Beetle .... Then, after that, we bought a Golf, and I was always fighting with him to say, "*Jinne*, Vernie, why must we always buy these cars that we struggle with?" And he said he cannot work in the community with a flashy car. And I said, "But just buy one of these box Toyotas. It's a second-hand car. How flashy is this?" But he just said he doesn't want to work in the community and be driving around with a car that makes people think he is better than others.'

June added that Petersen didn't even buy a new car during his time as national commissioner of correctional services. 'He always used what was there.'[8]

32

Into the lion's den

In 1990, the year Nelson Mandela exited the prison system, Vernie Petersen entered it. He was appointed as deputy national director of the South African National Institute for Crime Prevention and the Reintegration of Offenders (Nicro) in Cape Town, where he could truly put his passion for social welfare and justice to good use. The NGO works with young people in crime-ridden communities, inmates in prison and those who've been released, to integrate them back into society.

Petersen worked at Nicro for six years before being approached by Geraldine Fraser-Moleketi, then minister of social welfare and population development, to become her special advisor.

June Petersen recalled, 'I said, "Here [Lord], Vernie, you said you will wait and watch and only go and work for government after ten years of democracy when you see things have settled. He said things were still a bit *deurmekaar* [messy] in government and he wanted to wait and see. Then, of course, he was approached."[1]

Petersen filled that post for two years before accepting a position as chief director of social services, population and development in Mpumalanga. This put him in charge of the payment of social grants to the most vulnerable in society in that province – and it also brought him face-to-face with the predatory corruption that had engulfed government at all levels. He had fallouts with service providers who invited him to functions and events without declaring their intentions, and he realised that some of his comrades were in it for the money. His colleagues who blew the whistle received death threats. It all left Petersen disillusioned.

In 2004 he joined the DCS as regional commissioner for KwaZulu-Natal. He quickly moved through the ranks, first as regional commissioner of Gauteng, then as chief deputy commissioner in charge of corporate services, before replacing Linda Mti as national commissioner in May 2007.

Dudley Johnson, Petersen's brother-in-law and an advocate, remembered how he had to help Petersen get a copy of his ANC membership credentials before he was appointed as national commissioner. 'Vernie had to prove he was an ANC member. We had to get a letter from the Kuils River branch, from John van de Rheede.'²

After Mti's disgraceful exit from the DCS because of his clear links to Bosasa, it was a breath of fresh air to have a smart, straight guy to run the department. Shortly after his appointment, Petersen went to speak to an old friend and comrade in Cape Town who was working in the criminal-justice sector. June recalled, 'Vernie went to ask him, just how corrupt is correctional services? And he said to Vernie, "It is the weakest link in government. It is the most corrupt department. Don't get involved. Walk away." But he was already in.'³

So Petersen knew he would have a battle on his hands to clean up the DCS. He took the job well aware that his biggest challenges may be not only with the criminals in his prisons, but with the criminals in uniforms around him.

And Petersen took the job not as a step up the ladder of the civil service but because he really wanted to make a difference. He had huge insight into the role and purpose of correctional services in South African society to truly rehabilitate offenders and ensure that they could be reintegrated.

Introducing him to the media, Ngconde Balfour, then minister of correctional services and Petersen's old comrade, fellow community worker and brother in Christ, expressed his 'absolute confidence in Petersen's wealth of knowledge and experience in social activism, advancing democracy, good governance and service delivery improvement'.⁴

In Balfour, Petersen thought he had a comrade whom he could trust and who would support him in his endeavours to fix the department. 'And

Balfour probably thought he knows Vernie and they would have a good working relationship and that Vernie would listen to him,' said June. 'I think he underestimated Vernie.'

Vernie Petersen: my life insurance

'If something happens to me, these documents will show why.'[1]

33

Petersen's secret dossier

It didn't take long for Vernie Petersen to realise that he was in for the fight of his life. As the new national commissioner of correctional services, he was almost immediately obstructed from accessing certain documents pertaining to the Bosasa contracts, not included in certain meetings where Bosasa's tenders were discussed, and kept at arm's length by colleagues who were deeply embedded with service providers or union factions.

He decided to safeguard himself by building up a record of documents in secret that he believed would protect him if he was ever targeted by the capturers of the DCS. The documents were kept in an attache case safeguarded by good friend and comrade Neil Cole; a second set of the documents were kept by Petersen's friend Leon Scott.

In February 2019, after hearing Angelo Agrizzi's evidence at the Zondo Commission, about how Bosasa paid people to intimidate and target Petersen, June decided to share the documents with me. They included handwritten notes, memoranda of meetings, letters to and from Ngconde Balfour, communication with former ministers Trevor Manuel and Geraldine Fraser-Moleketi and with then President Thabo Mbeki's office, reports from the SIU, anonymous threatening emails, and two statements Petersen made telling his side of the story. There were also plenty of my articles connecting the dots of Bosasa's state capture and their collaborators in the DCS.

Working through the hundreds of pages gave me a glimpse of the tremendous pressure Petersen must have been under during his relatively short term of 18 months as head of correctional services, before being moved out by acting president Baleka Mbete in November 2008. Petersen had never stood a chance – but at least he'd tried.

What's clear from the documents is that it took him a mere two months to figure out something was very wrong in his department. By May 2007, when he took over the reins, Bosasa's first major tender with the DCS, to provide catering at prisons for R717 million over three years, was about to expire. The catering tender had become the single largest contributor to Bosasa's income sheet over the years, and made up the bulk of the R7 billion paid by the DCS to the company since 2004.

The department did very little to begin the process of putting out a new tender, and as a result was forced to extend Bosasa's contract by a year. An audit into the 'value for money' of the Bosasa contract – to determine whether the DCS should continue to outsource its catering services – should have been completed prior to the extension, but it wasn't.

Contained in Petersen's files were minutes of a meeting about the extension of Bosasa's catering tender that took place on 25 July 2007. The meeting was chaired by deputy commissioner Jenny Schreiner, a senior member of the SACP who'd been one of Mti's closest allies in the department. (Petersen was initially close to Schreiner, but later lost faith in her as he suspected her of being part of the faction to push him out.) In attendance were three other deputy commissioners, including Patrick Gillingham, who by then was receiving gifts and benefits from Bosasa.

When this meeting took place there'd been plenty of media reports about Bosasa's alleged corrupt relationship with Mti and the department, and it was known that the SIU had started to look into these tenders. But, according to the minutes, no mention was made of this: the written record reflects no deep discussion about the risks of extending the catering tender to Bosasa Operations. On the contrary, what is recorded is that Willem Pretorius of the procurement office made a presentation about why the contract should be extended, and that the committee agreed to the 12-month extension. Schreiner and her colleagues signed off on the decision and Bosasa continued to cook until July 2008.

Although national commissioners don't normally get involved in the nitty gritty of every tender, I found it odd that Petersen had been absent from such an important meeting. Clearly, he'd thought the same: at the top of the minutes was a hand-written notation by him in black ink: 'Where was I?'

This set the tone for the rest of Petersen's term at the DCS. He became deeply suspicious of the obvious favouring of Bosasa by the department and didn't know who to trust. 'He said to me there was nobody in the office that has his back. He doesn't have anybody,' June recalled.[2]

Petersen's 43-page statement, which he typed on 31 August 2008 and which was part of the dossier I received from June, revealed that in May that year, almost a year after the extension of Bosasa's contract, the value-for-money audit into the Bosasa catering tender had still not been done. At the same time, Balfour, the political head of the department, had sent Petersen a two-page document in which he'd motivated that Bosasa's tender be extended for a further 12 months. This document, Petersen discovered, had been created on a computer outside of the department.

Petersen soon realised that this wasn't an issue of incompetence. 'I requested a discussion on the matter but he [Balfour] appeared not to be interested,' he wrote in his statement.[3]

Petersen defied Balfour, allowing the contract to be extended for the shortest possible period. It was a move that marked the beginning of the end of his career as national commissioner of correctional services.

34

'Shona Malanga'

In May 2008 at least 62 people lost their lives in a spate of xenophobic attacks in South Africa's townships, originating in Alexandra, northeast of Johannesburg.[1] It was traumatic and embarrassing for the country, with then President Thabo Mbeki having to deploy the South African National Defence Force in domestic areas for the first time since 1994.

For Vernie Petersen, the attacks brought back bad memories of the 'witdoeke' attacks by apartheid state-sponsored vigilantes on the Cape Flats in the mid-1980s that had left 60 people dead and displaced over 60 000 others.[2]

Together with Ngconde Balfour and Petersen, the Anglican Church's Board of Social Responsibility intervened in the violence in Crossroads, a high-density township near Cape Town, and sought to negotiate an end to the unrest. 'On our way we encountered dead bodies and burnt shacks [and were] overcome by the smell of burnt human flesh.'[3]

As part of the justice, crime prevention and security cluster, Petersen also went on a site visit to some of the areas worst affected by the violence on the East Rand of Johannesburg. It coincided with Africa Day, the annual commemoration of the foundation of the Organisation of African Unity (OAU) on 25 May 1963, and at a celebratory function later, Petersen 'broke down emotionally and sobbed uncontrollably', which his doctor later diagnosed as post-traumatic stress disorder.[4]

Shortly afterwards, the department hosted the African Correctional

'SHONA MALANGA'

Services Association (ACSA) for the annual meeting of the continent's prisons ministers at Kievits Kroon country estate north of Pretoria. On 29 May 2008 the DCS hosted a gala dinner for visiting guests and Petersen found out at the venue that he was supposed to do the welcoming address. He went to the bar to get a glass of whiskey and soda. 'After having consumed the one drink, and while waiting for proceedings to start, Mr [Patrick] Gillingham [then regional commissioner for Limpopo, Mpumalanga and North West] offered me a glass of red wine. From then on he ensured that my glass was always filled.'[5]

Petersen started acting out of character, forgetting the words of a song that he mentioned in his speech, telling an inappropriate joke, and finally dancing and singing to the struggle song 'Shona Malanga' ('Let the sun go down'). 'However, as I heard people giggling, I left the stage, requesting Mr [James] Smalberger [a deputy commissioner] to allow Mr [Mnguni] Simelane, commissioner of Swaziland, to give a vote of thanks.'[6]

Petersen left immediately afterwards. June was asleep when he got home. 'He woke me up to say he is not feeling good. I asked him what he had to drink, and he said, "Just red wine."'[7]

The next morning Petersen was driving his son to school when they heard his name on the radio. And on her way to work, June 'saw the newspaper billboards saying "*dronk kommissaris*" [drunk commissioner] and I was like, "What?" I called Vernie and asked him, "What the fuck did you do?" He said he doesn't know.'[8]

Vernie called Smalberger to ask him if there was 'any reason I should not show my face this morning'. His response was, 'I suggest you speak to the minister,' and Petersen immediately knew something was wrong.[9] He called Balfour, who told him that he [Petersen] had embarrassed him and the ministers of defence, Mosiuoa Lekota, and home affairs, Nosiviwe Mapisa-Nqakula, who had, as a result, decided to leave the function early. 'Commissioner, I do not want you to attend the meeting [of African heads of prisons] this morning. Go to your office instead,' Balfour ordered.[10]

Extremely worried now, Petersen called Tozama Mqobi, the Gauteng regional commissioner (who became Balfour's third wife later that year) and asked her how she perceived the evening. 'With a chuckle she said,

"You told the minister [Balfour] last night, 'You can fire me, Minister, I don't care.'" This I knew to be untrue.'[11]

Petersen met with Balfour at Kievits Kroon. It was clearly a difficult meeting, and Petersen 'observed that during the discussion the Minister was extremely tense. His facial expression was strange, and he failed to make eye contact with me throughout this time.'[12]

Petersen explained to Balfour that he'd felt strange the previous evening. 'I do not understand it because I was having red wine at the table and, while I felt drunk, I was never affected in this way before. I reminded him that since I stopped smoking six weeks earlier, of my withdrawal symptoms ... He responded by saying that he knows how difficult it is because his good friend, the late former minister of safety and security Mr Steve Tshwete, complained that when he did so, he felt constantly drunk.'

Petersen told Balfour what a difficult week he'd had and how the xenophobic violence had physically upset him. 'I said to the Minister, I do not know what is happening, but if I have embarrassed his colleagues, I would like to apologise to them personally. I requested him to facilitate such a meeting with them and he undertook to discuss it with them.'[13]

Back in at his office, Petersen's office manager, Val Shabalala, told him something strange was happening. She'd overheard people talking in the corridors about the previous night, expressing shock. Mqobi had told her that Gillingham and Smalberger had called Balfour on their way home from the function to complain about Petersen's behaviour 'and how embarrassed they were'.[14]

Petersen told June that someone in his office had overheard senior officials saying, 'Nou het ons hom.' ('Now we've got him.') 'That is when he realised there was foul play.'[15]

June remembered her husband telling her that Nadira Singh, the department's chief financial officer, asked him, 'Why is Mr Gillingham continuously making sure your glass of wine is full?' 'She found it strange. There must have been a reason why she noticed.'[16] (Singh resigned the following month, following interference by Balfour and Gillingham in the finance department, and harassment from Bosasa about outstanding payments on a Sondolo IT tender for which the department hadn't budgeted.)

Petersen concluded that his drink had been spiked and called his doctor to conduct blood tests. But, June says, the tests were done too late – if a foreign substance had, in fact, been put in the wine, Petersen's body had already metabolised it and there was no sign of it left in his system – and his doctor didn't pick up any sign of a liver illness that may have explained the drunkenness.

With his doctor, Petersen 'discussed the events in the country over the past two weeks and the state of politics. He explained that he has developed an interest in the psychological side of health and that we often underestimate the power of the mind on our wellbeing. I explained to him my experience at the Africa Day dinner in relation to the Kievits Kroon gala dinner, and in his opinion, I was experiencing post-traumatic stress.'[17]

Petersen was, however, adamant that his condition was physical. '[The doctor] then suggested that we go to a nearby pathologist to draw more blood to test for diabetes and cholesterol levels, as this could also have had an effect. We waited for the results and [they were] clear except for minor signs of cholesterol. He prescribed tablets for the cholesterol and what he referred to as organic tablets for stress. He concluded that my condition is post-traumatic stress.'[18]

Three days after the incident the department's spokesperson, Manelisi Wolela, called Petersen to inform him that a journalist from *The Star* was in possession of a letter from an inmate who'd attended the Kievits Kroon gala dinner as part of the prison jazz band. The letter purported to be a complaint to Balfour about Petersen's 'drunken behaviour'.

Wolela told Petersen that the minister had asked him to respond with the following wording in a press statement: 'We confirm the unusual behaviour of the national commissioner. The minister views the matter in a serious light and will ask the Public Service Commission to investigate.'[19]

Ten minutes later Petersen got a call from Jenny Schreiner, who advised him to take leave. This information should be included in the press statement, she said, adding, 'I promise you, from my experience of how we handled the media around issues affecting former commissioner Mti, this is the way to handle it.'[20]

Petersen wasn't at all happy with any of these arrangements, and June agreed with him, advising him that under no circumstances should he take leave, as it would look like an admission of guilt. 'I said no, you go in there and claim your position. You don't stay away because you don't know what they are planning now.'²¹

Petersen informed Schreiner and Wolela that he would be back at work the next day.

On 2 June 2008 *The Star* published an article headlined '"Drunk" prisons boss embarrasses officials', quoting the letter from a prisoner in the jazz band. The gist of the story was that Petersen had embarrassed Balfour and Lekota during their speeches.²²

Petersen had a word with Wolela for responding to the media in a way that 'did not have my best interest at heart'. He then contacted Arthur Fraser, then deputy head of the NIA, whom he knew from when he was advising Geraldine Fraser-Moleketi, Fraser's sister, for advice and assistance.

35

Stranger things

In June 2008 dark stormclouds were gathering as Vernie Petersen travelled to Cape Town for the correctional services budget speech to be delivered in Parliament by minister Ngconde Balfour, just metres away from where he and Balfour had spent much of their youth as community workers at St George's cathedral on Wale Street.

Petersen now strongly believed that he was the victim of a dirty-tricks campaign for blocking the extension of Bosasa's catering contract for another year. He had nobody to trust and suspected his deputies of plotting against him. Even Schreiner, whom he'd initially thought was his ally, had started acting up: at a DCS function she hosted, she 'appeared to be extremely uncomfortable in my presence and demonstrated unusual nervousness during her presentation. Her mouth was dry, and she spoke with difficulty,' Petersen wrote in his statement.[1]

At his hotel in Cape Town, Petersen ran into Odette Ramsingh, head of the PSC. He told her that he was concerned about the integrity of his office in light of media reports about the 'drunken outburst' and wanted the matter investigated. She advised him to inform Minister Balfour about his intention to investigate all the circumstances surrounding the Kievits Kroon incident.

Petersen went to Balfour's office in Parliament and greeted him in a friendly way. 'I said, "Minister, I read in the media that you have instituted an investigation against me." He interrupted and said, "Commissioner, there is not going to be any investigation and we are not going to deal with the issue through the media." I said, "Well, Minister, in that case I want you to know that I am instituting an investigation."

'I requested him to excuse me from the media briefing and the meeting with stakeholders that he was going to have prior to the budget vote debate on that day, as I was consulting with counsel. I indicated that I will be at the budget debate.'[2]

This was Petersen drawing a line in the sand, telling Balfour that he would not be bullied into submission.

He was followed out of the office by Loretta Jacobus, deputy minister at the time. 'While still angry I told her I was going to take action against certain senior managers and was going to insist that Ms Schreiner takes leave.'

Petersen and his office manager, Val Shabalala, met with Petersen's old comrade and friend, Advocate Pat Gamble SC, who immediately suggested that Petersen's blood samples be tested for other substances. However, because the blood had only been drawn two days after the gala dinner, nothing was detected.

An email from Gamble to Petersen's private email address on 27 June 2008 highlighted the 'one central issue' for which Petersen was responsible: 'corrupt practices and/or other irregularities relating to departmental tender practices/contracts'.

The email continued:

> Your first choice of course is an easy one – pack up and move on. But we have discussed that one already and clearly it is not an option for you ...
>
> So what next? I think you need to define your objectives very clearly. Is it that you want to clean up and root out all of these malpractices/rotten eggs or do you rather want to bark a bit and hope they will back off? Knowing you I would suspect the former. As you explained to me, your department has some of the biggest tenders around and knowing the ways of the world, it is fair to presume that there are many who wish to get their snouts in the trough. I think one should move incrementally in the hope that one thing will lead to another.[3]

Gamble proceeded to advise Petersen that they should start by getting to the bottom of the Kievits Kroon incident; they needed to find out, the advocate said, if the letter supposedly written by the prisoner was real, and if so, how it had got to *The Star*. 'We know that such a line of investigation may ultimately point fingers at the executive, and if that happens, so be it. But your investigation should not be aimed at exposing any particular politician but rather cleaning up within the department,' Gamble advised.

The politicians (read: Balfour) would have no choice but to support Petersen if he adopted the right strategy to clean up the DCS. 'You have already done excellent work in that regard and it seems as if you can rely on solid support from the portfolio committee [as both the ANC chairperson Dennis Bloem and opposition MPs were supportive of Petersen's work],' Gamble concluded.

Later that morning Ngconde Balfour started calling Val Shabalala 'persistently', demanding that Petersen return to his [Balfour's] office. 'When I arrived, the minister led me to my office with an envelope in his hand. He was very nervous and explained that he spoke to Minister Fraser-Moleketi who agreed that he should give me a copy of his letter he forwarded to her. He left me with the letter.'[4] The letter was confirmation that Balfour had requested an investigation into Petersen's behaviour at Kievits Kroon.

Petersen then joined his colleagues for lunch, during which a regional commissioner asked Petersen what was happening. 'Earlier that day, he tells me, the minister [Balfour] spoke to them. He was crying as he spoke and was asking for Commissioner Mti, my predecessor, who was not there.' Presumably, Balfour longed to have his old commissioner back.

After Balfour's budget-vote speech, members of the correctional services portfolio committee, including those belonging to the ANC, spoke highly of Petersen and rejected the stories about him being drunk as a smear campaign.

Petersen flew back to Johannesburg for the preparation of his eldest son Ruari's wedding on Saturday 7 June 2008.

'Vernie was stressed. He couldn't really assist with the arrangements. I did all of that,' said June. 'He was very preoccupied, very preoccupied. And even at the function ... I mean, I did a speech at the function, not Vernie. He was very preoccupied at that function.'[5]

On the day of Ruari Petersen's wedding, the notorious Mozambican rapist and robber Ananias Mathe tried to escape from the high-security Ebongweni Prison in Kokstad. Two years before, Mathe had successfully escaped from the maximum-security division of Pretoria Central Prison.

Petersen was very suspicious about the timing. 'The minister [Balfour] was on the scene immediately and so was the media. When analysing the report, I became suspicious, especially when I was told that the head of the centre where the incident occurred was said to be leading the investigation [into the attempted escape], and the person who reported the escape was the minister's former driver. I phoned the minister to inform him that I will appoint the Departmental Investigation Unit and the NIA to become involved. I saw this as a sinister effort to divert attention away from the [positive] media reports around me [after the budget vote speech, during which MPs praised Petersen].'[6]

June Petersen says she realised 'trouble was brewing' on the day of her son's wedding. After the reception, she and her husband had gone home to the three-bedroom house they were staying in on the grounds of Pretoria Central Prison – Vernie had refused to move into the national commissioner's official residence because it had needed such extensive repair work, and he didn't want to waste the state's money.

At 01:30, June was woken up by some family members who were staying with the Petersens for the wedding and were registered as visitors at Pretoria Central. The family members had travelled together in a minibus, and the prison guards at the entrance of Pretoria Central were refusing to allow the vehicle in. In the wee hours of the morning, the family members had to get out of the minibus and walk 800 metres to the Petersens' house. Petersen was furious and humiliated.

A week later, the Pretoria area commissioner, Grace Molatedi, called Petersen to inform him that the 'inmate' who'd apparently witnessed and complained about his behaviour at Kievits Kroon didn't exist. 'There was no prisoner by that name who was part of the jazz band and they all denied having written the letter. A number of long-serving managers subsequently told me that inmates jealously guard the privilege of being able to attend such functions and would never jeopardise it. I requested Ms Molatedi to provide the information to Mr [Dennis] Bloem [chair of the portfolio committee on correctional services] which she did.'[7]

Following the revelation that the 'whistleblower' on Petersen was a fabrication, then defence minister Mosiuoa Lekota was quoted in the press denying that Petersen had insulted him and saying that, on the contrary, he'd received Petersen's comments on his speech 'warmly'.[8] Other prison bosses who'd been at Kievits Kroon on the night also made statements to confirm that Petersen hadn't been 'misbehaving'.

Encouraged by these developments, Petersen penned a message to the portfolio committee and his staff:

> It is now more than fourteen days since [Balfour told the media he would institute an investigation into Petersen] and I have not heard from the Public Service Commission about any such investigation ... I have since informed the minister of my intention to institute an investigation in my capacity as accounting officer of this department.
>
> I do not want to deal with the merits of the allegations but upon inquiry I have been informed by the area commissioner of Pretoria [Grace Molatedi] that, after much effort, no inmate with the name provided in the letter could be found who attended the function on 29 May 2008 as a member of the jazz band and who ... is reported to have written the letter.
>
> In any case, I shall not give much credence to the letter because, when analysing it, the letter goes far beyond the concern of an inmate complaining about 'the drunken behaviour' of the commissioner. The letter feeds into stereotypes. It presents me as a person with low morals, prone to drunken behaviour, with disrespect for authority and our institutions. The letter further suggests an element of opportunism on the part of the national commissioner by being disrespectful to three serving cabinet ministers.
>
> I reject these insinuations with the contempt [they deserve]!

> Whoever is behind [them] has discredited his or her cause, whatever it is.
>
> I know who is behind this letter and why it was written. Allow me to use this platform to warn them to stop with what they are busy. I am extremely proud of the vast majority of DCS staff – people of integrity with commitment to transformation, good governance and democracy.
>
> But I will not tolerate bad practices, neither for the sake of political expediency nor for the sake of being a popular manager.⁹

Petersen certainly suspected Balfour, some of his senior colleagues and Bosasa of trying to get rid of him for objecting to the extension of the lucrative catering tender, and he'd now declared himself up for the fight. He was by no means going to 'pack up and move on'.

36

The fear

'I remember his fear; he was afraid.'

Reverend Michael Weeder was casting his mind back to a cold Cape Town winter's evening in June 2008 when he opened the door to his home on St Phillips Street in Zonnebloem, and found his old friend Vernie Petersen standing there. 'He had two cars of security guards with him. I could see security, the driver and another security. When I looked about 50 metres down the street, I could see another car. And at the other block, there was another car. I thought to myself, that's a lot of security to be travelling with.'[1]

Vernie just started to talk, Weeder recalled. 'Talk and talk. He was talking about how our people were working with the old guard, with the Special Branch. They were in cahoots. And there [was] a lot of detail I can't remember now.

'There was never bravado in Vernie. If he could walk away from a fight, he would. But there was a steady determination in him that night. "It is wrong, and I can't walk away from this," he said. He was talking about fearing for his life and for his family.'[2]

After Grace Molatedi had reported to Petersen that the inmate who'd supposedly written the letter to complain about him didn't exist, she'd also told him that other members of the jazz band had wanted to talk. 'She undertook to visit them and to provide me with feedback. I advised her not to pursue them further as they may now want to exploit the situation. She did speak to them and afterwards informed me that they claim that inmate

Mr Eugene de Kock is showing a very keen interest in the matter. I was shocked as I knew that he was the master of dirty tricks.'[3]

Did Petersen believe the former Vlakplaas commander, who was a prisoner at Pretoria Central at the time, was somehow involved in discrediting him to ease the way for Bosasa's capture of the DCS? His statement didn't elaborate on whether he pursued this claim further and there was nothing else in his dossier that supported the claim. But it did explain his reference to the apartheid-era Special Branch in his fearful heart-to-heart with Weeder. (Someone close to De Kock told me it was 'nonsense' that he'd had anything to do with dirty tricks against Petersen.)

June said her husband had told her about threats targeting Dylan, their youngest son. 'Dylan used to cycle to the University of Pretoria. Vernie said to me Dylan was no longer allowed to cycle. I asked why. He said that he received a phone call to say, "We know your son cycles and we know what routes he takes, so watch it." So Dylan was no longer allowed to cycle.

'I asked Vernie, "What about us?" He just said we must be careful because they know what car we drive. At the time, we were sharing a car.'[4]

June talked calmly about this intimidation and it was clear to me that Petersen had downplayed the gravity of the threats to protect his wife and children. Also, growing up under apartheid had made them resilient – they'd had to deal with intimidation and threats and *impimpis* (informers) on an almost-daily basis. But this was supposed to be different, this democracy for which they'd given up much of their youth in the struggle against the oppression of apartheid.

After the Agrizzi bomb was detonated at the Zondo Commission, one of Petersen's bodyguards told June that Petersen had believed his life was in danger. 'He said, "My family's lives are in danger. I want you to be extra vigilant, and when I am away one of you will have to sleep at the house." When he [Vernie] used to go to Cape Town, he ... started taking this one bodyguard along. He didn't tell me why; he just said this guy has never been on a plane or has travelled and that's why he feels he needs to take him.'[5]

Included in Petersen's dossier was a threat analysis performed by Crime Intelligence after Vernie had received threatening calls in early 2009.

Although he'd already left the DCS and was working as director-general at the sports department by that time, this coincided with the period during which I also received threatening calls from men who identified themselves as Bosasa employees and who accused me of jeopardising their jobs as a result of the series of articles in the *Mail & Guardian* about Bosasa's corrupt relationship with the DCS. Did the masterminds behind the threats suspect Petersen of being my source for the articles? If they did, they were dead wrong.

I'd saved all the numbers from which threatening calls were made to my phone, and I compared them to the list provided by Petersen to the police. One of the Cape Town numbers identified by Crime Intelligence as that of a public phone at the Middestad Mall in Bellville was used to intimidate both of us. CCTV footage from the mall showed two men making calls from the phone on that specific date and time.

The Crime Intelligence report concluded: 'It should be noted that this office has conducted various enquiries related to similar telephonic threat activity. A common denominator relevant to some of them is contact with the company Bosasa. No specific individuals could however be identified.'[6]

Back at the office, Ngconde Balfour had ceased to communicate with Petersen and was cancelling their meetings. Petersen decided to establish a paper trail and wrote to Balfour about a proposal he'd submitted to him and on which he needed finality. 'I started to get the impression that he was bartering with me – [that he expected me to do] what he wanted me to do on the nutrition [Bosasa] contract in exchange for him approving the submission. His response was arrogant; he thanked me for reminding him how to do his work and [told] me that he will discuss it with the executive management committee.'[7]

At the same time, Petersen's deputy Teboho Motseki was pressurising him to extend the catering tender – if Minister Balfour said so. 'I did not trust [Motseki] as he informed me two years before that Mr Gillingham [had] arranged a job for his wife at one of the companies associated with Bosasa,' Petersen noted.[8]

The relationship between Balfour and Petersen continued to deteriorate. The minister threatened to veto some of Petersen's appointments and started to belittle him in front of his colleagues.

During a telephone conversation at one stage, Balfour reportedly asked Petersen why things between them were as bad as they were. 'Is it because [you think] I am corrupt, Commissioner?' he asked.

Petersen said that his response was to suggest that the minister and he discuss that face-to-face, 'to which he responded that he will call me for such a discussion'.[9]

Vernie Petersen: losing the battle

'When elephants fight it is the grass that suffers. Minister, I do not want to fight you, because I will not win.'[1]

37

'Something must break'

With each day closer to 31 July 2008, the day on which Bosasa's extended catering contract was due to expire, the relationship between Balfour and Petersen grew tenser and more acrimonious. The tender, which overshadowed everything else in the department, was a clear example of how a private company can capture a state institution: this wasn't 'mere' tender corruption or irregularities. The entire strategy, leadership and budget of the DCS were at stake.

A bid-adjudication committee meeting had already decided to extend Bosasa's contract by only six months, but Balfour was still motivating for a longer extension, even writing to then finance minister Trevor Manuel on why it was a good idea. Balfour was completely usurping the role and function of the department by interfering at this level.

At a senior management meeting on 28 July there was open war between Balfour and Petersen. Balfour, who'd arrived at the management meeting with a thick file on the Bosasa tender, was 'forthright' that he disagreed with Petersen about extending the contract for only six months while a feasibility study, which should have been completed more than a year before, was finished. Balfour shamelessly praised Bosasa's service and said everyone was happy with it.

Senior prison staff were 'astounded that he punted the service provider so directly and felt uncomfortable'.[2] Motseki even asked that no notes be taken of the discussion.

The minister reminded the commissioner that his performance

assessment was due. Petersen responded by reminding Balfour of their shared struggle roots in the ANC's underground in the 1990s. 'I stated that the minister has refused to meet with me since May for a one-on-one meeting.'[3] The senior managers decided that mediation was needed between the two.

Ultimately, Petersen defied Balfour, and on 31 July 2008 signed off an extension of only six months. On the same day he wrote a letter to Balfour in which he gave his reasons why outsourcing nutrition and catering may not be the best solution for the DCS going forward: it had a negative impact on farming activity at prisons and resulted in the underutilisation of farm produce, it reduced the opportunities for inmates to be involved in farming at prison farms, and it was detrimental to the department's budget.[4]

Petersen told Balfour he would fast-track a feasibility study and asked for the tender to be investigated by the departmental investigative unit. He informed National Treasury and the Auditor-General of his decisions, and said there would be no further extensions of the contract.

Balfour was furious. He instructed Petersen to appoint a task team, to be led by Patrick Gillingham, to draw up a new tender for the catering contract.

By this time, Carien du Plessis and I had reported on Bosasa's influence in the writing of tenders for the department, and Petersen knew where this was going. He refused to allow Gillingham to lead the process and forged ahead with the advertising of a new tender, while Bosasa finished its final six months in the kitchen.

After a meeting with the portfolio committee on 12 August 2008, where Petersen again received support for his actions, Balfour wrote a letter to Petersen: 'Commissioner, if we cannot trust and work together in this department, then something must break,' the letter read.[5] He instructed Petersen to cancel the new catering tender and anything to do with 'this issue of nutrition specifications'.

Petersen was 'really disturbed' by the tone of the letter and 'decided to give a copy to the chair of the portfolio committee to make him aware of the circumstances under which I am now working. He undertook to address the issue.'[6]

At the same time, Petersen was told by his colleagues that Gillingham and Balfour were meeting regularly at the minister's house.

Two days later, Balfour walked into Petersen's office, waving a document. 'He informed me that I did not understand him when he issues instructions. He could now confirm that this tender, being published, is already out there, being sold for R5 000. He had a witness who will be prepared to testify about this incident.' Balfour was claiming that the new tender document for catering, which Petersen had insisted be published, had been leaked and was already 'for sale' to the private sector without its having been advertised.

Petersen told Balfour to report this to the police and the SIU.

At a follow-up meeting with senior correctional services managers in August 2008, Balfour told Petersen he no longer believed they could work together. 'He accused me of undermining the collective and promoting cliques,' Petersen noted.

Balfour's supporters strongly argued that the tender should be cancelled. Petersen told Balfour that if he wanted the tender cancelled, he should put it in writing.

'I addressed myself to the minister, stating: "Minister, you have insulted and threatened me in the presence of my subordinates and in writing. I do not take kindly to that." I explained that as a Director-General we are sometimes viewed as deployees of the ruling party. I indicated that I am a member of the ANC as is the Minister and that I am willing to submit to the discipline of the party. I would welcome it if the Minister would initiate an approach to the leadership. However, I am a civil servant in the first instance and government has put in place structures and processes to manage discipline. I encouraged the Minister to follow that route.'⁷

A few days later, anonymous emails and text messages began circulating in the top management of the DCS. 'Commissioner Verne [sic], a law unto himself' was the title of one email that accused Petersen of being disrespectful to senior managers, overturning decisions made by the 'collective' and of having an 'apartheid rule' leadership style. Another text message, sarcastically noting *Siende jy deesdae so gelowig is* ('Since you're so religious these days'), quoted 2 Corinthians: 'We are hard pressed on every side, but not crushed; perplexed, but not in despair; persecuted, but not abandoned; struck down, but not destroyed.'[8]

Petersen wasn't ready to give up, and his resolve was strengthened after his departmental investigative unit presented him with evidence from a whistleblower that suggested Balfour's Volkswagen Touareg 4x4 had been financed by Kgwerano Financial Services, a company partly owned by Bosasa. 'A Mercedes 2004 was traded in as part of the deal. The trade-in value appeared to be excessively generous,' Petersen noted.[9]

38

Comradely betrayal

In 2004 the department of transport awarded a R100-million tender to Kgwerano Asset Finance, a joint venture between Wesbank and the Bosasa-owned Kgwerano Financial Services. The tender was for the supply of full maintenance operating leases to public-office bearers (POBs), such as ministers, premiers, speakers and MECs, and ran for a period of five years.

Evidence from a whistleblower in Petersen's dossier shows that Ngconde Balfour purchased two Volkswagen Touareg 4x4s through the Kgwerano scheme – a 5.0 V10 TDI model in March 2006 and a R5 2.5 TDI in November 2007. The vehicle statements provided to Petersen by the whistleblower showed that in October 2007 the account on the first vehicle was closed when R798 996 was still outstanding. A month later the account for the second vehicle was activated for an amount of R954 711. Another document from the dealership showed that in 2006 Balfour traded in his 2004 Mercedes-Benz E320 for R399 500; he'd bought it for about R450 000 in 2004.

Petersen, who was alarmed by the fact that another Bosasa-owned company was involved in the transaction, wanted to know who'd settled the account for Balfour's first Touareg before he'd purchased the second, more expensive model. Under the Protected Disclosures Act (which aims to protect whistleblowers), on 22 August 2008 he reported a suspicious transaction of fraud and corruption against Balfour to Geraldine Fraser-Moleketi, the then minister of public service and administration, the

SAPS, and Parliament's executive members ethics committee.

In his complaint he gave the background to the extension of Bosasa's catering tender and accused Balfour of 'instructing' him to further Bosasa's business in the department. He mentioned the Kgwerano vehicle financing as a 'conflict of interest in that a company associated to Bosasa, Kgwerano, has paid for the minister's motor vehicle'.[1]

In a report to the SAPS, Petersen wrote, 'It is suspected that the minister is/was involved in a corrupt relationship with Bosasa, the company rendering services to the department.'

On the same day, Petersen wrote to Balfour, asking him whether his 'something must break' letter had meant that it was his intention to terminate Petersen's services as a result of the decisions he'd taken on the Bosasa contract.

Three days later, at a meeting of the department's senior managers, Petersen handed Balfour an envelope containing the paperwork relating to the motor-vehicle purchases. Petersen had marked it 'secret' and asked Balfour not to open it in front of everyone. Nonetheless, the minister (who Petersen described as 'visibly shaking'), announcing that he had nothing to discuss with the commissioner outside of the meeting, opened it. 'He exclaimed: "This is my car! Are you investigating me, Commissioner?"'

Petersen told Balfour that he wasn't investigating him, but that he wanted to discuss the matter with him. 'I informed the meeting that I have requested an audience with the President [Mbeki].'[2]

Petersen's actions left Balfour spitting mad. After 'excusing' the commissioner from the meeting, Balfour issued a media statement in which he said he wouldn't 'hesitate to take head-on anybody who creates baseless stories like this with no facts whatsoever trying to achieve his motives'. He denied any impropriety, stating that he'd bought a black Volkswagen Touareg in 2006 as his personal car and had been paying off all the instalments 'till to date'. Curiously, Balfour didn't mention the second Touareg in his statement. 'I, Ngconde Balfour, a strong believer in clean governance, will never embarrass or humiliate my dead parents, my siblings and my children in whatever action,' he declared.[3]

A letter from Kgwerano Asset Finance CEO Brian Gwebu to Balfour, dated 25 August 2008, confirms that two vehicles were purchased by Balfour, 'one through the POB scheme and the other in the minister's private capacity. The vehicle purchased privately was financed through Kgwerano Asset Finance via Olive de Haas of Wesbank who has also confirmed to the Auditor-General previously that no additional discounts were provided to the minister other than those provided to the retail public. The vehicle purchased through the POB scheme was procured directly from a vehicle dealer at the manufacturer-recommended discounts to the retail public.'[4]

Parliament's ethics committee cleared Balfour of wrongdoing, declaring itself satisfied by an explanation from Wesbank that he'd regularly paid his monthly instalments. The financer told Parliament that the account on Balfour's first Touareg hadn't been closed but 'restructured'. Parliament didn't ask Balfour to submit his bank statements to show the monthly deductions on both vehicles and the matter of the two vehicles was never thoroughly clarified.

After the outcome Balfour said he would pray for Petersen, and that he was not corrupt; 'I am just a Christian,' he said.[5]

In the meantime, the SIU had delivered a briefing report to Petersen on three of the major tenders awarded to Bosasa, for catering, access-control systems and TV sets in prisons. The report confirmed what Petersen had suspected: that no feasibility assessments had been done on any of the tenders; that the process had been rushed through; that the tender specifications had been compiled outside of the department; and that security requirements had been built into the catering tender to the benefit of one supplier – Bosasa Operations. The report identified Patrick Gillingham as a key role player who was intimately involved in all three of the tenders.[6]

Petersen wrote to Balfour telling him that the report warranted the summary dismissal of Gillingham – the minister's confidant and ally, and Bosasa's key man in the DCS – but that a suspension would be the appropriate action in order to allow for further investigation. Petersen did suspend Gillingham, and a year later, after failing to halt his disciplinary hearing, Gillingham resigned in disgrace.

Petersen's action against Gillingham sent shivers through the department. For years Gillingham had been untouchable; he'd controlled the purse strings and had been instrumental in Bosasa's capture of the department. In return, he'd been blessed with home improvements, a new kitchen, cars and rugby tickets. And now he was out.

In September 2008 Thabo Mbeki was fighting for his political life. Judge Chris Nicholson had ruled (wrongly, as the Supreme Court of Appeal later found) that there had been political interference in the prosecution of Jacob Zuma, and Mbeki's head was on the ANC NEC's chopping block.

At the same time, his director-general, Frank Chikane, was deeply involved in the activities of the Ginwala Commission of Inquiry into the fitness of Advocate Vusi Pikoli to hold the office of NDPP.

A few months earlier, after the Kievits Kroon incident, Petersen had confided in Chikane and sought his advice – the two men had considered each other 'comrades'. 'He appeared to be under tremendous personal pressure, seemingly as a result of the Ginwala Inquiry and preparations for the budget vote of the Presidency,' Petersen wrote later in a statement. 'He suggested that I meet with Mr Trevor Fowler in the Presidency. I declined as I was concerned not to further feed into racial connotations. After half-heartedly listening to me, his only comment was, "Chief, the only advice I can give you is that when a Minister and DG fight, the DG always loses." I ended the discussion and left extremely disappointed in him.'[7]

Chikane says he doesn't recall saying this to Petersen. 'I remember that Mr Petersen told me that he had challenges with his Minister, that is, Minister Ngconde Balfour, and that their relationship was not good at all. As far as I can recall, it had to do with interference in his work as the director-general and expectations from him which he could not meet within his responsibilities and mandate. I do not remember the specific details about the matters that he was unhappy about. I do not have any written record relating to this matter and I'm afraid that my memory is not very helpful in this regard.'[8]

Fraser-Moleketi (then minister of public service and administration) called Petersen to a meeting and asked him about the status of his relationship with Balfour. 'I replied that I do feel bitter because I believe that he was complicit in the Kievits Kroon incident. We were comrades and he betrayed me.'

On 1 September 2008 Chikane phoned Petersen and told him Mbeki could meet him that evening in Pretoria. Of the meeting Petersen recalled, 'Not knowing how much time I would have, I started by giving a truncated account of events and then proceeded to fill in the gaps as I proceeded ... The president listened very intently and commented at the end that it seems to be a very complex situation. He undertook to speak to Minister Balfour.

'As they [Mbeki and Chikane] walked me to the door, I said, "Mr President, I am under tremendous pressure from various quarters to approach the ANC leadership at Luthuli House. I do not want to do so as I report to you as the president." His reply was, no, that would not be necessary.'[9]

Two days later Chikane called Petersen to another meeting, with him alone. 'He was keen to emphasise the president's intolerance to corruption.' Chikane then reportedly said, 'But Chief, directors-general don't have the luxury of an inquiry. The matter you reported to the ethics committee [about Balfour's cars] will take a long time before it is finalised. You know the president only acts on the basis of proven facts before him. Now we have to deal with the breakdown of the relationship between yourself and the minister. Chief, can you summarise for me this war between yourself and the minister?' Chikane asked Petersen to send them the file of correspondence with Balfour.

Petersen wrote he was shocked at Chikane's approach. 'What war? There is no war between the minister and myself ... Frank, if you want to approach this as a breakdown of the relationship I will resist you! There is no breakdown of the relationship, and the minister said it in so many words.' Petersen told Chikane that Balfour had said everything would go 'back to normal as it was before' if he cancelled the catering tender advert and extended Bosasa's contract for 12 months.[10]

'I expressed my disappointment in Dr Chikane for having prefaced his discussion with me in the way that he did ... I said that we should not pretend that he is interceding on my behalf. I reminded him of my own political track record – my wife and I hosted Dr Chikane at our house in Rocklands, Mitchells Plain when the UDF was launched 25 years ago and we are both signatories of the historic Kairos document.[11] I said I will take responsibility for defending my own integrity and lamented the fact that trust is often the first victim in situations like this.'[12]

Chikane certainly remembered that Petersen's relationship with Balfour was a 'source of great anxiety and stress for him' but he didn't recall the meeting with Mbeki. 'What I know is that I would have done everything possible to make sure that Vernie Petersen is given a fair hearing and appropriate support. This is a person I knew well from the days of our UDF activism. Both President Mbeki and I acted on whatever matters were brought before us in the most appropriate and expeditious manner possible. I have no doubt whatsoever that Vernie Petersen's matter would have been treated in the same way.'[13]

The inaction of Chikane and others to deal decisively with the Bosasa corruption allegations that Vernie brought to them made June, Petersen's widow, feel 'sad and betrayed'. 'When I read Vernie's statement and I hear the things Agrizzi [has] said, it's like Vernie died for me all over again and I couldn't make sense of it. I just felt an utter sense of loneliness and betrayal that he felt. I wish I can say to Vernie now, "You know when you told me at the time that I should know that you will lay down your life for the ANC? ... This [now] is not the ANC that we know."'[14]

'... What we learnt in the organisations, the underlying foundation of why we were involved in the civic, was respect, honesty, listening to others and caring for others, always putting yourself last, and these things that many of us still practise in our lives today. I practise it where I now manage people, and our boys, our children, live by those values.'

39

Departing

On 21 September 2008, Thabo Mbeki resigned as president of South Africa. 'I'm convinced that the incoming administration will better the work done during the past 14 and a half years so that poverty, underdevelopment, unemployment, illiteracy, challenges of health, crime and corruption will cease to define the lives of many of our people,' he said before leaving the stage.[1]

Ngconde Balfour was part of a group of outspoken pro-Mbeki ministers who resigned with the president.

Kgalema Motlanthe, Jacob Zuma's deputy in the ANC, was sworn in as president of South Africa. When he reappointed Balfour as minister of correctional services, Vernie Petersen knew he was out in the cold. It was now only a matter of time before the axe fell.

(Balfour remained in the portfolio until the May 2009 election, after which Nosiviwe Mapisa-Nqakula, in whose house Dyambu Operations had originally been formed, replaced him as minister of correctional services. Zuma appointed Balfour as high commissioner to Botswana.)

After returning to his portfolio, Balfour made it clear that he would be even more hands-on, and he was present at the opening of the tender box in September for the new catering contract. 'I'm the new minister in this department. I was gone for two days. I got reappointed. This is my department and I decide what happens in my department,' he was quoted as saying.[2]

Baleka Mbete, the former speaker of Parliament, was appointed by Motlanthe as deputy president of the country. On 22 October 2008, while

Motlanthe was in Benin on official business, Mbete, as acting president, signed a cabinet minute that ordered Petersen and Xoliswa Sibeko, director-general of the sports department, to swop jobs from the following week. Department insiders told me that shifting Petersen sideways like this was a huge victory for Balfour and Bosasa.

Devastated, Petersen wrote to Motlanthe requesting an urgent meeting before the matter was finalised. The meeting never materialised.

Although there's no proof she benefited from Bosasa's largesse, Mbete was a founding member of the Dyambu companies and had been chair of Dyambu Holdings before Gavin Watson 'bought' them out. There seems little doubt that she was aware of the fracas between Bosasa and Petersen.

Mbete said that she had no involvement in the negotiations of the transfer of the two director-generals, and that it was 'sheer coincidence' that she had signed the presidential minute.[3]

The DA's spokesperson on correctional services, James Selfe, said he was '99% sure' that Petersen's transfer was linked to his efforts to clean up the department, and particularly the Bosasa catering tender.[4]

In an interview at the time, Lukas Muntingh of the Civil Society Prison Reform Initiative said that Petersen was a remarkable prisons boss. 'All indications are that he is hard at work to unravel the deep-rooted interests that have caused this department so much misery,' Muntingh said. 'This departure from denialism, characterising previous commissioners, is remarkable. Recent actions relating to corruption allegedly involving senior officials, including suspending two, have also confirmed his commitment to rooting out corruption in the department.' For Petersen, according to Muntingh, the challenge lay in the extent to which he could trust his senior management team – 'Are they behind him or will the network of entrenched bureaucrats spin the web for his downfall? This is a high-risk endeavour and he had already lost the support of his political head [Balfour].'[5]

June Petersen recalled Balfour telling her husband that his skills were needed elsewhere and that he should go to sport. She said that Petersen 'contacted Sibeko and wanted them to challenge this. She agreed, but when she came to meet Vernie, she was already dressed in correctional services uniform. And he decided just to leave it. He was not fighting this. We had quite a laugh because Vernie was not a sports person at all. But he decided it was about managing the department and he moved there.'[6]

At the end of 2010, 52-year-old Petersen developed a cough, and June noticed 'how Vernie struggled to cover the pool'. 'Over Christmas, we always had fun with the kids and their music, dancing with the little ones. And he would always join in. That Christmas he just sat.'

In January 2011 Petersen went to the doctor. 'He came back with asthma medication, but I don't think it worked. I asked him to go back and ask for X-rays because this cough was getting really bad. He did and when they saw it, the doctor said, "Oh God, Vernie, one of your lungs is collapsing and your heart is enlarged."'[7]

The doctor sent him to a hospital, where he saw a physician. He was discharged the same day and allowed to travel for work. He went to Cape Town to give a speech at the District Six Museum, where he struggled to get through it. He returned to Johannesburg the next day for a meeting at OR Tambo International Airport about Cricket South Africa, where June saw him for lunch.

He had to fly to East London that evening for the funeral of a boxer which then sports minister Fikile Mbalula wanted him to attend. June was furious that he had to fly again and told him that he wouldn't even be able to carry his luggage.

'He said to me he will manage. He said one of the reasons he wanted to go that evening was that the hotel is near the beach and he wanted to hear the sea.'[8]

Vernie Petersen returned to Johannesburg for Johnny Issel's memorial service, and June was shocked by his deterioration. 'Vernie is much taller than me and normally walks much faster than I do. That day I was walking thinking, where is this man? He was walking with his hand against the wall. I knew something was not right. I said to Vernie, "I am going to the doctor with you [next] week."'

She accompanied him to a hospital in Pretoria where lung tests were done. The tests were inconclusive, and the doctors suggested a lung biopsy.

While waiting for the results, Petersen continued working, addressing a function at the German ambassador's home about a soccer donation. His friend Neil Cole, who accompanied him, remembered that he had a persistent cough. 'He struggled to get through the speech. Someone from the department came to take over the speech.'[9]

June took him back to hospital and the next day the biopsy showed that Petersen had interstitial pneumonia, 'progressive scarring of lung tissue' that can be caused by 'long-term exposure to hazardous materials, such as asbestos'.[10]

'We didn't tell friends; we didn't tell people because it's not serious; it's just a lung biopsy and he was going home,' June said.

But a week later Petersen was still in hospital. Concerned, his brothers travelled from Cape Town to see him.

On Saturday, after midnight, June was called by the hospital. 'The nurse said, "Your husband had a bad turn, come very quickly."'

June called her brother, Dudley Johnson, and asked him to come up to Pretoria from Cape Town. 'I don't think Vernie will see the sun rise,' she told him.[11]

When June arrived at the hospital, there were a number of people around her husband's bed. 'They ignored me. I pulled the one sister aside and asked her, "You guys called me. What are you doing here? What is wrong?"

'She asked me to just wait a minute, they are busy with him, there is no pulse. I'm thinking, God, what must I think? No pulse? It's like being in a dream.

'I phoned my eldest son [Ruari] and said, "Please, I don't know what is happening, you must come."

'I went into the room and asked the doctor, "What now?"

'The doctor says, "All we have to do now is to wait and see if he wakes up and cooperates with us." And they did X-rays and I heard this doctor behind me say, "Wow, look at this pneumonia." It was aggressive.

'There was a time when Vernie was linked to a breathing machine, but the machine was struggling to open up his lungs, because this disease hardens the tissue in your lungs. I just stood there, and I remember saying,

"Wake up, Vernie, wake up! This is not supposed to be happening. What am I going to do?"'

Ruari called in a bishop to give Vernie his last rites.

'We sat there, and you could see his organs shutting down. His heart was the last to shut down and then we realised they just came to take him off the machine.'[12]

At the Zondo Commission eight years later, Angelo Agrizzi testified that Bosasa had paid R1 million per month to the former prisons boss, Khulekani Sithole, and to members of the Police and Prisons Civil Rights Union to intimidate Petersen and ensure that he cooperated with the company. And during his testimony, Dennis Bloem, the former ANC MP and chair of the correctional services portfolio committee, broke down and pleaded with the commission to investigate Petersen's 'sudden' death.

For June Petersen, 'I've made peace. It is eight years. I've made peace with Vernie's death. It is very difficult because you know, when I wake up in the morning, I still look to … his side of the bed … We would sit on each of our sides of the bed and we are getting dressed and we would say, "O, *hier gaan ons altwee na onse kak jobs weer*" ("Here we are both going to our shitty jobs again"). But you know there is still a major gap in my life, because of who he was and what he meant to me and how close we were in terms of the kind of things we both wanted.'

But, she added, 'I really, really want to know what that million rand a month did. That is what I want to know. That must be investigated. And Balfour's role – he cannot get off scot-free.'[13]

After Petersen was moved out of the DCS, Bosasa faced no more obstacles in being reappointed to provide catering to prisoners in 31 of the country's largest prisons. In January 2009 the company was re-awarded the catering tender at a cost of R279 million per year. This was despite an intensifying corruption probe by the SIU into Bosasa's prisons tenders, which was public knowledge.

Xoliswa Sibeko, the new commissioner, was briefed on the SIU's findings and became concerned about Bosasa's presence in the department.

ABOVE LEFT: Gavin Watson during a public meeting in the mid-1980s in Port Elizabeth. The Watson family were staunch supporters of the ANC and the UDF. PHOTO: THE HERALD

ABOVE RIGHT: On 11 February 1990 Nelson Mandela was released from Victor Verster Prison outside Paarl, accompanied by his wife Winnie. Behind the Mandelas walked Hilda Ndude, the founding CEO of Dyambu, which became Bosasa. Ndude was an ANC activist from the Western Cape and one of the main organisers of the day of the release. PHOTO: ALLAN TANNENBAUM/GETTY

Angelo Agrizzi testified about several ANC events that were sponsored by Bosasa in cash or kind. The 2011 ANC Gauteng lekgotla was hosted on Bosasa's Mogale campus and fully sponsored by the company.

ABOVE LEFT: Lindie Gouws, who assisted with marketing and management at Bosasa and was widely thought to be Gavin Watson's mistress, often featured on the cover of Christian magazines. Bosasa funded her own magazine, *My World*, for a short time, at a loss.

ABOVE: Ronnie Watson (right) was the most politicised of the Watson brothers and played a key role in establishing Dyambu, which became Bosasa. He worked in the ANC's underground struggle alongside Chris Hani, Charles Nqakula and Linda Mti. Luke Watson (left) is the rugby-player son of Cheeky Watson, the youngest brother. Angelo Agrizzi testified how political pressure was put on the heads of SA Rugby to include Luke in the Springbok team.
PHOTO: SHARIEF JAFFER/GALLO

LEFT: Four-year-old Sinoxolo Hlabanzana died at Leratong Hospital after being illegally detained at Bosasa's Lindela repatriation facility, where his Congolese aunt was being held. According to his family, the boy wasn't fed or medically treated at Lindela. PHOTO: SUPPLIED/BHEKISISA

Bosasa CEO Gavin Watson and his colleagues with then ANC treasurer-general Zweli Mkhize at Luthuli House, after the company donated R3 million to the ANC's 2014 election campaign. Mkhize thanked Watson for Bosasa's 'ongoing support for our organisation'. From left: Papa Leshabane, Bosasa's director and spokesperson; Thandi Makoko, Bosasa's director of youth centres; Mkhize; Watson; Joe Gumede, Bosasa's chair; and Sesinyi Seopela, Bosasa's 'political fixer'.

Angelo Agrizzi testified at the Zondo Commission that Bosasa sponsored thousands of food parcels like these for ANC rallies.

Former Bosasa manager Retief van der Merwe shows his copy of the Bible that was given to staff members who attended Gavin Watson's morning prayer sessions.

Then home affairs minister Malusi Gigaba (left) during a visit to Bosasa's Lindela repatriation camp in Krugersdorp, with Bosasa's spokesperson Papa Leshabane and chief operations officer Angelo Agrizzi (right).

Bosasa sponsored at least two of former president Jacob Zuma's private birthday parties in Durban. Here, in April 2015, Zuma dances while Gavin Watson watches.

Former president Jacob Zuma celebrates his 72nd birthday in April 2014 with a cake baked by Bosasa and decorated by Angelo Agrizzi at the request of then minister Nomvula Mokonyane (left).
PHOTO: @LETHABOINJOZI/TWITTER

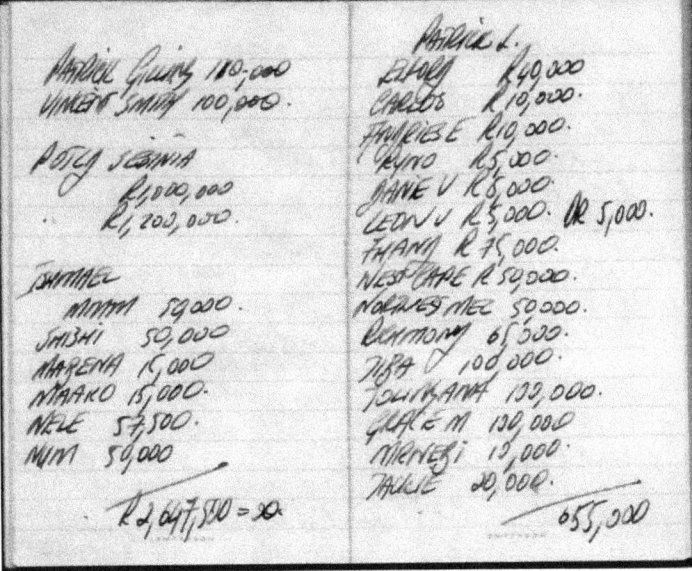

A couple of pages from Angelo Agrizzi's little black books, which he used to 'account' for the cash bribes paid to politicians and civil servants. The names of former prisons official Patrick Gillingham, ANC MP Vincent Smith, former prosecutions bosses Nomgcobo Jiba and Lawrence Mrwebi, and NPA secretary Jackie Lepinka appear on these pages.

Gavin Watson and Jacob Zuma in discussion at Zuma's Nkandla homestead in KwaZulu-Natal. Angelo Agrizzi testified that Watson had several meetings at Nkandla to discuss the criminal case against Bosasa and a shale gas project in which Bosasa was involved.

Then president Jacob Zuma visited Bosasa's Mogale campus in 2015, accompanied by Dudu Myeni and then deputy agriculture minister Bheki Cele. Back row, from left: unknown man, Papa Leshabane, Trevor Mathenjwa, Ishmael Dikani, Angelo Agrizzi and Joe Gumede; front row, from left: Myeni, Thandi Makoko, Zuma, Jackie Leyds, Gavin Watson, Lindsay Watson and Cele.

Former Bosasa COO Angelo Agrizzi, a Ferrari fanatic, owned two models of the luxury sports car, and turned his garage at his plush home in Dainfern into a Ferrari shrine.

ABOVE LEFT: Angelo Agrizzi commissioned a hand-crafted chess set featuring the 'good' and the 'captured' individuals in South Africa, with Agrizzi himself a character on the 'good' side along with President Cyril Ramaphosa and former public protector Thuli Madonsela. Gavin Watson featured on the 'bad' side with former president Jacob Zuma.

ABOVE RIGHT: Angelo Agrizzi's bombshell evidence before the Zondo Commission kicked off in January 2019 with the showing of a secretly recorded cellphone video taken inside Gavin Watson's private safe at Bosasa. In the video, millions of rands in cash, used as bribes (according to Agrizzi), is visible.
STILL FROM VIDEO BY ANDRIES VAN TONDER

This is how Zapiro portrayed Angelo Agrizzi after several days of intense testimony at the Zondo Commission, drawing inspiration from a Monty Python sketch. I am shown typing away, having been accused of embarrassing Bosasa.

Zapiro had a field day drawing all the politicians and civil servants implicated in state capture by Angelo Agrizzi.

On 5 February 2019 I gave evidence at the Zondo Commission about the intimidation and threats I'd faced from Bosasa while reporting on the company over the years.

Angelo Agrizzi's evidence before the Zondo Commission prompted friends and family of the late Vernie Petersen, who as prisons boss had tried to cancel Bosasa's contracts, to host a #Justice4Vernie rally in Cape Town.

On 26 August 2019, Gavin Watson died in a motor-vehicle accident at the entrance to OR Tambo International Airport in Johannesburg when his car crashed at high speed into a concrete pillar. PHOTO: EMPD

In 2009 a competitor to Bosasa challenged the awarding of the tender in court, and Sibeko received legal advice from two top advocates that she shouldn't oppose the application as there were solid legal grounds for the tender award to be set aside.

Not long afterwards Sibeko was suspended by Mapisa-Nqakula, the new correctional services minister, for renting a private house at R30 000 per month with public funds. A disciplinary hearing cleared her, but her contract was terminated nonetheless. Jenny Schreiner was appointed acting national commissioner.

In September 2009 the SIU handed its final report, which contained damning findings about Bosasa's tenders with the DCS, to Mapisa-Nqakula and Schreiner. The SIU handed a copy of its report to the NPA, in the hope that criminal proceedings would be instituted.

Mapisa-Nqakula said that it was sufficient to allow the NPA to handle the matter criminally and for disciplinary steps to have been instituted against Gillingham. 'I did not preoccupy myself with the issue of the contract,' she told me. 'If anything, I would have expected the contract to be cancelled by the accounting officer [the national commissioner] if it had to be cancelled ... I didn't think it was my business if there was still a legal process pending.' And she couldn't say why civil claims weren't instituted against Bosasa to recoup the money lost through corruption, which is the SIU's core function.[14]

On 7 December 2009 the NPA said in a press statement that it had forwarded the report to the police 'for further investigation. When the police investigation is finalised, they will submit the case docket to the NPA for a decision whether to prosecute or not.' (Nothing happened for another decade, until the Hawks finally started making arrests in 2019, following the testimony of Angelo Agrizzi at the Zondo Commission.)

In May 2010 Jacob Zuma appointed Tom Moyane as the new commissioner of correctional services. Moyane had come from the government printing works, where he'd been CEO reporting to Mapisa-Nqakula as home affairs minister.

Shortly after his appointment, I called Moyane to ask him what he intended do about Bosasa's continued presence in the department in light of the damning SIU report. He told me that he wasn't aware of the SIU report and hadn't seen a copy. I immediately couriered a copy to his Pretoria office.

Mapisa-Nqakula admitted to me that it was possible that she hadn't discussed the Bosasa matter with Moyane when he'd started. Her 'preoccupation, Gillingham, was gone ... how many contracts would I have had to discuss with [Moyane]? If I discussed the Bosasa contract with him, I would have had to discuss the other contracts too.'[15] She said this despite the fact that the Bosasa contracts were the largest contracts in the department by far, and that the company had been in the news for its alleged corrupt relationship with the department.

Mapisa-Nqakula reminded me that she'd found Bosasa at home affairs (Lindela) and at correctional services when she'd arrived as minister, implying that she couldn't have helped them to win the tenders. But she admitted to confiding in former home affairs director-general Jeff Maqetuka that it was 'very difficult' for her to oversee the Lindela tender. 'I knew it was run by a Watson brother; we are close to Ronnie Watson. I said to Maqetuka, "I am slightly uncomfortable being here [at home affairs]; I'm close to Ronnie Watson."'[16]

But she swore Ronnie had never asked her to do anything for his brother's company. According to her, Ronnie knew that she thought Gavin was 'arrogant', so he (Ronnie) would never raise Gavin's business issues with her.

When Tom Moyane left the DCS in September 2013, the multimillion-rand Bosasa catering contract was still firmly in place.

PART FOUR

Atonement

Angelo Agrizzi: going down

'In November 2017 I got a call from Brian Biebuyck to say he needs to see me urgently – there was a revolt in Bosasa. "You are implicated. If Gavin goes down, he's going to take you down with him."'[1]

40

The unlikely snitch

Of all the people I thought would blow the whistle on Bosasa over the years, Angelo Agrizzi was second-last on my list. Agrizzi was the quintessential yes-man, outrageously loyal to his boss, Gavin Watson, feverishly promoting and growing the Bosasa brand and company, and blinded by the extravagance of money and a lifestyle fuelled by business-class flights, Italian sports cars and fancy restaurants.

Some called Agrizzi a bullshitter, while others credited him for being the brain behind Bosasa's success. It was one thing to win tenders corruptly, but another when you actually had to deliver the services, and all former Bosasa employees I spoke to agreed that Agrizzi worked incredibly hard and was at Watson's beck and call literally all hours of the day. Watson had the political clout and struggle credentials, while Agrizzi brought the business acumen. He understood the power of access and information, and used charm to get his way.

I met Agrizzi and some of his colleagues in the early years of my investigation into Bosasa at the company's headquarters in Krugersdorp, when they still thought they could spin themselves out of trouble. He was a large, imposing figure who spoke convincingly and didn't let on when he wasn't entirely sure of what he was telling you. As an understudy to Watson – who wasn't at the meeting I attended at Bosasa, but whose presence could be felt throughout the company – he'd adopted many of the CEO's traits and behaviours in a mutually beneficial relationship built on the belief that Bosasa was part of a bigger calling by God to succeed; they had a shared ability to switch between Christian morality and naked depravity on a daily basis, and, of course, a love of money and influence.

Let there be no doubt that Angelo Agrizzi was part and parcel of the Bosasa state capture cult, and that his *mea culpa* at the Zondo Commission was both an act of atonement and a desperate attempt to reconstruct his legacy.

As chief operating officer of Bosasa, Agrizzi was second-in-charge at all times and benefited handsomely from the fruit of Bosasa's poisoned tree. In the process, the Germiston-born chef who'd dropped out of hotel school because his parents could no longer afford his studies became very, very rich. '[It was] very similar to being involved in a cult ... that you become so engrossed with what is happening and you actually start believing what is happening is right and that is why it took so long,' he said at the start of his bombshell testimony at the Zondo Commission of Inquiry into state capture. 'I became blunt in understanding what was happening at this stage and I became very accepting, but unfortunately it happens to a lot of people and my urge ... is for people out there, especially in Bosasa, to start coming forward as well ... I kept quiet and I should have exposed unlawful activities from day one.'[2]

Further explaining his *mea culpa* to chief evidence leader Paul Pretorius, Agrizzi referred to something that had happened to him at the end of 2016: 'I had a near-death experience where I was admitted into hospital and I had a tumour in my heart. I was in a coma and when I came out of the coma, myself and my family had made a conscious decision that we will clean up where we had made mistakes before.'[3]

I heard in 2016 that Agrizzi had fallen out with Gavin Watson, and at first I didn't believe it; I thought that it was probably just another ploy to distract me and other people investigating Bosasa from their criminal deeds. But as it turned out, miracles do happen, and knowing how deep he was inside the state capture machine that was Bosasa, I approached him in 2017 with a request to talk to me. He knew exactly who I was and invited me for a meeting at his posh house in Dainfern, north of Johannesburg.

I knew that Agrizzi had made some money from Bosasa but I was shocked at the sheer scale of the opulence I saw that day. His garages were a shrine to Ferrari, housing two Ferrari sports cars and a ton of memorabilia from Italy. Outside stood his BMW. Inside the house the walls were festooned with works by contemporary South African artists, and all the cutlery and glasses were shiny and new. A fan of personalised chess boards, Agrizzi had a 'state capture'-themed one, featuring himself as one of the 'good guys' alongside people like President Cyril Ramaphosa and the former public protector Thuli Madonsela, with Gavin Watson being on the 'bad' side with former president Jacob Zuma and Ajay Gupta. He also showed me his miniature monkeys. The Asset Forfeiture Unit, whose job it was to seize criminal assets, was going to have a field day with this lot, I kept thinking.

It was in this house that Agrizzi would later, in September 2018, be caught on tape making racist statements; and in the same taped conversation, he boasted to Watson's grownup children that I had visited him at his home with my children – he had clearly wanted to impress on the junior Watsons that he'd somehow succeeded in turning me, Bosasa's oldest nemesis. When the clip was published by *City Press* I was naturally furious and told Agrizzi that he'd had no right to lie about my children visiting his house. He apologised and told me that he'd wanted to 'shake them up' by lying about my family visiting his house.

The clip went viral on Twitter under the fiery stewardship of former journalist Pinky Khoabane, who was aggressively trying to undermine my reporting on Bosasa for reasons only she knew. Even after telling her that I'd never taken my children to Agrizzi's house – or on any work assignment, for that matter – she continued spreading the myth that I was a close friend of the corrupt and racist Agrizzi. Agrizzi told the Zondo Commission that Khoabane was one of the journalists on Bosasa's payroll, an allegation she strongly disputed.

Agrizzi was hesitant to talk to me on the day of my visit to his home, saying that he was working on putting together a bigger case to expose Bosasa. But he did admit to having been indoctrinated by Watson and his 'cult' through a combination of religion, money and fear.

Towards the end of 2018 I heard that Agrizzi was planning to go to the Zondo Commission and was working on a tell-all affidavit with his lawyers. I picked up rumours about a black book containing the names of all

Bosasa's blessees, and I expected Agrizzi to talk about the 'usual suspects' I'd exposed during my 13-year-long investigation into the company.

I had no idea of the enormity and scale of the files Agrizzi was about to drop. Bosasa had captured not only key state institutions, but also a large chunk of the governing ANC.

41

From the Guptas to the Watsons

On 16 January 2019 Angelo Agrizzi became a household name in South Africa when he blew open the largest state capture scandal in the country's history since the #GuptaLeaks, hard drives containing thousands of emails detailing alleged correspondence between the Gupta family, government officials and chief executives of state-owned companies which had been published in mid-2017.

Agrizzi's evidence before the Zondo Commission into state capture introduced an entire new dynamic to the state capture narrative. Unlike the Guptas, who were originally from India, it was a South African businessman with deep struggle roots who owned and ran Bosasa.

Gavin Watson and his brothers were well known ANC activists, particularly in the Eastern Cape, and the revelations forced the ANC to confront capture and corruption in its own bosom. It was easy to blame an Indian family for capturing 'our people'; it was exceedingly harder to confront the reality of crooked comrades who'd corrupted other comrades in their mutual pursuit of rent-seeking and self-enrichment.

And state capture was now no longer limited to Jacob Zuma and his tenure in office (although Zuma himself was implicated by Agrizzi in protecting and promoting Bosasa). Agrizzi's evidence sketched a frightening picture of how the ANC was for sale to the highest bidder and how a company could literally buy its way out of prison.

The other, major distinguishing factor between the Guptas and Gavin Watson was that Bosasa hadn't zoomed in on one politician and his family, as the Guptas had with former president Jacob Zuma, or on one project, such as the ill-fated R1.42-trillion nuclear deal Russia had tried to conclude with Zuma. Indeed, Bosasa had survived the tenures of Mbeki, Motlanthe and Zuma; and over many years Watson and his colleagues had cultivated mutually beneficial relationships with hundreds of civil servants and politicians at different levels of government to buy influence and access, making a fortune out of hundreds of smaller contracts and tenders in municipalities and provinces and from national departments.

Most of Bosasa's blessees weren't well known ministers, but lower-level officials who had access to the tender office, knew what a premier or mayor wanted done next, or could leak competitive information to Bosasa before a tender process had closed. 'I just buy them chicken,' Watson once told a former employee who asked him about his success in obtaining business from government.[1]

Although he was the least politically involved of the brothers, Gavin Watson used his ANC background as a ticket to ride the gravy train. 'My blood is green, black and gold,' he boldly declared to the Public Protector, Busisiwe Mkhwebane, during his interview about the R500 000 donation he'd paid to President Cyril Ramaphosa's presidential campaign.[2]

Most of the evidence led by the commission from its inception in August 2018 had concerned the Guptas and the Zuma era, but evidence leader Paul Pretorius, whom journalist Mandy Wiener dubbed 'South Africa's Robert Mueller', had different plans for 2019.[3] 'Agrizzi alleges that the senior management of a group of companies known as Bosasa, senior government employees, politicians and others are and were involved in criminal activities centred on tender fraud and corruption for the past 20 years. The amount of money involved in these illegal activities probably amounts to billions of South African rands. All those involved in these corruption practices received substantial cash and other gratuities,' Pretorius read from an affidavit by the commission's lead investigator, Frank Dutton.[4]

Pretorius told Judge Raymond Zondo that Agrizzi would testify to 'corporate and individual conduct over a period of many years, bordering on 20 years. He will testify to conduct involving bribery, fraud, corruption, money laundering and, arguably, even on his own version, state capture.'[5]

But, said Pretorius, Agrizzi's evidence should be approached with 'caution'. It could be 'entirely fabricated, exaggerated or distorted' and motivated by improper intentions, or it could be 'reliable and true and correct in part, material part or as a whole'.[6]

To balance the probability of Agrizzi telling lies, the commission sought corroborating evidence in the form of video recordings, other witnesses, documents and audio recordings – of which it found plenty, including my own evidence about Bosasa's attempts to silence me.

'[Agrizzi] implicates about 38 people, many of whom are persons of stature and influence, in alleged corrupt practices, money laundering and tax evasion. This includes bribery of public officials and politicians,' Pretorius continued.[7]

The nation was gripped, and Bosasa's blessers and blessees were shaking in their boots. Would Agrizzi drop their names?

The commission deviated from the usual practice of commissions of its type, of informing all implicated persons prior to evidence being given that their names would be mentioned. This was because of legitimate death threats made against Agrizzi, including one emanating from Bosasa in which a senior director was recorded as saying Agrizzi should watch his back 'because a prisoner could easily be released from Westville prison, kill someone and then be returned to the prison and have a solid alibi for the killing'.[8] Another threatening SMS read, 'Tell Agrizzi we have been patient and he needs to be careful. We do not want another funeral shortly.'[9]

Agrizzi decided that to testify in public was his best protection.

Agrizzi stated unequivocally that Bosasa didn't win any tender without paying bribes – there was literally not one tender that wasn't tainted by bribery and corruption, he testified. He provided the Zondo Commission with a table showing Bosasa's government contracts, their values, and the estimated value of the kickbacks paid annually to hold onto these tenders:

Agrizzi explained Bosasa's 'business model' to the commission as revolving around 'monthly payments'. 'Normally, if somebody is involved in bribery and they do a deal, what would happen is they would get a monthly payment instead of a lump sum. Or perhaps every second month they would get a monthly payment, because that way, according to the way

Contract name Company/ Department	Description	Contract value	Estimated annual bribes paid in cash
Correctional Services Bosasa Operations	Catering	R580 million	R15 million
Department of Transport Kgwerano Asset Finance	Fleet	R122 million	R3.6 million
Department of Justice Sondolo IT	Security systems	R700 million	R16.5 million
Correctional Services Sondolo IT	Access control and CCTV	R241 million	R4.2 million
Correctional Services Sondolo IT	Televisions	R300 million	R5 million
Correctional Services Phezulu Fencing	Fencing	R800 million	R10 million
North West Youth Bosasa	Youth services	R32 million	R4.5 million
Mogale Youth Centre Bosasa	Youth services	R14 million	R2.3 million
Airports Company South Africa Bosasa Security	Security guards	R32 million	R2.2 million
North West Youth Development Centres	Pre-opening expenses, fencing and software	R4.5 million	R2.2 million
Eskom Sondolo IT	Access control	Unknown (left when it started)	Unknown (left when it started)
Department of Home Affairs Lindela	Accommodation of undocumented migrants	R85 million	R7.2 million
Passenger Rail Agency of South Africa Sondolo IT	Access control	Unknown (left when it started)	Unknown (left when it started)

it was explained to me by my superiors at the time, you then have a hold over that person. Because they get their lifestyle accustom [sic] to that, so there were monthly payments.'[10]

Judge Raymond Zondo engaged Agrizzi on this, saying, 'And this way of bribing people – every month or at certain intervals continuously – are you able to say whether actually that would contribute to … making sure that, if I am in a government department or if I am in a company where Bosasa has a contract that is going to be coming to an end, and I have influence, and I know that if this contract of Bosasa is not extended or renewed, I will not be getting this extra cash, then, in all probability, I would be doing whatever I can for the contract to be renewed and to be extended, because if it is extended, then I continue to enjoy the lifestyle that I have become used to?'

'One hundred percent correct,' Agrizzi replied, adding, 'This is why we are in the situation we are in this country today.' He continued, 'You do not entrap somebody for life when you pay them a once off, because they take their money and they go, and they ... do something else, but once you start paying people – and I have realised that myself, the hard way – once you start paying people bribes on a monthly basis, for as long as that they are there, you control them one hundred percent.'[11]

Zondo remarked correctly that despite Bosasa's corruption allegations having been well publicised by me and other journalists for many years, the company had continued to receive government work. 'So this might provide the explanation, because people who may have had the power to stop the contracts did not stop them because they were continuing to benefit on a continuous basis, and if they stopped the contracts to Bosasa or did not renew them, they would be adversely affected in terms of the monetary value that they were getting from Bosasa.'

In this way Bosasa established long-term relationships with the enablers in the state departments from which they were scoring, helping the company to remain on the payroll for many years. In home affairs, for example, the Lindela contract had been with Bosasa since 1996.

Agrizzi testified that the first bribes-for-tenders corruption he was aware of in Bosasa was paid to employees of Sasol, the Post Office and the Airports Company South Africa.

He then introduced South Africa to the source of much of Bosasa's success and despair: Gavin's safe.

42

Monopoly money

'Gavin Watson would spend a lot of time in my office, and so would every other director, and normally I would be behind my desk and I had a small table and they would spend time there. So a lot of the times, directors would come in and ask Gavin for money because they [needed] to sort this person out or that person out, or they [needed] to literally pay bribes … So Gavin would then go to what I referred to specifically, and what everybody else did, as "Gavin's safe",' Agrizzi told the Zondo Commission.[1]

It was from Gavin's safe, situated in one of 'about eight' walk-in vaults at Bosasa, that the company conducted its cash-for-tenders business. 'If they wanted [money for] anything else other than bribing people, they would have gone to petty cash. I had very stringent forms in place. This was for bribes.'

Watson would put the money in a grey plastic bag, similar to a police evidence bag, and hand it over, according to Agrizzi. 'Cash was nothing in the company. It was just money. It was paper. Watson called it Monopoly money – it is just easily disposable.'

While most people would recognise the term 'Monopoly money' as referring to the play money used in the famous board game, Judge Zondo conferred on it an additional meaning. Asking Agrizzi for clarification, he said, 'So "monopoly" in the sense being, Bosasa wanted to monopolise state contracts?' to which Agrizzi responded, 'Correct.'

Agrizzi and Zondo became more relaxed with each other as his evidence continued, and I got a sense that the judge was extremely grateful to have a whistleblower who was that close to the fire at his commission.

After Bosasa's chief financial officer, Andries van Tonder, or a colleague had counted the money, it would go into a second safe nicknamed 'the oven'. 'This is where the bread [money] would cool down before being moved out,' Agrizzi testified.

Gavin's safe was refilled on a weekly basis to have a steady cashflow of money for kickbacks. Van Tonder later testified how he had to pick up the cash at a shopping mall close to Lanseria Airport on Johannesburg's West Rand.

During his testimony Agrizzi made it clear that at all times Watson was the one who had final say over who should be paid and how much. They would, however, sometimes debate whether an official should be a recipient of Bosasa's blessings or not, based on the person's 'usefulness' to and support for the company.

'"Support for" an organisation in this context meaning, will that person do what is necessary to get a tender for the company, is that what it meant?' Pretorius asked.

'You have hit the nail on the head,' Agrizzi said.

Bosasa spent between R4 million and R6 million a month on bribes through this cash scheme, Agrizzi said, and described these sums as 'a drop in the ocean' compared to the group's annual turnover.[2]

On Tuesday 28 March 2017, Andries van Tonder had had enough. Having worked for Bosasa for 22 years, the financial head was no longer able or willing to be one of Gavin Watson's henchmen. He'd got very rich from working for Bosasa – probably richer than he ever would've managed in a normal, 'clean', private-sector capacity – but he wanted to put an end to living a compromised life.

Van Tonder had seen henchmen come and go, doing Watson's dirty work because Watson wouldn't put his own signature to paper and hardly ever used a computer. These employees were expendable: Danny Mansell, Tony Perry and Angelo Agrizzi – all were senior Watson yes-men who'd ultimately got the boot. 'He used these people to do his corrupt and unlawful actions for him on his behalf, and then he would just dispose of them after they [had] served their purpose.'³

Van Tonder knew he was next for the chop, and he'd remained in close contact with Agrizzi, who by then had left Bosasa's employment. The two men were starting to build a case together. They knew they had to destroy Watson's plausible deniability that he knew nothing about the looting and bribery to win tenders worth hundreds of millions of rands from which he largely benefited. They needed Watson and his 'Monopoly money' on tape.

A plan was hatched. Van Tonder would use his cellphone as a recording device, putting it in his top pocket before entering Gavin's safe. 'Angelo Agrizzi asked me to take the video as [he'd] received information that Gavin Watson [would] place all the blame of possible illegal conducts on myself and Angelo Agrizzi, and Gavin Watson always boasted that he [had] never signed any document which might incriminate him,' Van Tonder later testified.⁴

On the morning of 28 March 2017, Van Tonder made the conscious break with the corrupt regime with which his life was ensnared. He put the phone in his top pocket, but quickly realised that the pocket was too deep. Removing the phone, he slipped an eraser into his pocket, and carefully reinserted the phone – the eraser gave the phone just enough lift to expose its lens.

Van Tonder was sweating and breathing heavily; he was feeling 'extremely nervous'. He'd heard the stories about how dangerous Watson could be, and later admitted to Zondo he was 'still fearful of' his ex boss. 'Gavin Watson is connected to very powerful people right up to the highest level in government, and many of those people actually visited the Bosasa head office and they were introduced to some of the staff,' he told the commission.⁵

Nonetheless, Van Tonder pressed the record button on his phone and entered Watson's walk-in safe. The resulting video was a masterstroke, providing corroborating evidence for Agrizzi's extraordinary testimony.

'Good morning, Gavin,' Van Tonder can be heard saying as he enters the vault, a small room sparsely furnished with a table, steel cupboards, a drop safe and two chairs. Van Tonder's heavy breathing is audible, and at some point Watson asks him if he is okay.

Joe Gumede, Bosasa's chair and head of its security company, BlackRox, is sitting with Watson. Papa Leshabane is standing talking on his cellphone, holding two bags of the type that Agrizzi testified were used for cash.

Van Tonder carries a cardboard box stashed with R1 million in crisp R100 notes packed in parcels of R100 000 each. The duct tape is ripped off the box and Watson removes the cash parcels, piling them onto the desk. Gumede can be heard asking Watson for R10 000 'to purchase two panic buttons', something Agrizzi interpreted as coded language for something else, probably more bribe money.

Narrating the video for the commission, Agrizzi pointed out a drop safe in the walk-in vault into which he would often deposit money for Watson when the latter wasn't around. He had bruises on his hands from all the times he'd had to drop cash there for Watson, Agrizzi testified, because the opening to the drop safe was too narrow for his large hands.

Agrizzi further identified two black books on the shelves in the vault, and the grey bags used for transporting the bribes. The bags of cash were dropped off by Watson, himself, other directors, or middlemen like Linda Mti (who Agrizzi claimed had been instrumental in keeping Bosasa out of court). The bags of money were handed over at offices, houses and restaurants, sometimes wrapped in newspaper.

Agrizzi testified that the grey bags stuffed with money were also given to Bosasa staff to keep them quiet. Van Tonder, for example, would receive R20 000 in cash monthly on top of his salary, which was paid by EFT.

In the video, Watson can be heard saying 'Here is your stuff, Andries,' which Van Tonder confirmed was his R20 000 'hush money'. Watson often reminded them 'that we are also compromised now'.

Crucially, in the video Watson implicates his long-time attorney Brian Biebuyck in continuing to pay cash to Patrick Gillingham, the disgraced former correctional services chief financial officer. 'Brian will handle him every month and then you can pay him every month,' Watson can be heard telling Van Tonder.

Agrizzi testified that previously he used to 'handle' Gillingham, looking after his cash and paying for his divorce and his children, but that he stopped fulfilling this role after he left Bosasa, which is when Gillingham was 'handed over' to Biebuyck.

Angelo Agrizzi: bookkeeping bribes

'I was tasked with recording the information and the amounts required, which I recorded in what became known as "the black book". The reason I was asked to do this was because of the number of withdrawals. I could not remember them all. I would have to account for any funds that were passed on to me, should I be questioned on the reconciliations by Gavin Watson.'[1]

43

The little black books

Angelo Agrizzi told the Zondo Commission that Gavin Watson had asked him to develop a checks-and-balances system for the payment of cash bribes from Gavin's safe.

For years I'd heard stories about Bosasa's secret lists and files with the names of corrupt people who were on their payroll, and I'd envisaged a room full of lever-arch files. In fact, Agrizzi said, he'd started by making notes on 'loose pieces of paper', using codes for the names of civil servants and politicians who'd received cash payments from the company to promote and protect its interests. But the paper system was inefficient, so Agrizzi began using little black books – A5 Moleskine journals.

Writing in black ink and capital letters, Agrizzi had penned the names of Bosasa officials, politicians and civil servants – mainly from the DCS – neatly on the crisp white pages.

Agrizzi attached copies of his little black books to his witness statement, apologising for smudges 'because I use a fountain pen and sometimes I slip'. A sample page read:

  PATRICK GILLINGHAM 110,000
  VINCENT SMITH 100,000
  JIBA 100,000
  GRACE M 100,000
  MRWEBI 10,000
  JACKIE 20,000
  PAPA LESH – Z. MODISE 1,000,000

THE LITTLE BLACK BOOKS

I wasn't surprised to see the correctional services names in the little black books – Bosasa had captured the department thoroughly and were blessing numerous employees, having started with Linda Mti when he was commissioner, moving through Patrick Gillingham, who remained on Bosasa's payroll even after leaving correctional services, and continuing right through to Tom Moyane's successor, Zach Modise, who, according to Agrizzi, had received up to R1 million in bribe payments.

The two names I hadn't expected to see on the lists were those of Jiba and Mrwebi – two of the most senior prosecutors at the NPA who had overseen almost a decade of inaction on the case. Both denied receiving bribes from Bosasa.

All forms of state capture are despicable and should be condemned, but the manipulation of the prosecuting authority is a special kind of evil.

I'd suspected foul play in the NPA's approach to the Bosasa matter since 2009, when the SIU had first handed over its report to the prosecuting authority. At that time the NPA had issued a terse statement, saying that the case needed more investigation and that it had been referred to the Hawks, the brand-new amalgamation of the police's serious organised crimes and commercial branches. With no focused anti-corruption capacity, however, it was a shadow of the Scorpions that it replaced.

The NPA's passing off the case, which was all but trial ready based on the SIU's own investigations, sent a clear message.

Over the years I'd sent the NPA countless media queries about the lack of progress on the case. The response was always the same: the Hawks were still investigating.

From insiders I heard that prosecutor Marijke de Kock, who'd been assigned to the case, was almost obsessively diligent. She wouldn't talk directly to me – the NPA has a centralised communications policy – but I suspected there was something more than the prosecutor's apparent lack of urgency that was keeping the matter out of court.

Agrizzi's evidence to the Zondo Commission confirmed that indeed it wasn't incompetence that had enabled Gavin Watson and Bosasa to avoid

193

the inside of a courtroom for over a decade: he painted a shocking picture of how Bosasa 'bought' case dockets and evidence using its connections in the ANC. He provided the Zondo Commission with copies of preliminary charge sheets, internal memorandums and NPA letters that the company had bought from the NPA over the years.

Linda Mti, Agrizzi testified, was the connector to Nomgcobo Jiba (known as 'the snake' at Bosasa), Lawrence Mrwebi ('the snail') and Jackie Lepinka. At the time, Jiba was a deputy NDPP, Mrwebi headed up the NPA's commercial crimes unit, and Lepinka was the executive assistant in the office of the NDPP, Menzi Simelane, which gave her access to sensitive documents. (Lepinka had worked as Mti's assistant at the DCS before he was moved to the 2010 Soccer World Cup local organising committee; according to their former colleagues, their relationship went deeper than a professional working arrangement.)

Agrizzi testified how Bosasa would deliver R130 000 every month to Mti for distribution to Jiba (R100 000), Lepinka (R20 000) and Mrwebi (R10 000). Agrizzi hadn't been present when the money was delivered, and Jiba and Mrwebi strongly denied receiving bribes from Bosasa. What is not in dispute, however, is that somehow the company received 17 confidential documents from within the NPA, and the Bosasa case never made it to court.

Bosasa received documentary support to which it wasn't entitled not only from within the NPA, but also at a political level. One of the documents leaked to Agrizzi and Watson from Simelane's office was the minutes of a special ministerial meeting in March 2010, convened after Simelane had told Glynnis Breytenbach, who then headed up the NPA's commercial crimes unit in Pretoria, to withdraw from the Bosasa matter. Present at the meeting were then justice minister Jeff Radebe, then correctional services minister Nosiviwe Mapisa-Nqakula and Simelane as head of the NPA. The minutes reflect an astonishing presentation by Simelane to the two ministers, laced with conspiracy theories and innuendo, during which he rubbished the SIU's investigation and report into Bosasa as unconstitutional and improper, without then SIU head Willie Hofmeyr being present to defend himself.

Simelane told Radebe and Mapisa-Nqakula that he'd identified a 'political vendetta/agenda' and that the public had been manipulated by the discussion of the SIU report in Parliament and in the media – in November 2009 Hofmeyr had given a presentation to Parliament's portfolio committee on correctional services during which he'd confirmed that the SIU had found evidence of criminality in the Bosasa tenders, and referred to Carien du Plessis' and my reporting on the probe.

'A concern on credibility of certain individuals and/or the effected [sic] organisation is a serious concern and might cost the NPA much with possible litigations,' Simelane said, and added that a 'predetermined element was identified as well as the race of both the investigators and prosecutors.'[2] The lead investigators from both the SIU and the SAPS, and the prosecutor working on the case, were white.

Simelane was effectively informing the ministers that the investigation by the SIU into Bosasa was one big conspiracy by white investigators and advocates (and probably journalists). The final sentence of his presentation is telling: 'Close monitoring is important to ensure fair trial and investigation, if any.' If any! Watson and co must have smiled broadly after this document was leaked to them.

Simelane's report read more like an amateurish attempt at a cloak-and-dagger intelligence note, steeped in conspiracy, than serious feedback from an NDPP. No wonder he was removed from his position a year later, when the courts upheld an application by the DA that his fitness for the position of NDPP hadn't been properly assessed by Zuma and Radebe before his appointment.

Unfortunately, Simelane's 'if any' comment didn't leave the NPA with him, as the case remained out of the courts for another decade. However, when the Bosasa matter did finally to go court in 2019, the same SIU report formed the bedrock of the NPA's charge sheet.

Mapisa-Nqakula said she had no recollection of the meeting with Simelane and didn't recall discussing the Bosasa matter with Simelane at all.[3]

Despite her initial criticism of the way the SIU had drafted its report, prosecutor Marijke de Kock was ready to submit her draft indictment against 27 accused persons and entities, including Watson, Agrizzi, Mti and Gillingham, to Jiba in the second half of 2013. She drew up a racketeering charge sheet, describing Bosasa as a criminal enterprise, and noted that, although the prosecution was at an advanced stage, a forensic audit and other investigative work were still outstanding.

Despite being so sensitive about document security that some of her colleagues called her 'crazy', all De Kock's important communiques with the office of the NDPP up to that point had been leaked to Bosasa via Mti. She testified at the Zondo Commission that she'd had a suspicion that confidential NPA documents were being leaked after having received correspondence from Bosasa's attorney Brian Biebuyck in which he displayed knowledge of information that could only have originated from the NPA's files.[4]

Included in Agrizzi's documents that he handed over to the Zondo Commission was a handwritten note from Mti in 2013 on 'what Jiba said they [Bosasa] should use' in challenging the legality of the Bosasa investigation. Points scribbled down included 'legality of the SIU report', 'evidence as contained in the report and how it was obtained', 'fundamental rights encroached upon', 'timelines', 'legal basis for the ongoing prosecution', 'relief sought' and 'approach and unethical conduct of the process'.[5]

In February 2016 then NDPP Shaun Abrahams removed De Kock from the case. Six years had passed, and he was reportedly unhappy with the lack of progress. Laughably, Jiba also blamed De Kock for 'messing up' the case, denying that she'd taken cash to stonewall the matter.[6]

A colleague of De Kock's defended her, saying 'she always maintained that the Bosasa case must and will be prosecuted. There was a lot of interference in this case.'[7]

(De Kock agreed in April 2019 to submit a supplementary affidavit to the Zondo Commission, detailing the interference in the prosecution. Until all this detail is known, it is difficult to say whether her 'slow' working pace or the leaking of her charge sheets and documents to Bosasa, or a combination of both, kept the case out of the courts for ten years.)

In September 2018, journalist Kyle Cowan obtained a copy of an audio recording of a meeting between Watson, Agrizzi and Mti in May 2015 in which they discussed Watson's approach to former president Jacob Zuma in a meeting they were scheduled to have. Watson was going to portray Bosasa as the victim of a plot by the media and anti-ANC forces. 'Mr President, we need to get this thing [the criminal investigation] closed down. We need the right people in the right place,' Watson could be heard saying, in preparation for what he'd say in his meeting with Zuma. '[Berning] Ntlemeza [the former head of the Hawks] is the right guy at that place, doing what he can. Now we need to get the right person at NPA.'[8]

This discussion took place shortly before the appointment of Shaun Abrahams as NPA head in June 2015. Abrahams strongly denied that Watson had anything to do with his appointment.[9]

44

A stuffed Louis Vuitton bag and a charge sheet

The relationship between the Watsons and former president Jacob Zuma was intriguing.

The brothers had met Zuma in exile, outside of South Africa, while he was part of the organisation's intelligence structures. In the Kristin Williamson biography of the Watsons, mention is made by Valence of their dealings with leaders 'like Jacob Zuma of ANC Intelligence … we found them to be gentlemen of integrity with a strong sense of justice and a commitment to peace'.[1]

After the unbanning of the ANC, the Watsons were instructed by ANC leaders like Zuma and Chris Hani to 'mingle with whites and find out what they could about their attitudes to a possible change of power in South Africa. They also had to convince the business community that their businesses would not be nationalised. Their task was to shed light on what the ANC was all about so as to counter the negative propaganda against it.'[2]

Under the Thabo Mbeki presidency, Bosasa had been strongly associated with ANC leaders from the Eastern Cape, where the Watsons were regarded as royalty. Ngconde Balfour, Linda Mti and Gibson Njenje all hail from the Eastern Cape and were close associates of the Watsons.

After Zuma took over the leadership of the ANC and presidency of the country in May 2009, Gavin Watson needed to rekindle the relationship with his old family friend. To get access to 'Number One', he solicited the assistance of two of the president's close associates, Dudu Myeni and Nomvula Mokonyane.

A STUFFED LOUIS VUITTON BAG AND A CHARGE SHEET

Myeni, a businesswoman from Richards Bay in KwaZulu-Natal who would go on to chair both South African Airways (SAA) and the Jacob G Zuma Foundation, had been romantically linked to Zuma for many years, despite denials by both. Her son, Thalente, lived in Zuma's Forest Town, Johannesburg house and once applied for an emergency visa on the basis that he was Zuma's son.[3] And Thalente Myeni had been a business partner of Sesinyi 'Commander' Seopela, Bosasa's political fixer, in a Prasa deal in which they'd scored R16.5 million.[4]

'Dudu Myeni was first introduced to me at the Sheraton Hotel in Pretoria,' Agrizzi stated in his affidavit to the Zondo Commission.[5] 'It was an informal introduction as I was with Gavin Watson coincidently at the time. I was well aware that Gavin Watson had committed to paying R300 000 a month in cash to Myeni for onward payment to the "Jacob Zuma Foundation". On occasions, I would have to pack the money for him in this regard. At this time, Dudu Myeni was the chair of the Jacob Zuma Foundation.'

Agrizzi testified that Watson said that he 'hoped she is giving it [the R300 000] to Zuma'.[6]

Agrizzi recalled an incident when Watson asked him how he could impress Myeni. 'He asked for my wife's advice. My wife said he should purchase her a nice handbag. She arranged with Louis Vuitton Sandton to procure one. The handbag was delivered. R300 000 in cash was placed in the bag. The bag was then given to her by Gavin Watson. I know this because of my discussions with Gavin Watson and because Dudu Myeni thanked me personally.'[7]

'Myeni would often call on Gavin Watson to arrange functions for President Zuma and his family,' Agrizzi recalled. 'Gavin Watson and directors of the Bosasa group would be invited. The cost of these functions extended to millions of rand per function.'[8]

Two of the functions Bosasa sponsored were Zuma's private birthday parties at Dube House, his official residence in Durban, in 2015 and 2016. In late 2017, the media were leaked pictures taken at the 2015 party of a dancing Zuma surrounded by family and friends, and being cheered on by Gavin Watson.

Bosasa forked out about R3.5 million for the parties through Myeni and the Jacob G Zuma Foundation.[9] Bosasa catered for 300+ people, erected a luxury marquee tent, and served prawns harvested at its (now defunct) aquaculture farm in Krugersdorp.[10]

'On behalf of the Patron of the Jacob G Zuma Foundation, His Excellency, the President of the Republic of South Africa, Mr Jacob Zuma, may we take this opportunity to thank you for the splendid birthday dinner planned at a short notice,' Myeni wrote to Watson and his colleagues in April 2016. 'The family was thrilled to have a memorable time with their father, intimately enjoying the wonderful dinner, prepared with care. The chef's creativity and professionalism was commended by everyone. Thank you for your generosity and time spent to ensure that the first family had the grandest birthday.'[11]

Leshabane, on behalf of Bosasa, said it was untrue that Bosasa had a 'special relationship' with Zuma and the ANC. 'African Global [Bosasa's new name] does interact with the ANC as the current ruling party of our Republic,' Leshabane said, conveniently failing to mention that Bosasa didn't only 'interact' with the ANC, but also donated money to its elections campaign, sponsored food parcels for its rallies, made its facilities available for the ANC's war room during elections, and blessed numerous ANC politicians in cash and kind.

(Three years after Jacob Zuma's R3.5-million party, Zuma's successor Cyril Ramaphosa was fighting the political battle of his life after having received a R500 000 contribution from Watson to his presidential campaign in 2017.)

The relationship between Myeni and Watson developed to such an extent that the then acting SAA chair managed to arrange a meeting with Zuma at his Nkandla homestead in KwaZulu-Natal in 2014 for Watson and prospective business partners interested in fracking for gas in the Karoo. Fracking, also known as hydraulic fracturing, is a controversial process that involves using a highly pressurised mixture of water and chemicals to drill into shale beds to release gas trapped inside the rocks.

'Bosasa had been approached by [businessman] Aneel Radhakrishna to become involved in the Karoo tracking transaction,' Agrizzi expanded in his testimony. '[Irish oil and gas company] Falcon Oil and Gas [chairman] Phillip O'Quigley, had expressed an interest to an attorney Lizel Oberholzer, who was a friend of Radhakrishna. He then brought the opportunity to Bosasa. I believe the reason that the opportunity was brought to Bosasa was that Radhakrishna had been told by me that Myeni was close to Gavin Watson. Myeni's influence over President Zuma was an important factor. Certain amendments to regulations were required to facilitate the transaction.'[12]

'It transpired that Dudu Myeni coordinated a meeting at Nkandla between Gavin Watson, O'Quigley and Oberholzer. It was the intention that at this meeting President Zuma would be persuaded to advise the minister of mineral resources to effect the legislative changes,' Agrizzi stated.[13]

O'Quigley confirmed attending a meeting with Zuma in 2014 that was facilitated by Bosasa.[14]

In early 2015 Zuma referred the Mineral and Petroleum Resources Development Act, which governs fracking, back to Parliament, which resulted in the promulgation of petroleum exploration and production regulations, under the Act, aimed at regulating fracking in South Africa.

(In 2019, the Supreme Court of Appeal set aside regulations in the Act that govern fracking, and Gwede Mantashe, Ramaphosa's mineral resources minister, announced that fracking would not happen, 'but we can access that gas if we use methodologies other than fracking, and that is what we are going to be focusing on.'[15])

The fracking meeting wasn't Watson's only sojourn at Nkandla. 'Myeni would coordinate numerous meetings at President Zuma's Nkandla residence to discuss matters with President Zuma. On one such occasion Gavin Watson was concerned that the R300 000 per month he was giving to Myeni was in fact not being delivered to President Zuma in full. He arranged to meet with President Zuma at Nkandla, and there personally handed the bag of R300 000 in cash to President Zuma. This was confirmed to me by both Gavin Watson and [Joe] Gumede who had attended the meeting,' Agrizzi said.[16]

In 2015 Watson told Agrizzi that he'd raised the Hawks' investigation into Bosasa with Zuma, who'd allegedly agreed to 'make a call to a senior official at the Hawks so that a meeting could be arranged between the Hawks and [Bosasa chair Joe] Gumede'.[17]

Gumede later told Agrizzi that the meeting with the Hawks had taken place.

What happened next placed Myeni firmly in the picture. Agrizzi recalled, 'One afternoon Gavin Watson asked that I attend a meeting with Myeni. He told me that she had important information regarding the Hawks investigation. She apparently also had had discussions at the NPA. She had told Gavin Watson that she had had long meetings at the NPA. Once more Gavin Watson prepared the R300 000. We proceeded to the Sheraton [hotel in Pretoria], where we were escorted to a private lounge area with stringent access control. I think it was a members-only lounge on the 6th floor.

'At the meeting Myeni briefed us. She said she was trying to arrange that the [Hawks] investigation be terminated. She produced a police case docket. She was insistent that I do not make copies.

'I asked Gavin Watson and Myeni if I could be excused to study the docket quietly and if I could make notes in my journal. Myeni conceded reluctantly on the basis that I would not make copies or [take] photos. She said that the docket had been obtained from the NPA. I took the docket to a quiet spot and took a few photos on my cellphone.'[18]

The photos, handed to the commission, show an Anti-Corruption Task Team (ACTT) progress and audit report into the Bosasa investigation. (The ACTT was established by the government to facilitate cooperation between the Hawks, the South African Revenue Service (SARS), the NPA, the SIU and other investigative agencies.) The carpet, visible in the photos, was confirmed by the commission's investigators as that of the Sheraton.

'I was interrupted by Myeni who seemed very nervous. I thought it best to appease her and return the docket to her,' Agrizzi said.[19]

At the meeting Watson asked Myeni to speak to President Zuma about the investigation 'as a matter of urgency'.[20]

Watson told Agrizzi and his colleagues about another meeting he'd had with Zuma at Nkandla, after it had been revealed that the state had paid almost R250 million for upgrades to the private homestead. According to

A STUFFED LOUIS VUITTON BAG AND A CHARGE SHEET

Agrizzi, '[Watson] would always go out of his way to let everybody know that he saw the president. So that made him feel good and important, so I let him have his say in front of all the executives. And he basically told them that he had been to Nkandla and he was shocked because there is no ways that place cost R250 million. And I remember the comments still; he said the toilet seats were like they were bought from Builders Warehouse.'[21]

Agrizzi testified he once heard Watson speaking to Zuma on the phone and that the Bosasa CEO 'believed that he had the support and protection of President Zuma'.[22]

Myeni was also a Bosasa blessee, having had security systems installed at her private house. Richard le Roux, the company's former head of special operations, testified how he'd had to buy security equipment with cash for installation at the houses of ANC politicians and Myeni, and that equipment worth around R250 000 had been installed at Myeni's Richards Bay house. The instruction for this, Le Roux said, had come from Bosasa director Trevor Mathenjwa, whom Agrizzi described as Myeni's 'handler', and Watson himself.[23]

In reaction to the evidence implicating her in a corrupt relationship with Watson and Bosasa, Myeni said she would apply to cross-examine Agrizzi. She called him 'a racist and bitter man' and challenged him to produce photos of the Louis Vuitton bag he'd bought her. Myeni didn't comment on the secret documents she'd leaked to Watson and Agrizzi, or any of the other detailed allegations against her.[24]

Angelo Agrizzi: the Energizer bunny

'When we first met Nomvula Mokonyane, we realised that she was extremely powerful. As a matter of fact, we, myself and Mr Watson, actually referred to her as an Energizer bunny. If we needed people spoken to, it would be done. If we needed protection, it would be done.'[1]

45

Braai packs and birthday cake

Nomvula Mokonyane was one of the founding members of Dyambu and was, according to Fanie van Zijl, the sole representative of the ANC Women's League at the meeting he and Gavin Watson had gone to, to conclude the sale of Meritum – Van Zijl's company – to Dyambu in the late 1990s.

Mokonyane, a former Gauteng premier known as 'Mama Action', came to national office after Zuma's inauguration as state president in 2009. Widely viewed as Zuma's closest political ally in Gauteng, she was sacked from Cyril Ramaphosa's cabinet after he became head of state in May 2019.

Over the years I'd heard stories about Mokonyane's close proximity to Watson and Bosasa but couldn't find proof of impropriety. On day four of his evidence before the Zondo Commission, Agrizzi dropped a bombshell: Mokonyane had been blessed with copious amounts of food and alcohol for her annual Christmas parties, with cash parcels and rental cars, and with various donations for the ANC where she served as head of election campaigns under Zuma.

In return, Mokonyane had provided Bosasa with clout – but it came at a price: 'if he [Watson] did not do what she wanted, we would not have protection and we needed her support to avert possible prosecution'.[2]

Frans Vorster, who headed up Bosasa's facilities and fleet, testified that it was clear to him that Mokonyane wielded 'a lot of influence and I am sure she opened a lot of doors for Mr Watson because we always had to jump when it was for her and make sure that she [got] special treatment. She did not wait for anything. If he said, "Do that," you would do it immediately and make sure whatever was asked was delivered.'³

Vorster, who said that Mokonyane was 'like an employee at Bosasa; she was there the whole time',⁴ had to 'drop everything' to attend to Mokonyane and her family 'and it became apparent over the years that she was the key person ... and had huge political contacts even to [Zuma].'⁵

Every Christmas since 2002/3, Agrizzi testified, Watson had provided him with a shopping list for Mokonyane. 'The list of items [was] the same more or less every year ... 120 cases of cold drinks, four cases of high-quality whiskey, 40 cases of beer, eight lambs, cut up obviously, 12 cases of frozen chicken pieces, 200kg of beef in various braai packs, and then numerous cases of premium brandy and some speciality alcohol.'⁶

Watson further tasked Agrizzi to pay for Mokonyane's family funerals during the year; to procure rental vehicles for her daughter, who was studying in China; to cater for the ANC's 'Siyanqoba' election rallies; to cater for Zuma's birthday party at Luthuli House and for his private birthday parties; and to perform upgrades at Mokonyane's house in Krugersdorp, including the installation of CCTV, electric fencing, generators, gates and lights.

Vorster recalled an incident when Watson desperately needed him to assist Mokonyane's daughter with a rental car. 'It was at the end of November 2015, Gavin called me and said Nomvula's daughter needed a Cabriolet. I searched the whole country for a Cabriolet but couldn't find one. Eventually I found an Audi A3 for her in Krugersdorp. After two or three weeks, the daughter phoned me and said she needed an extension of the rental. I phoned Gavin. He just said, "Frans, give her whatever she wants." At the end, we rented the car for her for two months.'⁷

The car, which was returned damaged to the rental agency, cost close to R100 000 to repair. When Agrizzi found out, he wanted to know who the vehicle had been for. 'Gavin Watson was very upset with me [for telling Agrizzi],' Vorster recalled. 'He phoned me and he shouted at me. I was so embarrassed. I had some of my managers sitting in front of me and they could hear the whole conversation. They felt so embarrassed that they stood up and they walked out of my office ... [Watson said] I was trying to create problems for him.'⁸

After this incident, whenever Watson walked past Vorster's office, he would belittle him, saying, 'Fat Fransie is creating problems for me and he is going to lose his job.'[9]

On top of the food, booze and cars, Mokonyane also received 'Monopoly money' – a monthly parcel of R50 000, according to Agrizzi. 'I would have to pack it and he would often deliver it in front of me ... If there was a serious matter to discuss [with Mokonyane] regarding the NPA, like at one stage he [Watson] wanted a senior person to withdraw the matter from the police, I was there because I would ... have to go back to the attorneys and tell the attorneys exactly what I had been told politically.'[10]

(Mokonyane has said she felt 'betrayed' by the Zondo Commission's decision not to pre-warn her that Agrizzi would implicate her, and has applied to cross-examine Agrizzi about his evidence. She has denied being corrupt.[11])

But perhaps the most revealing part of this evidence was Bosasa's intimate relationship with the governing party, the ANC. Agrizzi and Vorster testified about how they were instructed by Watson to sponsor the catering for the party's election rallies where 40 000 to 50 000 people attended (a photo shows polystyrene food boxes with a 'Bosasa proudly supporting the ANC' sticker on them); how the company set up a call centre for the ANC's 2014 national election campaign, manned by Bosasa staff and accompanied by a marquee tent with catering for the party's celebrations; and a 72nd-birthday cake for Zuma that was decorated by ex-chef Agrizzi himself, with Bosasa's logo on it, after a late-night call from Watson that Mokonyane had called to request it.

Here was a company, deeply implicated in corruption since 2006 in media reports, and being investigated for corruption since 2009 by the SIU, showering the ruling party with gifts in a grotesque act of bribery to avoid jailtime. Even Cyril Ramaphosa, deputy president of the ANC and the country at the time, admitted visiting the party's call centre at Bosasa's premises during the 2016 local government elections. Ramaphosa, who won the 2019 national election for the ANC on an anti-corruption ticket, nonchalantly stated in his affidavit to the Zondo Commission, 'I had no knowledge at the time of the source of funding for this centre as these matters were the purview of the elections team.'[12]

Had corruption become so normalised in the ANC, particularly during the Jacob Zuma era, that even Ramaphosa, who was supposedly in the vanguard of the ANC's return to the rule of law and constitutionalism, had become blind to such obvious signs of party capture?

46

Green, black and gold (and food parcels and cash)

On 31 March 2014, 37 days before South Africa went to the polls to return the ANC to power with a 62.15% majority, and eight years after Carien du Plessis and I had revealed former prisons boss Linda Mti's business links to Bosasa in our first exposé on the scandal, Dr Zweli Mkhize, treasurer-general of the ANC and former premier of KwaZulu-Natal, wrote a thank-you letter to Bosasa CEO Gavin Watson on an ANC letterhead.

Dear Mr Watson

This serves to acknowledge the receipt of R3,000,000.00 (Three Million Rand) donation to the AFRICAN NATIONAL CONGRESS.

On behalf of the African National Congress, I would like to express our sincere appreciation and gratitude to your organisation for this donation and for the continued financial support and contribution your organisation renders to the ANC.

Your ongoing support for our organisation is appreciated.

Kind regards
Dr Z Mkhize

Politics has become a lucrative business in democracies globally. In South Africa, parties that contest the national and local government elections are required to fork out hundreds of millions of rands every two to three years to successfully contest the polls – to pay for billboards, television-advertising campaigns, buses, stadiums and T-shirts. There's no way that they can raise this type of money from their membership fees alone, so parties go cap in hand to donors for funding. And because donor funding was unregulated for 25 years, the private donations were made in secret and the identities of the blessers remained opaque.

This is an international phenomenon with which academics, jurists and politicians have been grappling for decades. Félix Ulloa, a former magistrate and lawyer who was elected vice-president of El Salvador in June 2019, noted, 'The lack of transparency of private funding enables the great corporate interests that control the economy of our countries to impose their own agendas on governments, congresses and docile parliaments through the unlimited financing of parties and candidates, which will then represent their particular interests and not those of the people who elect them. This is a breeding ground for corruption in the public administration, since the representative is not accountable to his electors, but loyal to those who paid his campaign expenditures.'[1]

An inside source told *News24* that Bosasa had donated at least R40 million to the ANC over two decades.[2] The company, thanked by Mkhize for its 'continued' support of the ANC shortly before the 2014 election, had managed to avoid prosecution or any form of government sanction despite being continuously exposed for wrongdoing, not only by the media but also by a government agency specifically tasked to root out corruption. Watson and his colleagues knew exactly what they were buying when they sponsored the ANC with cash, food parcels, an election war room and cake: they were buying immunity against prosecution and imprisonment; their filthy lucre was being funnelled into a life-insurance policy provided by the ANC.

After Agrizzi and his fellow Bosasa canaries started to sing at the Zondo Commission at the beginning of 2019, more evidence emerged of the company's funding of the governing party. Mkhize, now serving as a cabinet minister, was forced to respond. 'As far as I can remember, Gavin Watson and members of his team had an introductory meeting with me at my office at Luthuli House in 2014. It was not "commonplace" for members of Bosasa to visit my office. I recall only ever encountering Mr Watson in passing on a few occasions, mostly at public and party events. These were not in my personal capacity. I can confidently say that I do not have a personal relationship with Bosasa's directors, and any inference of the sort will be treated with the contempt it deserves.'[3]

This was a disingenuous response by Mkhize by any standards: you had to have been living under a rock not to have been aware of the corruption scandal that had been hovering over Bosasa since 2006.

The evidence of Agrizzi and his former colleagues Richard le Roux, Frans Vorster and Andries van Tonder before the Zondo Commission laid bare the breadth and depth of Bosasa's capturing of the party, its politicians and civil servants.

Le Roux, head of special operations at Sondolo IT, told the commission that he'd received instructions from Watson, Agrizzi and other Bosasa directors to provide installation of CCTV, electric fencing and other security measures at the homes of ANC politicians. Le Roux was told by Watson to wear unbranded clothing and drive in unbranded vehicles when they were doing the installations,[4] and he was instructed to remove all serial numbers from security equipment, presumably to delete any Bosasa footprint.

Some of their projects had names: Project Blouberg was the upgrades to Mokonyane's house in Krugersdorp; Project Jones was security installations at the house of ANC MP Vincent Smith, who was the chair of the portfolio committee on correctional services; Project Bramley was deputy minister of correctional services Thabang Makwetla's house in Johannesburg; and Project Mantashe was installations done at the houses of then ANC secretary-general Gwede Mantashe in Johannesburg and the Eastern Cape.

Makwetla's response to Le Roux's revelations provided interesting insights into the power dynamics between Watson and the politicians. Makwetla admitted that Watson had organised for security equipment to be installed at his house after a break-in in 2016, but claimed that he'd wanted to pay. Makwetla's spokesperson told the press, 'When the deputy minister [Makwetla] spoke to Gavin about it, he said he doesn't expect himself to charge the deputy minister as a comrade for assistance that he can afford to offer without incurring any significant costs. Makwetla immediately disagreed with him for the obvious reason that perceptions of conflict of interest would be difficult to dispel because his company is doing business with DCS. Makwetla pleaded with Mr Watson, not once, not twice, not thrice, but continuously ever since, [and] Mr Watson has simply, flatly refused to send him the bill for the job.'[5]

Of course, Makwetla was in the wrong for agreeing in the first place to accept the security installation from Watson – paid or unpaid – because Bosasa was a major service provider to his department. But this was a classic example of the wily Watson at work, exploiting his relationship as a 'comrade' to compromise someone in a powerful position who could benefit him and his company.

The Mantashe case was just as interesting. The party heavy, now serving as minister of mineral resources in President Cyril Ramaphosa's cabinet, was deeply offended when his name came up at the Zondo Commission in relation to Bosasa. His version was that a family friend, Bosasa spokesperson Papa Leshabane, had paid for the security equipment installed at his three homes. Mantashe passionately denied receiving anything from Bosasa or doing anything for the company in return.

Mantashe's daughter Nombasa is married to MultiChoice CEO Calvo Mawela, who is one of Leshabane's closest friends; and Leshabane confirmed that he was a family friend of Mantashe. Leshabane initially told eNCA that Mantashe had called him for assistance after a break-in, but after the minister categorically stated that he'd never asked for the CCTV equipment, Leshabane changed his story and said he'd contacted Mantashe.[6]

Again, this showed a scheme at work to ensnare powerful politicians and compromise them in a way that could later be used against them. But Mantashe should have been smarter; he knew about Bosasa's links to corruption and controversy. Why on earth would he let anyone connected to the company install cameras in his most private spaces?

Bosasa firmly believed that every man had a price, so when Vincent

Smith, as chair of Parliament's portfolio committee on correctional services, was getting too critical of the company's DCS tenders, they roped in Cedric Frolick, a senior ANC MP and a close friend of Watson's brother Cheeky, to 'turn' him.

Frolick met Watson at Bosasa's head office on a tour of the operation, and the CEO slipped a packet of cash into Frolick's jacket pocket, Agrizzi testified.[7] Frolick was allegedly paid R40 000 a month.

Agrizzi and Gibson Njenje flew to Cape Town to meet Frolick in Parliament. He took them to a meeting with Smith, who was unimpressed at first. Later, however, and for reasons that aren't known, Smith softened up: he ended up being recruited as a blessee, and showered with cash payments, security equipment and a study bursary for his daughter.

Angelo Agrizzi: The end

'Lies and daily manipulation had become the order of the day, shrouded under the cloak of religion and political agendas. It was unbearable.'[1]

47

The chef who sold his Ferrari

There were two versions of Angelo Agrizzi's dramatic exit from Bosasa.

His fans and supporters believed that he'd reached the end of his tether with Gavin Watson's corrupt regime and wanted to come clean. This was the version that Agrizzi himself promoted.

The other version was that Agrizzi was planning a hostile takeover of Bosasa by getting rid of Watson and his allies, even drawing up a flow chart of how the systematic takeover would work.

The truth lay somewhere in between.

According to Agrizzi, the cracks in his relationship with Watson started to appear in 2013/14. He realised that Watson had changed. 'He was using people, ridiculing people. Gavin had become a totally different person. Gavin was a nice guy at some stage, he was very nice to me, but he started using and hurting people. I'm soft, that's my nature. My feeling was that I had to look after the staff. I was ridiculed because I looked after people. I would never forget when Gavin told me [in relation to a discussion about coming clean]: "You can come clean and then you can take the fall for me." This was playing in the back of my mind.'[2]

Agrizzi started to challenge Watson. The CEO wanted to take Bosasa international – 'He knew that government tenders ran out after ten to twelve years' – but Agrizzi strongly disagreed; they had to clean up their reputation in South Africa first before branching out, he felt. This included a *mea culpa* to the NPA, in Agrizzi's books.

In a board meeting in 2015 Watson questioned Agrizzi about Lindela's rising expenditure. Agrizzi retorted that it was because Lindela paid for the construction of luxury houses for his children, Lindsay and Roth.

Watson had become 'ultra-political', Agrizzi said, and had started ridiculing white staff in conversations and at functions. 'He was abrupt and got progressively worse ... He became so arrogant. When I questioned him, he would say, "Who pays your salary? Your wife?"

'Whatever Papa [Leshabane] and Joe [Gumede] told him became the gospel. I told him they were lying to him, but he was starting to meet them on their own.'[3] Agrizzi was no longer Watson's confidant.

Agrizzi's former colleagues say it was clear at this point that Watson was fuelling racial tension in the company. Agrizzi was positioned as the 'leader' of the white camp, while Watson pretended to promote black managers and directors, unofficially led by Leshabane. Denise Bjorkman recalled, 'Papa started calling Angelo "the cook" in meetings. He would say, "The cook thinks he runs the company now" or "The cook thinks he's got brains."'[4]

Then, in 2016, Agrizzi had a Damascus moment: ultimately, Watson would dump him. 'I told Andries [van Tonder] and mapped it out in my office, the people [he'd] got rid of. Who says he wouldn't do it to me?'

Agrizzi told the Zondo Commission, 'I realised that this was not a life to live. For 19 years I had been committed to Gavin Watson and had supported him. Gavin Watson continuously compromised people and hurt families in the manner he was conducting his business. People were easily disposed of and I no longer wanted part of this.'[5]

Agrizzi started to look for other jobs outside Bosasa and in mid-2016 he received an offer from a French company. He resigned and 'all hell broke loose'. 'Gavin was phoning me incessantly, sending me messages. I told him, "It's over Gavin. You cannot keep on doing what you are doing."'[6]

Agrizzi showed me one of the messages he received from Watson during this time. 'Angelo don't reject my calls,' it read. 'I have never rejected yours. As brothers in CHRIST this is not the way to handle this misunderstanding and confusion. Let's sit down and with respect, honesty and integrity speak to one another.' In another, Watson told Agrizzi not to throw away his 'inheritance which you have worked hard to accumulate for the last 20 years and do an injustice to yourself. GOD bless you will lead operations and keep your position pls. GOD bless.'

Brian Biebuyck, Watson's attorney, apparently cautioned Agrizzi 'as he always did, that we had to stick together because we will all end up in jail'.[7] (The Bosasa story is not short on irony: Biebuyck had once asked Agrizzi to remove a WhatsApp profile picture that read 'Blessed' because it upset the Watsons.)

When Agrizzi arrived home one day in mid-2016, Cheeky Watson was waiting for him in his driveway. 'I always had a soft spot for Cheeky. When he needed money for tyres, I would put it on the company books and [take] it off his salary.' (Cheeky Watson was paid R75 000 per month from Consilium – the front company used to pay senior white staff.) 'I spoke to Cheeky for hours on end. He told me, "The brothers have decided they cannot be without you. Bosasa will fold without you."

'At the time I hadn't threatened to blow the whistle yet. I told him that the corruption has to stop; we cannot pay R6 million per month in cash. How long are we going to continue with this?

'"We're going to clean up," Cheeky said. "The brothers are taking charge."'[8]

Cheeky tore up Agrizzi's new employment contract.

Agrizzi was promised a lump sum of R10 million, a monthly salary of R500 000 for five years, and shareholding in the company. 'I honestly believed Gavin was going to change,' he said.[9]

Agrizzi was allowed to address directors and staff at a bosberaad in Magaliesburg in August 2016. 'I told them we must get rid of all the hangers-on. All the biblical institutions, the bribery and corruption. I used the removal-truck image of the Stuttaford Van Lines ad, "There goes my only possessions", and dressed up as a doctor, doing surgery on the company. I tried to make it humorous.'[10]

At a meeting of company directors, Agrizzi told them the corruption must stop. 'But they were not happy because they probably took a haircut [a share] from the money [they were distributing to corruptees].'[11]

In November 2016, Agrizzi invited the Watson family to the wedding celebrations of his son Giancarlo. 'Gavin expected me to make him the highlight of the wedding, which I decided not to do.'

A week later, Watson told Agrizzi his shareholding had not been sorted out. 'Turbulent times' was Watson's excuse, to which Agrizzi responded, 'Well, then, we're in for a ride now.'

Going into Christmas, Agrizzi knew he was preparing for a fight with Watson. 'I knew a showdown was coming.'[12]

Through all of this, Agrizzi's health was taking a knock. 'I wasn't feeling well. I fell asleep [at] the wheel of my car. Once I almost drove into the back of a truck ... I fell asleep in meetings. My blood sugar wasn't under control. I felt progressively worse towards the end of December.'

During Christmas lunch at the Michelangelo Hotel in Sandton – a favourite venue of Watson, which he'd introduced Agrizzi to – Agrizzi felt very bad and battled to breathe. 'I was as white as a sheet. I looked in the mirror and said to myself, "Today is the day, brother." I told my brother and wife, "I am going to the hospital." I got a bit emotional. It's one of those times in my life where everything just came together, and I realised that things have got to change.'[13]

At the Life Fourways Hospital the doctor told Agrizzi that his blood-oxygen level was dangerously low. 'You are a walking dead,' the doctor told him. 'You are having a stroke right now.'

They called in a cardiologist who confirmed that Agrizzi's heart was double the size it should be. 'We're going to have to operate,' the doctor said.

A second cardiologist confirmed that there was a tumour on Agrizzi's heart.

The doctor called Agrizzi's family to a meeting and told them he had a 50/50 chance of surviving the operation. The tumour had grown over his aorta and he had water on his lungs. 'My wife and I broke down in ICU. I said to her, "Whatever happens, happens. You will be looked after." At that time, I had key man insurance [which companies take out on critical staff] and life insurance of about R40 million.'

The next morning, before the operation, Agrizzi called his senior colleagues to a meeting at the hospital to discuss the DCS catering tender that had just been re-awarded to Bosasa – the company had lost three management areas in the new contract and Agrizzi wanted to discuss their legal strategy. He asked them not to tell Watson about his medical condition.

After an eight-hour operation during which he 'flatlined twice', the tumour was removed.

His survival had a salutary effect on Agrizzi. 'I decided not to go back to Bosasa,' he said.

In January 2017, Agrizzi was back at his palatial Dainfern home, with a drip, an oxygen machine and a nurse. Watson wasted no time, arranging a meeting at Agrizzi's house about the prisons catering tender.

'Up pitches the entire Bosasa board and their lawyer, with Watson showing no compassion,' Agrizzi recalled.

During the meeting, Watson allegedly handed Agrizzi his cellphone to speak to ANC MPs Cedric Frolick and Vincent Smith about the tender. It was completely out of line for a company to speak directly to oversight politicians, who should only be concerned with keeping checks on the department's budget and good governance.

'After about an hour, I told [Watson], "Why don't you take your bunch of idiots and fuck off?"'[14] Thinking they had all gone, Agrizzi turned to his wife and commented, 'What a bunch of bloody criminals.' 'I didn't know Gavin was still standing behind me. He just looked me up and down.'

Back at work, Agrizzi wanted to get to the bottom of a mystery: shortly after he'd left hospital, his doctor had asked him why his wife had tried to claim his life insurance when he hadn't died. His wife had denied that it was her, and, indeed, Andries van Tonder told Agrizzi that it was Watson who'd tried to cash out his life insurance while he was gravely ill in hospital.

'I didn't believe Andries at first. So I phoned up Philip Putziger from Ambiton Financial Services in Port Elizabeth. Philip says to me, "Angelo, sorry to tell you but, yes, I had a call from Gavin on 30 December trying to claim your insurance. I was just following instructions from Gavin."'

This gave Agrizzi 'closure with Gavin because then I realised what type of a person he was'.[15]

A year later, at a meeting in Irene, Pretoria, Agrizzi challenged Watson about this. 'I said to him, "Why did you try to claim my insurance? Look me in my eyes and tell me, did you do it?"

'He said, "Yes, I did."

'I got up from the table and walked away. He tried to stop me and I said, "I want nothing more to do with you in my life." I still paid for the bill because I decided I wanted nothing from this man.'[16]

In March 2017 Bosasa bought Agrizzi out of his contract for R26 million and a consultancy fee of R200 000 a month. He claimed not to have received the settlement amount, and to have been paid the consultancy fee for only three months.

In November 2017 there was a revolt in Bosasa. Brian Biebuyck called Agrizzi to a meeting at a restaurant in Parkhurst, Johannesburg, where he told him that 38 Bosasa employees were threatening to blow the whistle on the corruption in the company. 'You have to help because senior staff don't want to believe Gavin [that everything was above board],' Agrizzi said the laywer told him.[17]

Agrizzi, who by that stage had been out of the business for some months, asked Biebuyck what he wanted him to do. 'You don't understand, my friend,' Biebuyck allegedly told Agrizzi. 'You are going to jail.'

Agrizzi told Biebuyck he wanted nothing more to do with Bosasa but the lawyer insisted, reportedly saying, 'They are all your people. If it doesn't work out [to keep the employees quiet], we'd rather liquidate the company and then no one will have jobs.'

(A little while later, Biebuyck apologised to Agrizzi in a text message for 'not listening to your warnings in the first place'. 'I was probably blinded by loyalty to the Watsons over many years. Gavin's conduct has left me gutted, but your kindness to me has restored a lot of faith in the "good" side of humanity.')[18]

Agrizzi met with his aggrieved former colleagues and they decided to make Watson an offer to buy out the DCS catering contract at R10 million per month for 48 months. 'That would have solved a lot of problems for the company and for Gavin because, believe it or not, I wanted Gavin to come clean. I sent him messages: "Gavin, you can't keep doing this."'[19]

Agrizzi and his colleagues ended up sending Watson a proposal by Crearis, Agrizzi's new company that he formed, on how to clean up Bosasa, by this stage called African Global Operations. Agrizzi insisted this wasn't an attempt to hijack the company, but on request from Watson. 'I said to Gavin, "Get these guys occupied – let them do a turnaround for you, clean up the corruption and open it up." That was the whole strategy: to say we had a problem, [but] we cleaned it up [and] it's not happening anymore; [to] be open about it. My main objective at that stage was to get people out of this shit.

'Gavin agreed that we go that route. It would be easier to clean it up, [to] go to the NPA and say we've done A, B, C and D wrong, we just want to tell you about it and we're prepared to pay a fine. But the business will still be okay. That was the strategy I had in mind for him.'[20]

But the deal didn't materialise, probably because Watson feared that Agrizzi was planning to hijack his company.

In 2018 matters escalated. On the evening of 21 August, after having received a threatening phone call, Agrizzi told his family, 'I have carried this burden long enough.' He then composed and sent out a media release via email headed 'Whistleblowing – Disclosures on Activities – AGO [African Global Operations] Bosasa Operations Pty Ltd Public Announcement':

> I have decided, pursuant to great thought, prayer and consideration, to provide comprehensive details on all the activities at the Bosasa Group of Companies and myself whilst I was employed there. I have tried to not report on the activities in an attempt to potentially save the jobs of the people concerned. It is however in my best interest to disclose the matters to all involved, and I think the most appropriate platform would be the Judiciary and the free press which I will be using.
>
> I am also fully aware that I have been fully aware of all the wrongdoings but will tender my full cooperation in resolving the matter, and bringing both clarity and truth to the matter regarding the racketeering, corruption and money laundering that I have been aware of over the last 18 years.
>
> The extent of the disclosures involve various high-level people,

government officials as well as public office bearers currently in government positions, parastatals and State Owned Enterprises.

I will be requesting that you will allow me the patience whilst I process the various information and make same available to all. I will also liaise with the relevant stakeholders in due course as to a press conference and open forum discussion that will be hosted. You will understand that I have been the subject of numerous threats, and thus we have made the requisite arrangements with various other sources.

I understand that my decision impacts on numerous people, but in the interest of our nation, it's imperative to clarify the points, and make full disclosures.

I remain yours truthfully
Angelo Agrizzi

The following evening brothers Ronnie and Valence Watson, Valence's son Jared, and Brian Biebuyck arrived at Agrizzi's house, and stayed until the early hours of the next morning. Agrizzi recalled, 'They were extremely apologetic and stated that they knew nothing of what I'd told them [about the revelations of corruption at Bosasa] ...'[21]

Later that day they were back to report that Gavin had denied Agrizzi's claims but would do anything to rectify the situation. And it was that night, after a few gin and tonics, that Agrizzi was recorded by Gavin Watson's nephew Jared, spewing racist language.

The next day, 25 August 2018, Biebuyck sent Agrizzi a draft agreement to 'buy' his silence. He would be paid R50 million plus R250 000 a month for five years if he retracted the press statement announcing his intention to blow the whistle. But 'I was not interested in any offer to secure my silence and advised the Watsons and Biebuyck [of this] in writing,' Agrizzi said.

Jared Watson, son of Valence, had a different recollection of the events that unfolded after Agrizzi released his tell-all press statement. According to him, it had been a clear attempt by Agrizzi to intimidate them and execute a takeover of Bosasa.

After having received the press statement on 21 August 2018, Valence Watson had phoned Agrizzi to ask him what was going on. 'Angelo asked my father [Valence] and Uncle Ronnie to come and see him,' Jared said.[22] According to Jared, he'd played the role of mediator, telling Agrizzi and the Watson brothers to 'kiss and make up'. Agrizzi had played along, Jared said, even suggesting that he [Agrizzi] and the Watson brothers should go for a retreat in Italy.

A few days later, Agrizzi's group had presented a proposal to the Watsons to buy Bosasa, to appoint Agrizzi as CEO and implement stringent cost-cutting measures.

They'd declined, said Jared; they'd believed Agrizzi was effectively black-mailing them into giving up the activities of Bosasa.[23]

Five months later, after many sessions with different attorneys, Agrizzi became the poster boy for whistleblowing in South Africa.

The entire experience left Angelo Agrizzi reflecting deeply on the value of material things. He said he regretted not spending more time with his children when they were growing up, while he was chasing and cooking tenders with Watson.

'How many pens can you have? How many watches can you have? How many houses do you need? How many cars can you drive?' asked the man who started selling his assets, including one of his Ferraris, to pay his bills and those of his former colleagues who were struggling to put food on the table. 'It's just not worth it. All the hard work – for what? It's not worth it.'[24]

48

Enter the Ramaphosas (by Kyle Cowan)

I first came across evidence that the web of corruption and state capture woven by Bosasa may have extended to newly elected president Cyril Ramaphosa while digging into alleged tax dodges surrounding some of Gavin Watson's projects.

In the latter part of 2018 I was given an affidavit by Peet Venter, a former SARS official who had left the tax service in 2004, in the midst of an audit by SARS on Bosasa.

Venter had joined the Krugersdorp-based audit firm Bester Viljoen. The firm later changed its name to Maseng Viljoen, and then to D'Arcy-Herrman. Within a few years, as the company's external auditor Venter had become an integral part of the Bosasa machinery. He compiled the tax returns of the directors and assisted prisons boss Linda Mti and financial chief Patrick Gillingham to square their affairs with SARS.

Venter would later take over the running of Consilium, the Bosasa front masquerading as a labour broker. The conflict was profound: at the same time, Venter worked for the audit company responsible for ensuring Bosasa's books were being kept in order.

Venter's affidavit, ostensibly compiled while he was part of the group of whistleblowers led by Agrizzi who were gearing up to oust Watson, was explosive. It revealed that when Watson was asked to pay the legal fees of disgraced SABC chief operations officer-turned-politician Hlaudi Motsoeneng in August 2017, Venter was called on to make the R1.1-million payment to Zola Majavu Attorneys. Venter was also called

ENTER THE RAMAPHOSAS (BY KYLE COWAN)

on to make three payments of R450 000 each to an obscure company named Moroka Consultants, linked to Israel Thoka, long-time friend and ally of then North West premier Supra Mahumapelo. The payments were made through another front company called Miotto Trading and Advisory Services. Miotto's sole director at the time was Venter's sister, Margaret Longworth. Longworth said she'd had nothing to do with the day-to-day running of Miotto; Venter, she said, managed the bank account.

In October 2017, Watson asked Bosasa company secretary Natasha Olivier to transfer R3 million from his personal account to Miotto. R500 000, Watson told Venter, was to be paid into an account for the 'Andile Ramaphosa Foundation'.[1] The remaining R2.5 million was to be paid towards a house for Watson's alleged mistress Lindie Gouws, who later instructed Venter to repay the funds to Watson.

Attached to the affidavit was proof of payment to an account named 'EFG2' which Venter was led to believe belonged to Cyril Ramaphosa's businessman son, Andile. Venter stood by this version when testifying before the Zondo Commission.

However, it seems that either Watson lied to Venter, or Venter lied in his affidavit. The EFG2 account was an attorney's trust account belonging to Sandton-based law firm Edelstein, Farber and Grobler Attorneys, and was used to house donations to Ramaphosa's CR17 presidential bid in the ANC's 54th national elective conference held at Nasrec, Johannesburg in December 2017.

I mulled over Venter's affidavit for several weeks. Its contents insofar as Motsoeneng's legal bill had been confirmed, leaving me in little doubt the rest could be relied on. But the Andile Ramaphosa Foundation didn't exist. I ran searches with the Master of the High Court's office, where all foundations and trusts are registered. They came up empty.

This left me with little to go on other than the bank account number. With the assistance of sources, I set about trying to confirm who the recipient account belonged to. While I was trying to make sense of this anomaly, on 6 November 2018, a question-and-answer session in Parliament blew the matter wide open.

Standing in the national assembly, DA leader Mmusi Maimane waved Venter's affidavit at President Ramaphosa to a chorus of jeers from the opposition benches. Ramaphosa, who had run his campaign for president on a clean-governance, anti-corruption agenda, was suddenly thrust into the spotlight.

'We can't have family members benefiting, Mr President,' Maimane said.

A seemingly confident Ramaphosa started to respond. Yes, he knew of the matter. It was part of a business contract his son Andile had with Bosasa. It was all above board, Ramaphosa said. If his son had done something illegal, he would personally hand him over to the police.

I was surprised. Ramaphosa had answered Maimane confidently and without hesitation. He had been prepared for this, I thought, despite the Bosasa question not being part of the written follow-up questions. He had also, crucially, confirmed that a relationship did exist between his son and Bosasa.

Smelling a rat, I immediately called Ramaphosa junior. 'Your father has just confirmed you are in business with Bosasa, but the foundation mentioned in the affidavit doesn't seem to exist. What is going on?' I asked him.

Andile denied that the R500 000 in question had ever been paid to him. He'd never seen a cent of that money, he said.

Had the president of South Africa just lied to Parliament?

I pushed Andile for details on the business relationship, but he remained tight-lipped. 'I have absolutely nothing to do with this. I have never received such a payment,' he insisted.

It was bizarre – the president's son had directly contradicted what his father had told the national assembly just hours before.[2]

The following week President Ramaphosa stunned the nation when he made a U-turn on his explanation. He wrote a letter to then speaker Baleka Mbete, correcting his oral reply to Maimane's question. He said he'd responded incorrectly to Maimane, and that the payment by Watson had in fact been a donation to his CR17 presidential campaign. His campaign managers had informed him of this after the fact, he said.

ENTER THE RAMAPHOSAS (BY KYLE COWAN)

Essentially, he'd confirmed his son's version – with an added and explosive revelation over the funding of his campaign. The funding of political parties and party candidates is a hugely contested issue in South Africa and the fact that the CEO of a corruption-implicated company had donated money to CR17 immediately raised red flags.

It was manna from heaven for Ramaphosa's political foes, and immediately sparked a complaint to the Public Protector from the DA followed by one from the Economic Freedom Fighters' Floyd Shivambu.

In mid-December 2018, forensic investigator Paul O'Sullivan published a report on the Ramaphosa/Bosasa business deal debacle, saying that he'd inspected the agreement between Ramaphosa Jr and Bosasa and had found it all to be above board. He published a redacted 'advisory mandate' between Ramaphosa Jr's company, Blue Crane Capital, and African Global Operations which didn't shine much light on the affair other than providing further confirmation that pen had been put to paper.

The advisory mandate itself, now public but redacted, raised further suspicions. It was devoid of specifics and brought me no closer to understanding what exactly Ramaphosa Jr and Bosasa's deal was in aid of – other than 'advisory services' from Ramaphosa Jr and his business partner, John Mathwasa. (Mathwasa was part of the team that drove undersea data-cable company Seacom, funded in part by Ramaphosa Sr's Shanduka.)

O'Sullivan's report added limited value, but it held a crucial clue: it named as a key player China's Dahua Technology, the world's second-biggest surveillance-equipment manufacturer. Ramaphosa Jr wanted to bring the company's high-tech solutions to Africa. All he needed was a company with a proven track record in tackling large projects.

During Angelo Agrizzi's headline-grabbing testimony before the Zondo Commission in January 2019, I went back to key Bosasa sources and started pushing them for more details. Within a few weeks one source had relented, and over copious cups of cappuccino at a noisy coffee shop in a mall on the edge of the West Rand, the story of Dahua and Andile Ramaphosa was revealed. More specifically, the source was able to trace an invaluable timeline and sketch some new characters in the story.

I could now reach out to Ramaphosa Jr for a sit-down interview, to check these new facts and information I had painstakingly pieced together over three months.

Andile Ramaphosa was open to the request but hesitant to act without a green light from the office of the presidency, now occupied by his father. After weeks of requests going unanswered, I fired off an email to Ramaphosa Jr with several questions and a final plea for a sit-down. We spoke at length over the phone, as I pushed, prodded and pulled him into seeing the need for a full disclosure.

Two weeks later, I met with the president's son and his business partner, the managing director of Blue Crane, Gavin Singh; they were chaperoned by a former spin doctor for Jacob Zuma, Vincent Magwenya, who'd left in the early days of Zuma's turbulent administration to start his own firm.

I had sent the main points of discussion ahead of the time and had kept it germane. Hitting too hard too early could spell disaster. Another sit-down interview over such a controversial topic would not be in the offing any time soon.

The conversation was cordial but guarded. Ramaphosa Jr laughed easily and often but behind the jovial exterior, I sensed a well-practised readiness. Often, almost imperceptible cues from Magwenya, who was seated to my right, would send the conversation in a different direction.

During the hour-long interview, Andile Ramaphosa told me about his time in China, where he'd spent eight years studying and working for Standard Bank. He was surprisingly open, confirming amounts and dates, and confidently stating his version of events.

I revealed the ace up my sleeve: a text message from Bosasa employee Riaan van der Merwe to Angelo Agrizzi saying that Dahua wished to set up a meeting between Ramaphosa Jr and Agrizzi. 'They [Ramaphosa Jnr's company] will use their influence to secure projects,' was the main thrust of the text.

Ramaphosa, Singh and Magwenya were surprised by this information, and following the interview they addressed it specifically, denying that Ramaphosa Jr was ever planning to use his influence to secure projects.

Our story, published on 27 March 2019, detailed R2 million in accumulated monthly payments Blue Crane had received from Bosasa in exchange for Ramaphosa Jr opening up a 'pipeline' of more than 20 projects in East Africa, including Uganda and Kenya, potentially worth billions.[3] (He later backtracked on this, saying the true value of the projects was never fully realised.)

The article also detailed how Dahua representatives had introduced Ramaphosa Jr to Bosasa. Andile Ramaphosa said he regretted going into business with Bosasa and that it had been an oversight on his part.

49

The curtain falls

Like the Guptas, Gavin Watson learnt the hard way that your shop shuts the day the banks close your accounts. In mid-February 2019, after listening to nine days of Angelo Agrizzi's riveting evidence before the Zondo Commission, FNB and Absa finally pulled the plug on Bosasa, Watson and a number of other Bosasa directors and entities. The company could no longer pay salaries, receive money or service its debts.

This decision was long overdue. South Africa's banks had, despite years of negative publicity about their clients' financial affairs, continued to let them trade, right up until it became absolutely indefensible in the eyes of the public to do business with the likes of the Watsons and the Guptas.

FNB, which had been Bosasa's main banker for many years, said it would investigate wrongdoing by any of its employees. But what about all the years, from at least 2006, when Bosasa was linked to tender corruption, I wondered. Why had the bank been willing to take the company's dirty money for over a decade before it acted, and then only because of bad publicity emanating from the Zondo Commission?

In the Bosasa case, it wasn't only the integrity of the state and the private sector that had failed, but the system of checks and balances inherent in a capitalist society that had broken down. Neither Bosasa's banks nor the company's auditors or lawyers blew the whistle and took the appropriate action expected of these professionals when confronted by evidence of wrongdoing. In fact, auditor Peet Venter and lawyer Brian Biebuyck were seemingly active participants in and beneficiaries of what turned out

THE CURTAIN FALLS

to be the great Bosasa scam – after leaving formal legal practice in 2017, Biebuyck continued to receive monthly consultancy fees, while Venter cashed in millions through his work for Bosasa.

On 12 February 2019 Bosasa's board of directors resolved to place the group of companies under voluntary liquidation. The rumour was that the directors had a specific liquidator lined up and were planning to move the company's assets and contracts into new entities where they could begin to trade anew. They desperately needed a bank account through which to operate again.

This plan was rudely upset when a number of creditors insisted on the appointment of liquidator Cloete Murray, who has a reputation for being as tough as nails. As soon as he had his certificate of appointment from the Master of the High Court, Murray moved into the Mogale Business Park premises.

According to a source with knowledge of the liquidation, Murray and the liquidators didn't waste any time suspending the company's directors and taking charge of the finances and operations. 'He [Murray] chased them all, Watson included, out of their offices. Watson said he was going home. Murray told him that he would have to organise a lift home, because his car was not leaving the premises. Watson's BMW X5 was a company vehicle. Watson was fuming and caught a lift with his daughter, Lindsay.'¹

When the liquidation process didn't go their way, Watson and the board made new plans. Realising that the liquidators were going to close down Bosasa and possibly hold insolvency enquiries that would get to the bottom of the corruption in the company, and that they had everything to lose, Bosasa's directors filed an urgent application in the Gauteng High Court in Johannesburg, arguing that they had acted on flawed legal advice when they'd placed Bosasa into voluntary liquidation and that the resolution did not conform with the Companies Act. In a surprise judgment, acting Judge Goolam Ameer agreed with Bosasa and overturned the liquidation on technical grounds.

The liquidators immediately filed an appeal, which suspended the implementation of the reversal.

Then Murray dropped a bombshell in court when his preliminary report revealed that Watson had been paid a 'performance bonus' of R5 million on top of his monthly salary of R5.7 million two weeks before the company was placed in liquidation – and in the middle of Agrizzi's devastating evidence to the Zondo Commission. Clearly, it was still raining Monopoly money at Bosasa, amidst the real prospects that 4 500 employees would be retrenched as a result of Watson and co's looting over many years.

Jared Watson denies that his uncle Gavin ever earned R5.7 million per month. The most he ever earned was R5 million per year. 'Gavin's monthly salary received between AGO and Consilium was R236 075. He received a bonus of R3 535 205 in 2018,' Jared said.[2] Hopefully, the ongoing SARS inquiry will clarify how much money Watson made from his salary and shareholding in Bosasa, and what he did with the funds.

Murray and his co-liquidators returned to Bosasa to start wrapping up the contracts, including trying to find purchasers for Bosasa's projects and properties. There, they were forcibly grabbed by Bosasa employees and frogmarched off the premises. The employees were singing and dancing, and holding up posters that read 'Fokof Cloete'. Watson was standing at the back of the singing crowd.

Murray tried to explain to the employees what his role was and that there was no turning back. Eventually, Watson had to escort Murray safely off the Bosasa campus.

In February 2019, after many attempts by the likes of Vernie Petersen over the years to end the DCS catering contract, the DCS abruptly gave Bosasa 30 days' notice to get out of the prisons. Under the new prisons boss Arthur Fraser, with whom Watson had bumped heads when he was deputy director-general at home affairs, Bosasa was booted out as the liquidation came into force and the department returned to insourced cooking by DCS staff and inmates.

By September 2019 the liquidators had almost completed their work of wrapping up most of the company's government tenders. Some government departments insourced some of Bosasa's functions, while others advertised for new service providers.

The Watsons were bitter about the way the Zondo Commission had conducted its hearings into the Bosasa matter, without pre-warning them that they would be implicated. The family believes their rights were infringed on by allowing Agrizzi and others to testify without warning them, and said they didn't intend to participate in the commission's work.[3]

Angelo Agrizzi's revelations in January 2019 had serious ramifications for many players who'd enabled Bosasa's capture of the state to happen over almost two decades.

On 6 February the Hawks finally arrested Agrizzi, Mti, Gillingham, Van Tonder and other Bosasa employees who'd been instrumental in the illegal outsourcing of key DCS functions to Bosasa. This was the same case that the SIU had finalised ten years before and on which the NPA had been sitting since 2009.

Watson wasn't one of the suspects when the case appeared in court but it was expected that the NPA would add him as a co-accused before the case went to trial.

(The Hawks have instituted numerous other probes based on Agrizzi's testimony that are expected to see more politicians and civil servants appearing in court for their roles in Bosasa's state capture.)

In March Peet Venter testified how the loss-making prawn farm company SeaArk had been used to procure products and services for other, unrelated Bosasa companies, to avoid paying tax.[4] Investigators and tax officials tracked the outflow of money to accounts and trusts inside and outside of South Africa, and it was reported that some of Bosasa's money may have flowed to tax havens like Guernsey.[5]

SARS instituted a massive probe into allegations of tax dodging and fraud against Watson, Bosasa and 83 other individuals who'd been involved in fleecing taxpayers out of millions of rands. These proceedings took place under lock and key, but SARS was expected to file its claim against Watson and co towards the end of 2019, and insiders said they wouldn't be surprised if it ran into the hundreds of millions.

Nomvula Mokonyane, 'Mama Action', was left out of President Cyril Ramaphosa's cabinet after the May 2019 national elections. She resigned as an MP and took up a position at Luthuli House, the ANC's head office.

Vincent Smith didn't return to Parliament as an ANC MP after the May 2019 elections.

Maseng Viljoen, one of Bosasa's external auditors, shut its doors in June 2019 after reputational damage to the firm. Director Johan Kirsten denied that the closure was linked to Bosasa, but said in a letter to staff that the 'environment has changed drastically over the last year, with ever-increasing risks for the firm and directors in their personal capacity'.[6]

Hogan Lovells, where Brian Biebuyck had been a partner before he retired in 2017, shut its local firm in August 2019, and Biebuyck's former colleagues from Routledge Modise, the local firm that had teamed up with the US-based Hogan Lovells, formed a new entity. According to insiders, this was directly linked to the negative publicity Hogan Lovells had had to face as a result of the Zondo Commission. A much smaller, remaining group of attorneys continued to practise under the Hogan Lovells brand.

And Lindie Gouws was there to the end. One day, while the liquidators were busy going through Bosasa's books, they received a call from a source, tipping them off that Gouws was at his shop, attempting to make a mirror copy of a laptop that had previously belonged to Gavin Watson. Unfortunately for Gouws, the same specialist was delivering services to the Zondo Commission and he quickly blew the whistle when he realised what was going on.

The liquidators' representatives told the specialist to lock the doors so that Gouws couldn't escape and rushed to the shop. When they arrived, Gouws gave them a tongue-lashing and proceeded to the fire escape to try and dodge them. After running around the shop for a while, Gouws realised she wasn't going to be able to escape, and pushed Watson's laptop under a security door into the shop next door.

By this time, investigators from the Zondo Commission had also arrived. Gouws, finally accepting that the game was up, she took them to her car and handed over more of her own laptops that she'd stored there. The next-door shopkeeper, who coincidentally also had a link to the Zondo Commission, retrieved Watson's laptop and handed it to the investigators.

Watson arrived on the scene to calm Gouws down.

Gouws's version of this incident was that she'd been planning to hand over Watson's laptop to the Zondo Commission's investigators, but had wanted to make a mirror copy of it first because she believed someone had impersonated Watson in emails stored on the laptop. She told me she was cooperating with the commission's investigation.[7]

After years of impunity, the net was finally closing in on Bosasa.

50

'We were prostitutes'

At the end of most of my interviews with ex-Bosasa employees, I asked them the same question: 'How did you manage to live this life of lies and hypocrisy for so long? How did you reconcile the religious façade – the plaques with Bible verses and the morning prayers – with the depravity and corruption that pervaded Gavin Watson's company for so many years?'

I got different answers. For some, it was about the money. Others said they'd been brainwashed or manipulated by Watson's religious overtures. Others claimed ignorance: 'We didn't know.' All of them were conflicted about how to deal with their own culpability and how to package their memories of Bosasa – the good and the bad.

Jason Stoltz, who headed up marketing at a time I was publishing article after article implicating Bosasa in corruption, said, 'My job was to counter the articles you wrote. … Gavin Watson said to me, "We are not corrupt. It's all chequebook journalism. It's all anti-competitive, anti-political smear campaigns to try and discredit this amazing empowerment organisation. The white guys can't handle the fact that a black organisation could be so successful." It was all that kind of stuff that we were told. And you know, you get sucked into it and you believe it. Because you see the good work that we're doing at the youth centres, you see the training in the kitchens, and you are told by head office, "Guys, we don't do this stuff [corruption], we've never done it."

'So my job was to build the brand. When more and more articles came online, it evolved into a strong online reputation-management function. We had about 190 web properties. The idea was to publish the good stories about the things that we do so that we could flush the negative off Google's first page and we could tell the good stories, tell about the positive. And that was the drive.'[1]

Despite being immensely proud of what he and his team built during their time at Bosasa, Stoltz – who admitted 'I always thought where there's smoke, there's fire' – now carries the Bosasa brand as a burden. He's struggling to find work and, like many of his former colleagues, doesn't know where next month's rent and food budget will come from.

Denise Bjorkman took pride in the good work the wellness centre did and the young employees she and her colleagues assisted to graduate and upskill. But she admitted having compromised her own values to remain in the system and told a story to illustrate this. 'A man hires a secretary who can't do anything but is very beautiful. Every day she comes to work and he says, "Oh my God, you're so beautiful, I'm so lucky to have you." Then one day he says, "Look, I can't take it any more. I'm absolutely in love with you. Will you sleep with me if I give you a million rand?" She says okay, so they do the horizontal dirty deed. Afterwards he gets up and puts ten rand on the table. Outraged, she says, "What do you think I am?" He says, "We know what you are; now we're just negotiating the price."

'I always said to Thembi [Modungwa, her colleague], "We are prostitutes." Because despite all our incredible values, we are doing exactly the same as that secretary, so it was a joke throughout the company. Everybody knows we used to say we are prostitutes for Bosasa.

'Did we make a difference? Profoundly. We saw so many people do their degrees, we did all their research, developed their careers. We had a cleaner who became a commercial pilot so, yes, Thembi and I did a lot of good.

'Could we have done it elsewhere? We were in our 70s; I don't think people were in a hurry to employ us. We knew our age, and Gavin never let me forget that too. He expected loyalty from you. You know, it is not easy to find jobs out there.'[2]

Dennis Bloem:
We must save this country

'The reason why I have decided to come to this Commission, I really want to see anybody who [is] guilty of corruption or any other crime ... imprisoned. They must go to jail.

'Chairperson, the reason why I am saying so is because Nelson Mandela and many other leaders went to prison for a very long time. Many people went into exile for a very long time. Other people have paid with their lives for this freedom that we are enjoying today.

'We cannot allow this thing [to] happen when we are still alive. I do not want my children to live a life under a corrupt society. We must save this country and I have full confidence in you. You are the hope of South Africa as we speak now.'[1]

51

The wounded buffalo

The actions of Bosasa wrecked many lives, careers and businesses. It's the story of a poisoned tree: until it's demolished, it will taint and endanger everyone and everything it touches.

And so it was with President Cyril 'the Buffalo' Ramaphosa. During all my years of investigating Bosasa, I'd never come across Ramaphosa as someone who'd helped them to capture R12-billion worth of tenders from the South African state. But in a moment of foolishness, one of his CR17 campaign managers, James Motlatsi, asked Gavin Watson to donate to the campaign. Whether Watson did this out of goodwill or with an ulterior motive is unknown, but the mere fact that Ramaphosa's campaign was now tainted with Bosasa's money dented Ramaphosa's image as a clean anti-corruption crusader. And the fact that his son Andile's business dealings with Bosasa went deeper than he'd originally declared didn't help his cause either.

In July 2019 Public Protector Busisiwe Mkhwebane found that Ramaphosa had violated his oath of office by deliberately misleading Parliament about the R500 000 donation to his CR17 campaign received from Watson. The fact that Watson had seemingly tried to hide the payment through a series of opaque transactions further muddied the water.

Watson's interview with Mkhwebane, which she included in her report on the Ramaphosa donation, provided interesting insights into Watson's state of mind and how he viewed himself as an ANC benefactor and victim.

Mkhwebane: Yeah, because we had two candidates [for the presidency – Cyril Ramaphosa and Nkosazana Dlamini-Zuma (NDZ)]. Hence, I was … asking you – did you pay into somebody's campaign or you paid into the ANC? … Did you donate to the NDZ campaign? No? [Laughing] You know why?

Watson: You know, my sister, these things that you are asking … [chuckles] I don't want to get myself into trouble. Let me tell you, you've seen what's been said in the newspapers.

Mkhwebane: Yes, I have.

Watson: Indeed, I am the polony in the sandwich here. I am the polony, okay, I mean, you can see that now.

Mkhwebane: You are.

Watson: I am being used … I am a small, little company on the West Rand. I was warned 6 months ago from people from Parliament. Now I am being lambasted.

Mkhwebane: Indeed you are, because as far as the public is concerned, you are taking work away from other people. You asked why I am asking this question. I am still going back to 'your blood is green, black and gold'.

Watson: Sure, ja.

Mkhwebane: I'm asking now, in relation to the statement that you made that your blood is green, black and gold: you had two people coming from the same organisation eyeing to emerge victorious – have you found yourself in this kind of situation before?

Watson: You see, my sister, I helped them both. I helped them both. So, I don't want to get into the semantics of those things but I helped them both and they are both aware of that as can be seen from the newspaper reports, but I seem to be the one being used as a scapegoat in this whole thing. This whole thing is very wrong. Truly.[2]

On receipt of the transcript of the interview, Watson's attorneys wrote to Mkhwebane, saying that she had 'misconstrued' his statement that he helped them both to mean he gave money to both the Ramaphosa and

Dlamini-Zuma campaigns. Watson denied giving money to Dlamini-Zuma, which led Mkhwebane to recommend that Watson be prosecuted for perjury.

Mkhwebane used the Bosasa complaint against Ramaphosa to gain access to the full bank statements of his CR17 campaign, which have since been selectively leaked to certain journalists and on social media. At the time of writing, Ramaphosa was challenging Mkhwebane's findings in court while his detractors were using the Bosasa report as their weapon of choice in their fightback against Ramaphosa's clean-up of the Zuma years – bear in mind that the criminal case, the SARS investigation and the liquidation of Bosasa all happened on Ramaphosa's watch.

One thing remains certain: there are no permanent friends or enemies in this game. Although Watson started out being blessed by the Eastern Cape faction of the ANC, he quickly switched allegiance to Zuma after he became president, and then moved swiftly on to get Andile Ramaphosa on the books after he saw the winds of Nasrec blowing. If you could help him to build his kingdom, you would be blessed by Gavin Watson.

Author Mark Gevisser put it succinctly in his feature about the Watsons for *The Guardian*: 'The whistleblowers' testimony sketches one of the most troubling dynamics of post-apartheid South Africa: as some freedom fighters went into politics and others went into business, support networks morphed into patronage networks, which in turn became criminal syndicates.'[3]

This is how crony corruption works, and the ANC has fallen victim to the same modus operandi time and again. As in the case of Shaik and Zuma, or Agliotti and Selebi, Watson bought politicians and civil servants to serve his private interests.

It remains to be seen whether Ramaphosa has the persistence to fundamentally change the ways of the ANC, or if Watson succeeded in fatally maiming the Buffalo – and maybe even the liberation movement to which he and his family dedicated their young lives.

Epilogue

At 13:56 on Thursday 22 August 2019, I had enough evidence and information for this book to approach the main protagonist, Gavin Watson, for his side of the story. I sent Watson a text message, which he read.

The Watson brothers were gathered in Johannesburg for the birthday celebration of a grandchild and Gavin discussed my request for comment with his brother Valence.

My message to Gavin apparently angered Valence. 'What was this person [myself] wanting to know from Gavin when he knows the hateful, toxic articles that he's written over the many, many years?' Valence said.[1]

Gavin told Valence that he wanted to send me a short message: 'Jesus loves you.'

Valence told his brother that on no account would he do that while he was there, and Gavin Watson never replied to my text.

Gavin Watson used the rest of the weekend to finalise his response to a tax inquiry by SARS that was scheduled to resume on Tuesday 27 August. Watson and a number of former Bosasa directors, including Agrizzi, had given evidence to the inquiry, which had been instituted after the Zondo Commission had learnt about large-scale tax avoidance and tax fraud at Bosasa. Those involved speculated that SARS could issue Bosasa with a fine running into the hundreds of millions of rands. If this happened, it would completely ruin what was left of Bosasa's assets, and Watson stood to lose his personal assets too. There was also a good chance that SARS

EPILOGUE

would institute tax-fraud charges against all those involved.

On the afternoon of Sunday 25 August, Gavin Watson called a friend to pick him up in Sandton, where the family was gathered and where Watson was preparing for the following week's SARS inquiry, and take him to the Bosasa head office in Krugersdorp for a prayer meeting. Watson's metallic-blue BMW X5 was parked at the company's office – his family said the liquidators had declined to let Watson use the BMW, which was owned by Bosasa.[2]

The friend dropped Watson at Bosasa, and Watson proceeded to partake in Holy Communion with Bosasa directors and staff present. According to an inside source, Watson told his colleagues that all people make mistakes and that he'd forgiven Agrizzi, presumably for breaking their secret pact of 20 years not to speak out.

After the prayer meeting, Watson asked one of the Bosasa fleet managers if he could borrow a company vehicle, and was provided with a white Toyota Corolla Quest with a manual gearbox. Watson preferred automatic cars (like his BMW X5), and someone present noticed how he struggled to reverse the Corolla when he left the Bosasa premises.

According to Jared, his uncle returned to his family in Sandton, and left the party around 20:00, presumably heading to his upmarket house in Constantia Kloof on the West Rand.[3] Watson was supposed to meet Jared the next morning between 07:30 and 08:30 in Sandton, so that they could drive together to their attorneys in Pretoria, to prepare for Tuesday's SARS inquiry.

But for reasons not yet known, Gavin Watson instead left his house early on Monday morning and drove to OR Tambo International Airport. (Rumours abounded for weeks that he'd planned to skip the country, but he didn't have an air ticket.) Shortly before entering the airport premises, Watson crashed into a concrete pillar at high speed.

'Gavin Watson dead in car crash,' read the text message I received from a contact around 10:00 on Monday 26 August.

I couldn't believe my eyes. This wasn't how the story was supposed to end. Instantly, the country had been deprived of hearing Watson's version of why he'd done what he'd done. My questions would forever remain unanswered.

The days that followed Watson's death were a mad frenzy, filled with conspiracy theories and allegations of foul play. His family didn't believe that Watson had died in an innocent car crash, and appointed an independent team of investigators to probe the cause of the accident.

I received photos from the crash scene and was able to confidently identify Watson's body in the wreck. Agrizzi identified the shoes Watson was wearing as a pair he'd bought for him in London. And police detectives and investigators made numerous visits to the Germiston mortuary to make sure it was indeed Gavin Watson's body that had been retrieved from the Corolla. The story was too important to take any chances or let anything slip.

Irrespective of his many faults and misdeeds – for which he would now never face justice – nobody deserved to die this way and I felt sorrow for Watson, his family and children.

I also felt deep anger towards South Africa's criminal justice system that had allowed Watson and Bosasa to evade justice for so many years. Had the NPA and the Hawks done their work better and faster, the country would have known much more about the origins and optics of this state capture cult.

If Watson's aim had been to escape justice and die a hero, he'd succeeded, at least in the eyes of the ANC. The governing party's statement following his death completely ignored the litany of cases, charges and allegations levelled at him, and lauded 'Cde Gavin Watson' as a philanthropist, activist and hero of the struggle against apartheid. The party didn't have the courage or ability to admit Watson's wrongdoing, including the fact that he'd stolen the BEE shares of black investors in a manganese mine.

'There is no doubt that Watson used his political connections, forged during an honourable struggle against a criminal system, to further his personal and the ANC's fortunes,' I wrote in the wake of his death. 'This is where the two worlds collide. [Linda] Mti, for example, was the commander to Watson's brothers in Umkhonto we Sizwe. The noble relationship continued after 1994, but was corrupted when Mti accepted bribes from Bosasa in exchange for tenders from his department ... Until the ANC has found a way of shaming the likes of [Tony] Yengeni, [Gavin]

EPILOGUE

Watson, [Schabir] Shaik and [Jackie] Selebi without diminishing their role as freedom fighters, any government efforts or policies to curb corruption will ring hollow.'[4]

Gavin Watson's memorial service was held four days after his death. Besides his family, the service was attended by about 200 people made up of Bosasa employees and people like Nomvula Mokonyane, Linda Mti and Kevin Wakeford, who'd been implicated at the Zondo Commission for accepting bribes from Watson.

The speakers chose to speak only about Gavin Watson's good deeds – the creches he funded in Orange Farm south of Johannesburg, the upliftment of West Rand communities around Bosasa, and his time and effort spent at Bosasa's youth centres. Those of us who were critical about Bosasa were called 'enemies' and compared with the apartheid regime that hated the Watsons because they were white people siding with the ANC.

Speaking at the service, Valence Watson and Nomvula Mokonyane (who was back at Luthuli House as a senior ANC employee after having been dropped by President Cyril Ramaphosa from his cabinet) launched a stinging attack on me for my reporting on Bosasa and Watson over the years. Misquoting from the film *Braveheart*, Valence Watson said, 'History is written by journalists who have hanged heroes.'

Mokonyane, who said she was Watson's friend, compared him to Jesus Christ and Chris Hani. 'My friends and comrades who have been persecuted because they have never been made by the media, they have never been loved by the media; those who wanted to kill us and still want to kill us today,' said Mokonyane in a reference to Watson. 'They never loved you because of your conviction. They still will not love you today. They will never forgive you for who you are … just like Jesus Christ, who was persecuted.'

The night before the memorial service, I'd sent Mokonyane a list of questions to answer for this book. She told those attending the memorial that she would tell her story 'one day' but that it wouldn't be through my book. Representing the 'genuine members of the ANC', Mokonyane referred to one of my questions – why she'd frequented the Bosasa head office – by saying Bosasa was friendly to the ANC. 'Some of us in the ANC are running away from identifying with our old dear friends. This is a family [the Watsons] that never shied away from Nomvula.'

Her final words, before receiving a standing ovation, were: 'Love them all, but trust no one.'

At the time of the memorial, the liquidation of Bosasa was at an advanced stage and thousands of employees had been retrenched. The company's contracts were wrapping up and being taken over by other companies or state departments. The Zondo Commission had issued Watson with a notice asking him to respond to the allegations made by Agrizzi and others against him, and the NPA was looking to add Watson as an accused to the corruption case against Agrizzi and his former Bosasa colleagues. With the SARS inquiry going into its final phases, the net was closing in on Watson and his companies, and it was clear that the end had arrived.

All that was left to fight for were his and Bosasa's legacy.

At Watson's funeral in Port Elizabeth, former president Jacob Zuma delivered the eulogy and called Watson his 'brother'. Without any reference to the numerous allegations of corruption against Watson or Bosasa, Zuma had only praise for Gavin and cast doubt on whether his death really was an accident. Zuma said a number of comrades close to him were 'being removed' and said he hoped that Watson 'is not one of those who were cleverly removed'.[5]

Infuriated by the use of religion to deify Watson, former Bosasa employee and devout Christian Retief van der Merwe sent me a message the next day. 'I believe the bitter taste that the Bosasa cult try to justify was purely corruption deodorised with Christianity,' he wrote. 'Like the devil, they quote the Bible to hide away the unbelievable harm and injustice they [have] done to South Africa, its government and its people. They try to justify it by saying they were struggle stalwarts and freedom fighters. That fight is done and over and has been celebrated for 25 years. You cannot justify your corrupt actions and the harm you are doing to a young democracy after 25 years and not be held accountable.'[6]

I share his views. As much as I have respect and admiration for what people like Gavin Watson, his brothers, Nomvula Mokonyane and Jacob Zuma did in the struggle against apartheid, we now live in a democracy based on principles of the rule of law and human rights. This is what they struggled for – a society ruled by a Constitution that underscores the importance of freedom of expression.

It's this freedom that I've exercised over the last 13 years to tell the sordid story of Bosasa's state capture cult.

Acknowledgements

My clever and beautiful wife Cecile has been on the Bosasa journey with me for 13 years, including witnessing some of the threats I received as a young reporter. She has been a rock in supporting me to tell this story from day one, despite the late-night calls, trips at strange hours to meet sources on the West Rand of Johannesburg, and turning our guest bedroom into a 'nerve centre' complete with whiteboard and copious notes unscrambling the Bosasa empire. Thank you, love, for always believing in me.

I'm privileged to have had incredible colleagues working alongside me on the Bosasa story through the years. Carien du Plessis was there in the beginning when nobody had yet heard of the company and we first broke the story – thank you for sharing your byline, notes and tips with me, comrade. Yolandi Groenewald was a thorn in Bosasa's side with her fearless reporting into the prawn farm saga, and Kyle Cowan has been at the forefront of exposing the company's capture of the ANC and its links to the Ramaphosa family.

I'm extremely grateful to my brave editors over the years at *Beeld*, the *Mail & Guardian* and *City Press*, who allowed me to pursue the Bosasa story with rigour and verve: Peet Kruger, Nic Dawes and Ferial Haffajee, thank you for seeing the potential in the story and for encouraging me to stay on it all the way.

The Basson, Clark, Nel and Koen families have been a constant source of support and inspiration over the years. I am incredibly blessed to have you in my life.

ACKNOWLEDGEMENTS

To my colleagues at News24, who supported me and encouraged me to write this book: thank you for the words of support and cappuccinos when I burnt the midnight oil.

The lawyers and advocates who defended me over the years against Bosasa's attempts to silence me: you gave me a great sense of comfort and strength to keep on digging. A special thanks to Dario Milo, Pamela Stein and Willem de Klerk.

To all the interviewees for this book, thank you for entrusting me with your stories. I've tried my best to reflect history as accurately as possible. A special word of thanks to June Petersen for sharing Vernie's personal stories and documents with me.

Jeremy Boraine of Jonathan Ball Publishers and my editor Tracey Hawthorne were absolute professionals in getting the manuscript print-ready at breakneck speed.

And lastly, to all the whistleblowers who've assisted me through the years to tell the Bosasa story: thank you. This is your story and your victory. Some of you made great sacrifices and paid a painful price. I always believed that the truth would one day be revealed and here we are. Your trust meant the world to me and kept me going when days were dark.

Author's notes

Right to reply

I've attempted to source comment from everyone named or implicated in this book. Where I didn't receive a response, I tried my best to source opposing views from public records and incorporate these.

I contacted the following people but they declined to comment or didn't respond to my questions: Patrick Gillingham, Nomvula Mokonyane, Ngconde Balfour, Gibson Njenje, former president Thabo Mbeki, Brian Biebuyck and James Motlatsi.

South African prisons

South Africa has 243 prisons with 119 134 available beds. Overcrowding is a massive issue, and at the end of March 2017 our prisons had 160 280 inmates.[1] A large proportion of prisoners – up to 8 000 – are awaiting-trial detainees who can't afford bail.

In general, South Africa's prisoners are served three meals per day: porridge for breakfast; meat, a starch and vegetables for lunch; and bread, margarine and jam for dinner. In 2004 catering at the country's biggest prisons was privatised and outsourced to Bosasa. The contract came to an end in 2019.

Whistleblowers

I'm eternally grateful to the brave and selfless whistleblowers who put their lives and careers at risk to assist journalists in uncovering the truth. Not all sources are equal – some have axes to grind or only tell you half of the story to protect their own interests or cover their tracks. It's a favourite spin technique of government officials and politicians caught with their hands in the till to blame whistleblowers and media sources for being 'disgruntled' – but wouldn't you be disgruntled too if you saw how taxpayers' money is rampantly wasted and/or stolen day after day?

The good cops and prosecutors

I have the greatest admiration and respect for the hundreds of good, clean and dedicated police officers, prosecutors, investigators, analysts, forensic experts and legal advisors who've dedicated their professional lives to fighting crime and corruption when they could have made much more money in the private sector. It's easy to blame the law-enforcement agencies and the NPA for the poor state of South Africa's criminal-justice system – lots of them fell victim to state capture – but the truth is that hundreds, even thousands of hard-working civil servants tried their best to do the right thing. Some have been obstructed to the point where they had to resign, while others remained in the system but were prevented by their superiors from digging through the dirty linen of politically connected individuals and families.

Notes

Preface
1 'Thuma Mina' ('Send me') is a song about solidarity, compassion and renewal, composed in 2007 by Hugh Masekela, Sello Twala and Peter Mokoena. In his inaugural State of the Nation address in February 2018, President Cyril Ramaphosa used 'Thuma Mina' as a slogan for South Africans to find new inspiration and hope in a common humanity, ubuntu, duty and service.

1. The first fight
1 Witpoortjie means 'white gateway'; colleagues tell me that today the neighbourhood is jokingly being called Swartpoortjie – 'black gateway' – because of the large number of new middle-class black families who've made it their home.
2 A referendum was held on 17 March 1992, asking only white South Africans whether or not they supported the negotiated reforms begun by State President FW de Klerk two years earlier, in which he proposed to end apartheid. The result was a large victory for the 'yes' side.

2. Getting hooked on Bosasa
1 The Strategic Defence Package, or 'arms deal', was a multibillion-rand military acquisition by the South African government. Finalised in 1999, it was the ANC's first major foray into the world of multimillion-rand tenders and ended up costing the state over R70 billion. Out of it arose allegations of large-scale bribery and corruption, with millions of rands of public money lost to bribery and other irregularities. ANC chief whip Tony Yengeni was found guilty in 2003 of fraud in a case linked to the corruption investigation into the arms deal, when he didn't declare to Parliament a discount given to him by Daimler-Benz.
2 Chin, J (2015) 'The Costs of Malay Supremacy', *The New York Times*, 27 August. https://www.nytimes.com/2015/08/28/opinion/the-costs-of-malay-supremacy.html Accessed 19 August 2019.
3 I know Carien through mutual friends and have immense respect for her family and the role her father, Professor Lourens du Plessis, played in the writing of South Africa's Constitution and the Bill of Rights.

3. Meet the Watsons
1. Valence Watson's eulogy at the memorial service for Gavin Watson, 30 August 2019.
2. Craven was president of the whites-only South African Rugby Board between 1956 and 1993.
3. Email interview with Vusi Pikoli, 1 May 2019.
4. Kebble was a mining owner who allegedly stole millions of rands from shareholders; he died in an assisted suicide in 2005 before he could face trial.
5. In 2007 then Saru boss Oregan Hoskins forced Springbok coach Jake White to include Luke Watson in the national team; White revealed in his biography that the Watsons promised him an extension of his contract if he picked Luke.
6. Published in Australia, the book was never released in South Africa and it's very hard to find a copy. I found one in the Unisa library in Pretoria, and finally managed to import one from a small Australian bookshop.
7. Interview with Angelo Agrizzi, Johannesburg, 25 April 2019.
8. Williamson, K (1997) *Brothers To Us – The Story of a Remarkable Family's Fight Against Apartheid*. Penguin Books, Australia.
9. Ibid.
10. Ibid.
11. Ibid.
12. Sparks, A (1986) 'Rugby stars on defensive for stand against apartheid', *The Washington Post*, 23 September. https://www.washingtonpost.com/archive/politics/1986/09/23/rugby-stars-on-defensive-for-stand-against-apartheid/35bf37fb-7c60-4d6d-90df-33c2ada154e5/ Accessed 19 August 2019.
13. Oliveria changed her name from Carol Mkele after they were divorced.
14. Interview with Frans Vorster, Krugersdorp, 21 June 2019.
15. Williamson, K (1997) *Brothers To Us – The Story of a Remarkable Family's Fight Against Apartheid*. Penguin Books, Australia.
16. Ibid.
17. Interview with Angelo Agrizzi, Johannesburg, 25 April 2019.
18. Ibid.
19. Ibid.
20. Williamson, K (1997) *Brothers To Us – The Story of a Remarkable Family's Fight Against Apartheid*. Penguin Books, Australia.
21. Ibid.

4. 'I sold my company to the ANC'
1. Telephone interview with Fanie van Zijl, 20 February 2019.
2. Pienaar, W (2016) 'Author celebrates rich SA athletics history', *Potchefstroom Herald*, 13 August. https://potchefstroomherald.co.za/20239/author-celebrates-rich-sa-athletics-history/ Accessed 20 August 2019.
3. Interview with Frans Vorster, Krugersdorp, 21 June 2019.
4. Telephone interview with Fanie van Zijl, 20 February 2019.
5. Interview with Frans Vorster, Krugersdorp, 21 June 2019.
6. The SBDC trades today as Business Partners.
7. Telephone interview with Fanie van Zijl, 20 February 2019.
8. Interview with Angelo Agrizzi, Johannesburg, 25 April 2019.

9 Interview with Frans Vorster, Krugersdorp, 21 June 2019.
10 Interview with Angelo Agrizzi, Johannesburg, 25 April 2019.
11 Ibid.
12 Telephone interview with Fanie van Zijl, 20 February 2019. Van Zijl wouldn't speak to me again after this, and asked that I not mention him in a book about Bosasa – he wanted nothing to do with the unfolding scandal of capture, corruption and deceit that threatened to bring the ANC to a fall. I explained that I couldn't erase history.

5. The forgotten comrade

1 The Province of the Cape of Good Hope encompassed the old Cape Colony; in 1994 it was split up into the new Eastern Cape, Northern Cape and Western Cape provinces, along with part of the North West.
2 Du Toit, P (2010) 'Mandela demanded to walk out', *News24* archives, 11 February. https://www.news24.com/SouthAfrica/News/Mandela-demanded-to-walk-out-20100210 Accessed 20 August 2019.
3 Charles Nqakula would later serve as Thabo Mbeki's minister of police.
4 Interview with Nosiviwe Mapisa-Nqakula, Kempton Park, 13 August 2019.
5 Nqakula, C (2017) *The People's War: Reflections of an ANC Cadre*, Real African Publishers, Johannesburg.
6 'Richman' and 'Gibson Makhanda' were the noms de guerre of Linda Mti and Lizo Njenje, respectively.
7 Email interview with Mavivi Myakayaka-Manzini, 25 July 2019.
8 Interview with Nosiviwe Mapisa-Nqakula, Kempton Park, 13 August 2019.
9 Ibid.
10 Angelo Agrizzi's evidence to the Zondo Commission, 16 January 2019.
11 Interview with Nosiviwe Mapisa-Nqakula, Kempton Park, 13 August 2019.
12 Nqakula, C (2017) *The People's War: Reflections of an ANC Cadre*, Real African Publishers, Johannesburg.
13 Interview with Hilda Ndude, Cape Town, 1 March 2019.
14 Email interview with Nozuko Pikoli, 2 May 2019.
15 Email interview with Mavivi Myakayaka-Manzini, 25 July 2019.
16 In the end, there were three Dyambu entities: Dyambu Trust, Dyambu Holdings and Dyambu Operations. The women were under the impression they owned 100% of all three entities, but Gavin Watson and Danny Mansell originally owned 90% of Dyambu Operations, which became Bosasa Operations, and later African Global Operations.
17 Interview with Nosiviwe Mapisa-Nqakula, Kempton Park, 13 August 2019.
18 Interview with Hilda Ndude, Cape Town, 1 March 2019.
19 Ibid.
20 Ibid.

6. 'We need to make money. The struggle is over'

1 Interview with Hilda Ndude, Cape Town, 1 March 2019.
2 Chief evidence leader Paul Pretorius at the Commission of Inquiry into State Capture, 16 January 2019.

NOTES

3   Van Hees, B (2015) 'Former Cope treasurer sentenced for fraud', African News Agency, 30 November. https://www.iol.co.za/news/former-cope-treasurer-sentenced-for-fraud-1952928 Accessed 20 August 2019.
4   This information was corroborated by Agrizzi during his testimony at the Zondo Commission.
5   Interview with Hilda Ndude, Cape Town, 1 March 2019.
6   Ibid.
7   Email interview with Nozuko Pikoli, 2 May 2019.
8   Email interview with Mavivi Myakayaka-Manzini, 25 July 2019.
9   Ibid.
10 Interview with Nosiviwe Mapisa-Nqakula, Kempton Park, 13 August 2019.
11 Interview with Hilda Ndude, Cape Town, 1 March 2019.
12 Angelo Agrizzi, who joined the company in 1998, testified at the Zondo Commission that Watson would bribe trade-union leaders on the mines to ensure they pressurised management to move catering and cleaning tenders to Dyambu.
13 Interview with Hilda Ndude, Cape Town, 1 March 2019.
14 Email interview with Nozuko Pikoli, 2 May 2019.
15 Email interview with Mavivi Myakayaka-Manzini, 25 July 2019.
16 Interview with Hilda Ndude, Cape Town, 1 March 2019.
17 Interview with Nosiviwe Mapisa-Nqakula, Kempton Park, 13 August 2019.

7. Betrayal

1   Interview with Hilda Ndude, Cape Town, 1 March 2019.
2   Ibid.
3   Interview with Angelo Agrizzi, Johannesburg, 25 April 2019.
4   Interview with Hilda Ndude, Cape Town, 1 March 2019.
5   Angelo Agrizzi's testimony to the Commission of Inquiry into State Capture, 16 January 2019.
6   Interview with Hilda Ndude, Cape Town, 1 March 2019.
7   Interview with Nosiviwe Mapisa-Nqakula, Kempton Park, 13 August 2019.
8   Email interview with Nozuko Pikoli, 2 May 2019.
9   Email interview with Mavivi Myakayaka-Manzini, 25 July 2019.
10 Email interview with Baleka Mbete, 9 September 2019.
11 Interview with Hilda Ndude, Cape Town, 1 March 2019.
12 Interview with Nosiviwe Mapisa-Nqakula, Kempton Park, 13 August 2019.
13 Interview with Hilda Ndude, Cape Town, 1 March 2019.

8. Selling out

1   Letter to Hilda Ndude from Gavin Watson dated 1 August 2000.
2   Interview with Hilda Ndude, Cape Town, 1 March 2019.
3   Email interview with Mavivi Myakayaka-Manzini, 25 July 2019.
4   Email interview with Nozuko Pikoli, May 2019.
5   Interview with Hilda Ndude, Cape Town, 1 March 2019.

9. Old networks, new money

1. Interview with Frans Vorster, Krugersdorp, 21 June 2019.
2. Interview with Angelo Agrizzi, Johannesburg, 25 April 2019.
3. Ibid.
4. Frans Vorster's evidence, Commission of Inquiry into State Capture, 30 January 2019.
5. Interview with Retief van der Merwe, Krugersdorp, 24 February 2019.
6. Frans Vorster's evidence, Commission of Inquiry into State Capture, 30 January 2019.
7. Ibid.
8. After restructuring and renaming the business, Watson bought out Mansell's shares and kept him on as a 'consultant' on strategic government projects. Years later, after the house of cards had started to tumble, Mansell fled to Austin, Texas, where he set up a fencing business called Safe As Fences with his son Jarrod. Watson still paid him a 'retainer' of $7 000 per month, Agrizzi testified, to keep quiet.
9. SIU report, 'The irregular awarding of contracts by the Department of Correctional Services to Bosasa Operations and its affiliated companies', September 2009.
10. Basson, A (2006) 'Hy bestuur R9 mjd – met net matriek', *Beeld*, 1 December. Gillingham was only removed from his post after Bosasa's links to the DCS were revealed in 2006.
11. Frans Vorster's evidence, Commission of Inquiry into State Capture, 30 January 2019.

10. 'Oh Lord, won't you buy me a Mercedes-Benz?'

1. Frans Vorster's evidence, Commission of Inquiry into State Capture, 30 January 2019.
2. Ibid.
3. Ibid. A shelf company is one that has been created and left 'on the shelf', with no activity.
4. Andries van Tonder's evidence, Commission of Inquiry into State Capture, 30 January 2019.
5. Basson, A (2013) 'Bosasa faces dti fronting investigation', *City Press*, 22 September. https://www.news24.com/Archives/City-Press/Bosasa-faces-dti-fronting-investigation-20150429 Accessed 21 August 2019.
6. Agrizzi's evidence led to Empowerdex's Broad-Based Black Economic Empowerment accreditation being suspended by the South African National Accreditation System for three months in April 2019.
7. Frans Vorster's evidence, Commission of Inquiry into State Capture, 30 January 2019.
8. M&G online reporter (2007) 'Yengeni release "is national disgrace"', *Mail & Guardian*, 15 January. https://mg.co.za/article/2007-01-15-yengeni-release-is-national-disgrace Accessed 21 August 2019.
9. Frans Vorster's evidence, Commission of Inquiry into State Capture, 30 January 2019.
10. Ibid.
11. Ibid.
12. SIU report, 'The irregular awarding of contracts by the Department of Correctional Services to Bosasa Operations and its affiliated companies', September 2009.
13. This caused a major issue for Biebuyck's then employer, Hogan Lovells, which instituted a forensic investigation into whether its trust account had been used for illegal purposes.
14. Angelo Agrizzi's evidence, Commission of Inquiry into State Capture, 28 March 2019.

11. Connecting the dots

1. In his testimony before the Zondo Commission, MP Dennis Bloem said that even after Bosasa was awarded the catering tender, inmates at some prisons still did the cooking. When Bosasa's catering tender was cancelled in 2019, prison staff and inmates took over the kitchens again.

12. The smoking gun
1 Paton, C (2010) 'Corruption is out of control', *Financial Mail*, 26 May.

13. Richman
1 Basson, A and Du Plessis, C (2006) 'Tronkhoof verbind met tenderfirmas', *Beeld*, 31 March.
2 Williamson, K (1997) *Brothers To Us – The Story of a Remarkable Family's Fight Against Apartheid*. Penguin Books, Australia.
3 South African Government (2006) 'Correctional Services commends L Mti', 9 November. https://www.gov.za/correctional-services-commends-l-mti Accessed 21 August 2019.
4 Angelo Agrizzi's evidence, Commission of Inquiry into State Capture, 28 March 2019.
5 Du Plessis, C and Basson, A (2006) 'DKD soek hard na "klikker"', *Die Burger*, 6 April.
6 Basson, A and Du Plessis, C (2006) 'Tronkhoof verbind met tenderfirmas', *Beeld*, 31 March.

14. Smoke and mirrors
1 Njenje, a top spy, served under Thabo Mbeki and Jacob Zuma, first as a deputy director-general of the National Intelligence Agency and later as director-general of the State Security Agency's domestic branch.
2 Basson, A (2009) 'Spy boss haunted by tender probe', *Mail & Guardian*, 9 October.
3 Letsoalo, M and Molele, C (2013) 'Ex-spy boss slams Cwele over Guptas', *Mail & Guardian*, 17 May. https://mg.co.za/article/2013-05-17-00-axed-spy-vows-to-expose-guptas Accessed 21 August 2019.
4 I have no proof that Njenje was involved in any of Bosasa's illegal activities or assisted them with the surveillance of journalists or staff, except for a Bosasa-sponsored flight ticket I found among leaked documents while he was employed by the NIA. I asked Njenje if I could interview him for this book; he ignored my request.
5 Interview with Denise Bjorkman, Johannesburg, 25 February 2019.

15. Red flags
1 Du Plessis, C and Basson, A (2006) 'Waarom leen DKD geld as begroting nie bestee is?', *Die Burger*, 3 May.
2 Cowan, K (2018) 'Top ANC MP Vincent Smith got cash, CCTV', *News24*, 2 September.

16. Gambling with state money
1 Affidavit of Angelo Agrizzi, 15 January 2019.
2 Stock Exchange News Service (2006) 'Simmers – Issues of Shares for cash', 21 July.
3 Interview with Andries van Tonder, Roodepoort, 11 September 2019.
4 A derivatives broker trades in futures or options that are reliant on the performance of an underlying asset.
5 According to Investopedia, single stock futures are contracts between two investors. The buyer promises to pay a specified price for shares of a single stock at a predetermined future point, while the seller promises to deliver the stock at the specified price on the specified future date. https://www.investopedia.com/articles/optioninvestor/06/singlestockfutures.asp
6 Curator's report, Executive Officer of the Financial Services Board in re the business of Dealstream Securities (Pty) Ltd, High Court of South Africa, Transvaal Provincial Division, 6 February 2009.

17. Mti resigns

1. Du Plessis, C and Basson, A (2006) 'Tronkhoof bedank na volgehoue druk', *Die Burger*, 10 November.
2. Interview with Retief van der Merwe, Krugersdorp, 24 February 2019.
3. Interview with Angelo Agrizzi, Johannesburg, 25 February 2019.
4. South African Government (2006) 'Correctional Services commends L Mti', 9 November. https://www.gov.za/correctional-services-commends-l-mti Accessed 21 August 2019.
5. Ibid.

18. The smoking bazooka

1. Basson, A and Du Plessis, C (2006) 'Skryf self tender – en kry kontrak!', *Beeld*, 16 November. I was extremely proud of this story and it set the tone for the rest of our Bosasa investigation. When Carien and I won the Taco Kuiper award for investigative journalism for our 'Prisongate' series, the judges remarked that it was a 'remarkable piece of enterprise journalism ... the stuff of powerful, thorough and ground-breaking reporting'. See Wits Journalism Department, (2007) 'Taco Kuiper 2006 Winners Press Release', 26 April, http://journalism.co.za/taco-kuiper-2006-winners-press-release/ Accessed 21 August 2019.

19. The Mbeki links

1. Email interview with Vusi Pikoli, 1 May 2019.
2. Basson, A and Du Plessis, C (2006) 'Onthul: Die hoë name agter konkelfirma', *Beeld*, 30 November.
3. Du Plessis, C and Basson, A (2006) 'Mamoepa maak aandele weg', *Beeld*, 2 December.
4. Van Dyk, J (2019) 'Cost of corruption – How a toddler died at Bosasa's detention centre', Bhekisisa, 1 February. https://bhekisisa.org/article/2019-02-01-00-cost-of-corruption-how-a-toddler-died-at-bosasas-detention-centre-zondo-agrizzi Accessed 21 August 2019.
5. Email interview with Vusi Pikoli, 1 May 2019.
6. Basson, A (2009) 'Selebi playing victim, says Pikoli', *Mail & Guardian*, 5 October. https://mg.co.za/article/2009-10-05-selebi-playing-victim-says-pikoli Accessed 22 August 2019.
7. Moosajee, A (2009) 'Pikolis deny Selebi allegations', Politicsweb, 5 October. https://www.politicsweb.co.za/party/pikolis-deny-selebi-allegations Accessed 22 August 2019.
8. Email interview with Nozuko Pikoli, 2 May 2019.
9. Ibid.
10. Ibid.
11. Ibid.

20. Crash and burn

1. Affidavit of Angelo Agrizzi to the Inquiry into State Capture, 15 January 2019.

21. Enter the Cobras

1. Interview with Nosiviwe Mapisa-Nqakula, Kempton Park, 13 August 2019.
2. Ibid.
3. Ibid.

NOTES

4 Clint Oellermann's evidence to the Commission of Inquiry into State Capture, 1 April 2019.
5 Ibid.
6 Interview with Nosiviwe Mapisa-Nqakula, Kempton Park, 13 August 2019.
7 NPA press release on Bosasa investigation, 7 December 2009.

22. #BosasaLeaks

1 Basson, A (2009) 'Prisons graft: Here's the proof, minister', *Mail & Guardian*, 30 January.
2 Guardiar went on to become a global fencing company, while SA Fence & Gate later that year started competing with Bosasa in the department, becoming embroiled in its own corruption scandal. At the time of writing, the SIU was investigating a R1.4-billion fencing tender awarded by the DCS to SA Fence & Gate involving allegations of tender irregularities and corruption.
3 Basson, A (2009) 'Linda Mti's Bosasa bonanza', *Mail & Guardian*, 6 February.

23. Burner phones and death threats

1 Interview with Angelo Agrizzi, Johannesburg, 25 February 2019.
2 Bell Pottinger was a British PR company headquartered in London which in 2016/2017 ran a 'dirty campaign' in South Africa, playing on racial animosity by creating fake news (among other tactics), in order to benefit its client Oakbay Investments, which was controlled by the Gupta family. The much-disputed term 'white monopoly capital' can refer to an oligopoly owned by a super-wealthy white elite that dominates large sectors of the economy, or business groups critical of corruption and state capture within the administration of former South African president Jacob Zuma.
3 Angelo Agrizzi's evidence to the Commission of Inquiry into State Capture, 28 January 2019.
4 Staff reporter (2019) 'How spin doctor tried to "influence" reporting on Bosasa', *News24*, 29 January. https://www.news24.com/SouthAfrica/News/how-spin-doctor-tried-to-influence-reporting-on-bosasa-20190129 Accessed 22 August 2019
5 Herald reporter (2019) 'Angelo Agrizzi's claims "the fabric of lies", insists Kevin Wakeford', *HeraldLIVE*, 29 January. https://www.heraldlive.co.za/news/2019-01-29-angelo-agrizzis-claims-the-fabric-of-lies-insists-kevin-wakeford/ Accessed 22 August 2019.
6 Sergeant, B (2013) *The Assault on the Rand*, Zebra Press.
7 Ibid.
8 Ibid.
9 Interview with Denise Bjorkman, Johannesburg, 25 February 2019.
10 Telephone interview with Jason Stoltz, 16 August 2019.
11 Telephone interview with Alec Hogg, 25 July 2019.
12 Hogg, A (2019) 'Valence Watson – My brother Gavin, Agrizzi and Bosasa', *Biznews*, 1 August. https://www.biznews.com/undictated/2019/08/01/valence-watson-gavin-agrizzi-bosasa Accessed 22 August 2019.
13 Hogg, A (2019) 'Bosasa: explosive evidence exposes "whistleblower" Agrizzi's true motives', *Biznews*, 23 September.

24. Protecting my sources

1 Bosasa Operations (Pty) Ltd v Basson and Another (09/29700), 26 April 2012, South Gauteng High Court.

2 Parker, F (2012) 'M&G fights to protect its sources from Bosasa', *Mail & Guardian*, 13 February.
3 Bosasa Operations (Pty) Ltd v Basson and Another (09/29700), 26 April 2012, South Gauteng High Court.
4 Sapa (2012) 'Judge rules on media sources', IOL, 26 April. https://www.iol.co.za/news/south-africa/judge-rules-on-media-sources-1285157 Accessed 22 August 2019.
5 Holmes, T (2013) 'ConCourt rejects Bosasa's appeal to expose M&G sources', *Mail & Guardian*, 1 February.

25. The affair
1 Interview with Denise Bjorkman, Johannesburg, 25 February 2019.
2 Exodus 20:14.
3 Interview with Lindie Gouws, Roodepoort, 11 September 2019.
4 Interview with Angelo Agrizzi, Johannesburg, 25 April 2019.
5 Interview with Lindie Gouws, Roodepoort, 11 September 2019.
6 Interview with Andries van Tonder, Roodepoort, 11 September 2019.
7 Interview with Lindie Gouws, Roodepoort, 11 September 2019.
8 *News24* (2019) 'WATCH: Bosasa's Gavin Watson: "Put God at the centre of everything"', 22 February. https://www.news24.com/SouthAfrica/News/watch-bosasas-gavin-watson-put-god-at-the-centre-of-everything-20190222 Accessed 22 August 2019.
9 Interview with Angelo Agrizzi, Johannesburg, 25 April 2019.
10 Interview with Lindie Gouws, Roodepoort, 11 September 2019.
11 Interview with Denise Bjorkman, Johannesburg, 25 February 2019.
12 Ibid.
13 Ibid.
14 Interview with Lindie Gouws, Roodepoort, 11 September 2019.
15 Interview with Angelo Agrizzi, Johannesburg, 25 April 2019.
16 Ibid.
17 Interview with Retief van der Merwe, Krugersdorp, 24 February 2019.
18 Interview with Lindie Gouws, Roodepoort, 11 September 2019.
19 Interview with Denise Bjorkman, Johannesburg, 25 February 2019.
20 Interview with Lindie Gouws, Roodepoort, 11 September 2019.
21 Ibid.
22 Interview with Andries van Tonder, Krugersdorp, 11 September 2019.
23 Interview with Retief van der Merwe, Krugersdorp, 24 February 2019.
24 Interview with Denise Bjorkman, Johannesburg, 25 February 2019.
25 Skype interview with Jared Watson, 12 September 2019.
26 Interview with Andries van Tonder, Roodepoort, 11 September 2019.
27 Affidavit of Petrus Stephanus Venter, 18 December 2017.
28 Ibid.
29 Interview with Lindie Gouws, Roodepoort, 11 September 2019.
30 Interview with Denise Bjorkman, Johannesburg, 25 February 2019.
31 Interview with Lindie Gouws, 11 September, 2019.
32 Ibid.

26. Let us pray
1 Interview with Retief van der Merwe, Krugersdorp, 24 February 2019.
2 Ibid.
3 Ibid.
4 Interview with Denise Bjorkman, Johannesburg, 25 February 2019.
5 Angelo Agrizzi's testimony, Commission of Inquiry into State Capture, 16 January 2019.
6 Ibid.
7 Interview with Retief van der Merwe, Krugersdorp, 24 February 2019.
8 Ibid.
9 During their testimony at the Zondo Commission, Angelo Agrizzi and Andries van Tonder disclosed how Bosasa would issue fake invoices to Jumbo Liquor and a chicken supplier to maintain a steady cash-flow that would be used for bribes.
10 Interview with Retief van der Merwe, Krugersdorp, 24 February 2019.
11 Ibid.
12 Ibid.
13 Email interview with Denise Bjorkman, 8 July 2019.
14 Ibid.
15 Psalm 35: 1-3.
16 Interview with Retief van der Merwe, Krugersdorp, 24 February 2019.
17 Interview with Denise Bjorkman, Johannesburg, 25 February 2019.
18 Interview with Retief van der Merwe, 31 August 2019.
19 Ibid.
20 eNCA (2019) 'Gavin Watson persecuted like Jesus: Nomvula Mokonyane', 30 August. https://www.enca.com/news/watson-was-freedom-fighter-nomvula-mokonyane Accessed 11 September 2019.

27. The Donald Trump of Krugersdorp
1 Interview with Denise Bjorkman, Johannesburg, 25 February 2019.
2 Interview with Retief van der Merwe, Krugersdorp, 24 February 2019.
3 Interview with Denise Bjorkman, Johannesburg, 25 February 2019.
4 Ibid.
5 Ibid.
6 Interview with anonymous source.
7 Interview with Denise Bjorkman, Johannesburg, 25 February 2019.
8 Interview with anonymous source.
9 Interview with anonymous source; and Cillizza, C (2019) 'Donald Trump bullied a man as overweight, then didn't apologize', CNN, 16 August. https://edition.cnn.com/2019/08/16/politics/donald-trump-fat-new-hampshire-rally/index.html Accessed 11 September 2019.
10 Email interview with Denise Bjorkman, 8 July 2019; the CCMA is a dispute-resolution body established in terms of the Labour Relations Act, 66 of 1995
11 Interview with Angelo Agrizzi, Johannesburg, 25 April 2019.
12 Interview with Denise Bjorkman, Johannesburg, 25 February 2019.
13 Ibid.
14 Interview with Retief van der Merwe, Krugersdorp, 24 February 2019.
15 Interview with Denise Bjorkman, Johannesburg, 25 February 2019.
16 Interview with Retief van der Merwer, Krugersdorp, 24 February 2019.

28. Sex on the desk
1 Interview with anonymous source, Johannesburg, March 2019.
2 Ibid.
3 Ibid.
4 Ibid.
5 Ibid.

29. The k-bomb
1 Interview with Retief van der Merwe, Krugersdorp, 24 February 2019.
2 Pijoos, I (2018) 'Vicki Momberg sentenced to an effective 2 years in prison for racist rant', *News24*, 28 March. https://www.news24.com/SouthAfrica/News/vicki-momberg-sentenced-to-an-effective-2-years-in-prison-for-racist-rant-20180328 Accessed 23 August 2019.
3 Interview with Denise Bjorkman, Johannesburg, 25 February 2019.
4 Cowan, K (2019) '"Dishonest" Bosasa boss Gavin Watson ordered to pay back millions in BEE mining shares', *News24*, 27 June. https://www.news24.com/SouthAfrica/News/dishonest-bosasa-boss-gavin-watson-ordered-to-pay-back-millions-in-bee-mining-shares-20190627 Accessed 23 August 2019.
5 Fengu, M (2018) 'Bosasa scandal 1: Big boss in k-word tirade', *City Press*, 2 September.
6 Interview with Denise Bjorkman, Johannesburg, 25 February 2019.
7 Basson, A and Cowan, K (2018) 'Bosasa executive to blow the whistle on corruption', *News24*, 22 August. https://www.news24.com/SouthAfrica/News/exclusive-bosasa-executive-to-blow-the-whistle-on-corruption-20180822 Accessed 23 August 2019.
8 Interview with Jason Stoltz, Johannesburg, 27 March 2019.
9 Cowan, K (2018) 'Bosasa scandal 2: Top ANC MP Vincent Smith got cash, CCTV', *News24*, 2 September. https://www.news24.com/SouthAfrica/News/bosasa-paid-top-anc-mp-20180901 Accessed 23 August 2019.
10 Basson, A (2018) 'Bosasa affair shows that corruption and racism must fall', *News24*, 3 September. https://www.news24.com/Columnists/AdriaanBasson/bosasa-affair-shows-that-corruption-and-racism-must-fall-20180903 Accessed 23 August 2019.
11 Ngqakamba, S (2019) 'Agrizzi agrees to pay R200k to charity for using the k-word', *News24*, 2 June. https://www.news24.com/SouthAfrica/News/agrizzi-agress-to-pay-r200k-to-charity-for-using-the-k-word-20190627 Accessed 23 August 2019.
12 Ngqakamba, S (2019) 'SAHRC guns for Gavin Watson's children over Agrizzi's k-word recording', *News24*, 27 June. https://www.news24.com/SouthAfrica/News/sahrc-guns-for-gavin-watsons-children-over-agrizzis-k-word-recording-20190627 Accessed 23 August 2019.
13 Skype interview with Jared Watson, 12 September 2019.
14 Interview with Jason Stoltz, Johannesburg, 27 March 2019.
15 Ibid.
16 Interview with anonymous source, Krugersdorp, April 2019.
17 Interview with Denise Bjorkman, Johannesburg, 25 February 2019.

30. Rape and death
1 Interview with Denise Bjorkman, Johannesburg, 25 February 2019.
2 Ibid.

NOTES

3 Ibid.
4 Pretorius, K (2019) 'South Africa is not overrun by immigrants – experts', *Weekend Argus*, 14 April.
5 Van Dyk, J (2017) 'Did Bosasa illegally detain kids while working for the department of home affairs?', Bhekisisa, 13 December. https://bhekisisa.org/article/2017-12-13-00-children-illegally-detained-under-bosasas-watch-at-lindela-as-health-care-crumbles/ Accessed 23 August 2019.
6 Van Dyk, J (2019) 'Cost of corruption – How a toddler died at Bosasa's detention centre', Bhekisisa, 1 February. https://bhekisisa.org/article/2019-02-01-00-cost-of-corruption-how-a-toddler-died-at-bosasas-detention-centre-zondo-agrizzi/ Accessed 23 August 2019.
7 Interview with anonymous source, Krugersdorp, March 2019.

31. The Mitchells Plain Youth Movement

1 Interview with June Petersen, Pretoria, 24 February 2019.
2 Ibid.
3 Ibid.
4 Interview with Michael Weeder, 26 June 2019.
5 Ibid.
6 Interview with June Petersen, Pretoria, 24 February 2019.
7 bid.
8 Ibid.

32. Into the lion's den

1 Interview with June Petersen, Pretoria, 24 February 2019.
2 Interview with Dudley Johnson, Cape Town, 16 April 2019.
3 Interview with June Petersen, Pretoria, 24 February 2019.
4 Department of Correctional Services (2007) 'Minister Balfour welcomes a new national commissioner of correctional services', 3 May.

33. Petersen's secret dossier

1 As related by June Petersen in an interview in Pretoria, 24 February 2019.
2 Interview with June Petersen, Pretoria, 24 February 2019.
3 Statement by Vernie Petersen, 31 August 2008.

34. 'Shona Malanga'

1 Reuters (2008) 'South Africa violence toll rises to 62', 31 May. https://www.reuters.com/article/us-safrica-violence-deaths/south-africa-violence-toll-rises-to-62-idUSL31541720080531 Accessed 24 August 2019.
2 Statement by Vernie Petersen, 31 August 2008.
3 Ibid.
4 Ibid.
5 Ibid.
6 Ibid.
7 Interview with June Petersen, Pretoria, 24 February 2019.

8   Ibid.
9   Statement by Vernie Petersen, 31 August 2008.
10 Ibid.
11 Ibid.
12 Ibid.
13 Ibid.
14 Ibid.
15 Interview with June Petersen, Pretoria, 24 February 2019.
16 Ibid.
17 Statement by Vernie Petersen, 31 August 2008.
18 Ibid.
19 Ibid.
20 Ibid.
21 Interview with June Petersen, 24 February 2019.
22 Flanagan, L (2008) '"Drunk" prisons boss embarrasses officials', *The Star*, 2 June.

35. Stranger things
1   Statement by Vernie Petersen, 31 August 2008.
2   Ibid.
3   Email from Pat Gamble SC to Vernie Petersen, 27 June 2008.
4   Statement by Vernie Petersen, 31 August 2008.
5   Interview with June Petersen, 24 February 2019.
6   Statement by Vernie Petersen, 31 August 2008.
7   Ibid.
8   Ibid.
9   Ibid.

36. The fear
1   Interview with Michael Weeder, Cape Town, 26 June 2019.
2   Ibid.
3   Statement by Vernie Petersen, 31 August 2008.
4   Interview with June Petersen, Pretoria, 24 February 2019.
5   Ibid.
6   Statement by Vernie Petersen, 31 August 2008.
7   Ibid.
8   Ibid.
9   Ibid.

37. 'Something must break'
1   Statement by Vernie Petersen, 31 August 2008.
2   Ibid.
3   Ibid.
4   Letter from Vernie Petersen to Ngconde Balfour, headed 'Full Facilities Management Services', dated 31 July 2008.

5 Mkhabela, M (2008) 'Balfour goes up against his prisons boss', *Sunday Times*, 17 August.
6 Statement by Vernie Petersen, 31 August 2008.
7 Ibid.
8 These printed messages and emails were included in Petersen's dossier provided to me by his wife June.
9 Statement by Vernie Petersen, 31 August 2008.

38. Comradely betrayal

1 Letter from Vernie Petersen to Geraldine Fraser-Moleketi, headed 'Obligation to report suspicious transaction of fraud and corruption', dated 21 August 2008.
2 Statement by Vernie Petersen, 31 August 2008.
3 Department of Correctional Services (2008) 'Minister Balfour responds to allegations of failure to disclose a gift to Parliament', 26 August.
4 Letter from BS Gwebu, CEO of Kgwerano Financial Services, to Minister BNM Balfour, headed 'Public office bearers, full maintenance operating lease tender', dated 25 August 2008.
5 Mafela, N and Mkhabela, M (2080) 'Cleared Balfour in forgiving mood', *Sunday Times*, 16 November.
6 Memorandum from Faiek Davids, deputy head of the SIU, to Vernie Petersen, headed 'Briefing report on the High Value Contracts Awarded to the Bosasa Group of Companies', dated 5 September 2008.
7 Statement by Vernie Petersen, undated.
8 Email response by Frank Chikane to questions from author, 19 August 2019.
9 Statement by Vernie Petersen, undated.
10 Statement by Vernie Petersen, undated.
11 The Kairos Document was a theological statement issued in 1985 by a group of mainly black South African theologians challenging churches' response to the vicious policies of the apartheid regime under the state of emergency declared in July 1985.
12 Statement by Vernie Petersen, undated.
13 Email response by Frank Chikane to questions from author, 19 August 2019.
14 Interview with June Petersen, Pretoria, 24 February 2019.

39. Departing

1 Mbeki, T (2008) 'Thabo Mbeki's resignation speech', Politicsweb, 21 September. https://www.politicsweb.co.za/news-and-analysis/thabo-mbekis-resignation-speech Accessed 26 August 2019.
2 Basson, A (2009) 'Kitchen confidential', *Mail & Guardian*, 23 January.
3 Email interview with Baleka Mbete, 9 September 2019.
4 Basson, A (2008) 'Why was I shifted, Kgalema?', *Mail & Guardian*, 26 October.
5 Ibid.
6 Interview with June Petersen, Pretoria, 24 February 2019.
7 Ibid.
8 Ibid.
9 Interview with Neil Cole, 20 February 2019.
10 Mayo Clinic, 'Interstitial lung disease', https://www.mayoclinic.org/diseases-conditions/interstitial-lung-disease/symptoms-causes/syc-20353108 Accessed 26 August 2019.

11 Interview with Dudley Johnson, 16 April 2019.
12 Interview with June Petersen, Pretoria, 24 February 2019.
13 Ibid.
14 Interview with Nosiviwe Mapisa-Nqakula, Kempton Park, 13 August 2019.
15 Ibid.
16 Ibid.

40. The unlikely snitch
1 Interview with Angelo Agrizzi, Johannesburg, 25 April 2019.
2 Angelo Agrizzi's evidence, Commission of Inquiry into State Capture, 16 January 2019.
3 Ibid.

41. From the Guptas to the Watsons
1 Interview with anonymous source, Krugersdorp, April 2019.
2 'Report of the Public Protector on an investigation into allegations of a violation of the Executive Ethics Code through an improper relationship between the president and African Global Operations, formerly known as Bosasa', July 2019.
3 Wiener, M (2019) 'Paul Pretorius: Guiding SA through the morass of corruption', News24, 1 February. https://www.news24.com/Analysis/paul-pretorius-guiding-sa-through-the-morass-of-corruption-20190131 Accessed 26 August 2019.
4 Affidavit of Frank Kennan Dutton, Commission of Inquiry into State Capture, 15 January 2019.
5 Ibid.
6 Chief evidence leader Paul Pretorius at the Commission of Inquiry into State Capture, 16 January 2019.
7 Ibid.
8 Ibid.
9 Ibid.
10 Angelo Agrizzi's testimony to the Commission of Inquiry into State Capture, 16 January 2019.
11 Ibid.

42. Monopoly money
1 Angelo Agrizzi's testimony to the Commission of Inquiry into State Capture, 16 January 2019.
2 Ibid.
3 Andries van Tonder's testimony to the Commission of Inquiry into State Capture, 29 January 2019.
4 Ibid.
5 Ibid.

43. The little black books
1 Affidavit of Angelo Agrizzi, 15 January 2019.
2 Minutes of a Special Extended Ministerial Meeting between Advocate Menzi Simelane and Ministers Jeff Radebe and Nosiviwe Mapisa-Nqakula, Cape Town, 9 March 2010.

3 Interview with Nosiviwe Mapisa-Nqakula, Kempton Park, 13 August 2019.
4 Marijke de Kock's testimony to the Commission of Inquiry into State Capture, 2 April 2019.
5 Notes by Linda Mti, attached to Angelo Agrizzi's affidavit to the Commission of Inquiry into State Capture, 15 January 2019.
6 Cowan, K (2018) 'New life for Bosasa prosecution after 8-year delay', *News24*, 12 October. https://www.news24.com/SouthAfrica/News/new-life-for-bosasa-prosecution-after-8-year-delay-20181012 Accessed 27 August 2019.
7 Ibid.
8 Cowan, K (2018) 'How Bosasa bragged about Zuma, NPA influence', *News24*, 26 September. https://www.news24.com/SouthAfrica/News/exclusive-how-bosasa-bragged-about-zuma-npa-influence-20180926 Accessed 28 August 2019.
9 Cowan, K (2018) 'I was not appointed to protect anyone – Shaun Abrahams on links to Bosasa bosses', *News24*, 26 September. https://www.news24.com/SouthAfrica/News/i-was-not-appointed-to-protect-anyone-shaun-abrahams-on-links-to-bosasa-bosses-20180926 Accessed 27 August 2019.

44. A stuffed Louis Vuitton bag and a charge sheet

1 Williamson, K (1997) *Brothers To Us – The Story of a Remarkable Family's Fight Against Apartheid*. Penguin Books, Australia.
2 Ibid.
3 amaBhungane and Letsoalo,M (2014) 'Jacob Zuma links to "untouchable" SAA boss', *Mail & Guardian*, 7 November. https://mg.co.za/article/2014-11-06-jacob-zuma-links-to-untouchable-saa-boss Accessed 27 August 2019.
4 Myburgh, P (2016) 'Exclusive: Myeni and co's R16m Prasa "freebie"', *News24*, 11 September. https://www.news24.com/SouthAfrica/News/myeni-and-cos-r16m-prasa-freebie-20160911-2 Accessed 27 August 2019.
5 Affidavit of Angelo Agrizzi, 15 January 2019.
6 Angelo Agrizzi's testimony to the Commission of Inquiry into State Capture, 28 January 2019.
7 Ibid.
8 Affidavit of Angelo Agrizzi, 15 January 2019.
9 Groenewald, Y (2017) 'Exclusive: "Corrupt" company sponsored Zuma's birthday parties', *Fin24*, 7 November. https://www.news24.com/SouthAfrica/News/exclusive-corrupt-company-sponsored-zumas-birthday-parties-20171106 Accessed 27 August 2019.
10 Ibid.
11 Ibid.
12 Angelo Agrizzi's testimony to the Commission of Inquiry into State Capture, 28 January 2019.
13 Affidavit of Angelo Agrizzi, 15 January 2019.
14 Corcoran, B (2019) 'Dublin-based firm drawn into South African corruption scandal', *The Irish Times*, 31 January.
15 Mathe, T (2019) 'Gwede keeps options open despite anti-fracking ruling', *Mail & Guardian*, 12 July. https://mg.co.za/article/2019-07-12-00-gwede-keeps-options-open-despite-anti-fracking-ruling Accessed 27 August 2019.
16 Affidavit of Angelo Agrizzi, 15 January 2019.
17 Ibid.
18 Ibid.
19 Ibid.

20 Ibid.
21 Angelo Agrizzi's testimony to the Commission of Inquiry into State Capture, 28 January 2019.
22 Affidavit of Angelo Agrizzi, 15 January 2019.
23 Richard le Roux's testimony to the Commission of Inquiry into State Capture, 31 January 2019.
24 eNCA (2019) 'Dudu Myeni: Agrizzi is a bitter man', 28 January. https://www.enca.com/news/dudu-myeni-agrizzi-bitter-man Accessed 27 August 2019.

45. Braai packs and birthday cake
1 Angelo Agrizzi's evidence to the Commission of Inquiry into State Capture, 21 January 2019.
2 Affidavit of Angelo Agrizzi, 15 January 2019.
3 Frans Vorster's testimony to the Commission of Inquiry into State Capture, 30 January 2019.
4 Interview with Frans Vorster, Krugersdorp, 21 June 2019.
5 Frans Vorster's testimony to the Commission of Inquiry into State Capture, 30 January 2019.
6 Angelo Agrizzi's testimony to the Commission of Inquiry into State Capture, 21 January 2019.
7 Interview with Frans Vorster, Krugersdorp, 21 June 2019.
8 Frans Vorster's evidence to the Commission of Inquiry into State Capture, 30 January 2019.
9 Ibid.
10 Angelo Agrizzi's testimony to the Commission of Inquiry into State Capture, 21 January 2019.
11 Smit, S (2019) 'Mokonyane slams Zondo commission amid Bosasa allegation', *Mail & Guardian*, 22 January. https://mg.co.za/article/2019-01-22-mokonyane-slams-zondo-commission-amid-bosasa-allegations Accessed 27 August 2019.
12 Statement by the President of the Republic of South Africa, Matamela Cyril Rampahosa, to the Commission of Inquiry into State Capture, 2 July 2019.

46. Green, black and gold (and food parcels and cash)
1 Casas-Zamora, K (2005) *Paying for Democracy: Political Finance and State Funding for Parties*, ECPR Press, UK.
2 Cowan, K (2019) 'ANC accepted Bosasa millions for years', *News24*, 19 February. https://www.news24.com/SouthAfrica/News/anc-accepted-bosasa-millions-for-years-20190219 Accessed 27 August 2019.
3 Ibid.
4 Richard le Roux's testimony to the Commission of Inquiry into State Capture, 31 January 2019.
5 Madisa, K (2019) 'Thabang Makwetla wants to correct Bosasa allegation against him', *The Citizen*, 13 February.
6 Cowan, K (2018) 'I didn't lie about Bosasa – Mantashe', *News24*, 27 November. https://www.news24.com/SouthAfrica/News/i-didnt-lie-about-bosasa-mantashe-20181127 Accessed 27 August 2019.
7 Angelo Agrizzi's testimony to the Commission of Inquiry into State Capture, 29 March 2019.

47. The chef who sold his Ferrari
1 Affidavit of Angelo Agrizzi, 15 January 2019.
2 Interview with Angelo Agrizzi, Johannesburg, 25 April 2019.
3 Ibid.
4 Interview with Denise Bjorkman, Johannesburg, 25 February 2019.
5 Affidavit of Angelo Agrizzi, 15 January 2019.

NOTES

6 Interview with Angelo Agrizzi, Johannesburg, 25 April 2019.
7 Ibid.
8 Ibid.
9 Ibid.
10 Ibid.
11 Ibid.
12 Ibid.
13 Ibid.
14 Ibid.
15 Ibid.
16 Ibid.
17 Ibid.
18 WhatsApp messages sent by Brian Biebuyck to Angelo Agrizzi in 2017.
19 Interview with Angelo Agrizzi, Johannesburg, 25 April 2019.
20 Ibid.
21 Affidavit of Angelo Agrizzi, 15 January 2019.
22 Skype interview with Jared Watson, 12 September 2019.
23 Ibid.
24 Interview with Angelo Agrizzi, Johannesburg, 25 April 2019.

48. Enter the Ramaphosas (by Kyle Cowan)
1 Affidavit of Petrus Stephanus Venter, 14 November 2017.
2 Cowan, K (2018) 'Ramaphosa's son denies receiving R500 000 Bosasa payment', *News24*, 6 November. https://www.news24.com/SouthAfrica/News/ramaphosas-son-denies-receiving-r500-000-bosasa-payment-20181106 Accessed 28 August 2019.
3 Cowan, K (2019) 'Exclusive: Andile Ramaphosa admits Bosasa paid him R2m', *News24*, 27 March. https://www.news24.com/SouthAfrica/News/exclusive-andile-ramaphosa-admits-bosasa-paid-him-r2m-20190327 Accessed 29 August 2019.

49. The curtain falls
1 Interview with anonymous source, 13 August 2019.
2 Skype interview with Jared Watson, 12 September 2019.
3 Ibid.
4 Affidavit by Petrus Stephanus Venter before the Commission of Inquiry into State Capture, 19 March 2019.
5 Pheto, B (2019) 'Sars goes after ANC top brass in Bosasa scandal', *Sunday Times*, 28 April.
6 Brown, J (2019) 'Former Bosasa auditor to shut down', *City Press*, 7 July.
7 Interview with Lindie Gouws, Roodepoort, 11 September 2019.

50. 'We were prostitutes'
1 Interview with Jason Stoltz, Johannesburg, 27 March 2019.
2 Interview with Denise Bjorkman, Johannesburg, 25 February 2019.

51. The wounded buffalo

1. Dennis Bloem's testimony to the Commission of Inquiry into State Capture, 1 February 2019.
2. 'Report of the Public Protector on an investigation into allegations of a violation of the Executive Ethics Code through an improper relationship between the president and African Global Operations, formerly known as Bosasa', July 2019.
3. Gevisser, M (2019) 'State capture corruption investigation that has shaken South Africa', *The Guardian*, 11 July. https://www.theguardian.com/news/2019/jul/11/state-capture-corruption-investigation-that-has-shaken-south-africa Accessed 28 August 2019.

Epilogue

1. Valence Watson's eulogy at the memorial service for Gavin Watson, 30 August 2019.
2. Skype interview with Jared Watson, 12 September 2019.
3. Alec Hogg, 'Jared Watson: Shining new light on Gavin Watson's untimely death', *BizNews*, 28 August 2019. https://www.biznews.com/interviews/2019/08/28/jared-watson-gavin-untimely-death.
4. Basson, A (2019) 'In life and death: The meaning of Gavin Watson', *News24*, 29 August. https://www.news24.com/Analysis/adriaan-basson-in-life-and-death-the-meaning-of-gavin-watson-20190829.
5. Manona, N (2019) 'Zuma worries about "enemy agents", hopes Gavin Watson was not "cleverly removed"', *News24*, 3 September.
6. Text message from Retief van der Merwe, 31 August 2019.

Author's notes

1. Africa Check (2017) 'Factsheet: The state of South Africa's prisons', 18 July. https://africacheck.org/factsheets/factsheet-the-state-of-south-africas-prisons/

Index

Abrahams, Shaun 196, 197
access-control systems 58, 164, 184
accommodation, payments for 74–75, 84
African Global Operations (AGO) 12, 123
African National Congress (ANC) xvii–xix, 6–7,
   10–11, 65, 130, 133–134, 167, 181, 198–200,
   207–212, 240–241, 244–245,
   picture section p.1, 3
African National Congress Women's League
   (ANCWL) 15, 17–18, 21, 23–24, 29–30,
   126, 205
Agrizzi, Angelo
  on Arthur Kotzen 13–14
  at Bosasa 95, 177–179
  #BosasaLeaks 82–83
  death threats against 183
  exit from Bosasa 121, 176, 215–223
  Gavin Watson and 10, 18, 64, 115–117, 197,
   243–244
  on harassment 85
  health of 178, 218–220
  on Hilda Ndude 31
  on Lindie Gouws 99, 101–103, 105
  photos of xii, *picture section p.4, 6*
  racism 121–124, 179, 222
  on religion 107, 109–110, 177–178
  SARS tax inquiry 242
  SIU report 41
  at Zondo Commission xvii, 12, 22, 32, 38–39,
   44–45, 47, 53, 57, 60–61, 72–76, 80–81, 83,
   88–91, 124, 172, 178–194, 196, 199–207,
   213–214, 216, *picture section p.7*
Agrizzi, Debbie 124
Airports Company South Africa 27, 184, 185

alcohol 108
'Andile Ramaphosa Foundation' 225
Anti-Corruption Task Team (ACTT) 202
apartheid 5, 131, 142
  Archie Mkele Business Trust 12
arson court case 11–13
Assault on the Rand, The 89–90
assaults at youth centres 125–128
Auditor-General 64, 159, 164

Balfour, Ngconde xiii, 54, 59, 63, 65, 83, 133,
   136–137, 141–152, 155–156, 158–169, 172, 198
Bancar Investment Holdings 71
bank accounts of Bosasa 49, 230
Barnard, Niel 57
Barney Mokgatle Foundation 122
Beeld 54, 67, 87
Bekaert Bastion *see* Betafence
Bester, Gerrie 107
Bester Viljoen Inc 53–54, 224
Betafence 60–61, 83
Biebuyck, Brian 14, 47, 75, 79, 86, 176, 189–190,
   196, 217, 220, 222, 230–231
birthday parties of Jacob Zuma 199–200, 206,
   207, *picture section p.4*
Biznews 91
Bjorkman, Denise xiii, 57, 90, 98, 101–105, 107,
   109, 111, 113–116, 120–121, 124–126, 216, 237
'black books' 191–193, *picture section p.5*
black economic empowerment (BEE) 17, 44, 50,
   120–121, 123
Blake's Travel 74–75
Bloem, Dennis 8, 48, 59, 149, 151, 172, 238
blogs, by Gavin Watson 116

271

Blom, Pastor Theuns 109
Blue Crane Capital 227–229
Board of Social Responsibility 133, 142
Bonifacio, Carlos 45
#BosasaLeaks 82–84, 86
Bosasa Security 22, 184
Botes, Corrie 67
Botox 113, 115
Brothers To Us 10–11, 14, 52, 198
Buchan, Angus 103
BuildAll 13–14
Bumiputera model of affirmative action 7
Burger, Die 54, 87

call centres, ANC 207–208
catering services 27, 39–41, 49, 58, 64, 82–83, 140, 158–161, 164, 172–174, 184, 218–219, 232
CCTV equipment 58, 65, 67–68, 184, 206, 211
cellphones, used for harassment 85
Chabula, Mamisa 71
chess set, personalised 179, *picture section p.6*
Chikane, Frank 71, 165–167
City Press 76, 121–122, 179
Cole, Neil 132, 139, 171
Companies Act 231
conflict within Bosasa 116–117, 216
Congress of the People (Cope) 27, 37
Consilium Business Consultants 44, 75, 104, 124, 217, 224
Cowan, Kyle 121–122, 197, 224–229
Crearis 220–221
Crime Intelligence 154–155
Cwele, Siyabonga 57

Dahua Technology 227–229
Dan Watson American Imports 10–11
D'Arcy-Herrman 224
Dawes, Nic 94
Dealstream 62
deaths, at Lindela repatriation camp 127–128
death threats *see* threats
De Haas, Olive 164
De Kock, Eugene 154
De Kock, Marijke 193, 195–196
Democratic Alliance (DA) 195, 227
Department of Correctional Services (DCS)
    Bosasa and 8, 17, 43, 46, 58–62, 65–68, 71, 77–83, 173–174, 184, 192
    catering services 39–40, 49, 53–54, 64, 82–83, 158–161, 172–173, 218–219, 232
    leadership of 38, 53–54, 65–66, 136–141, 158–161

Department of Home Affairs 21, 39, 126–128, 174, 184
Department of Justice 184
Department of Trade and Industry 44
Department of Transport 162, 184
destroying of evidence 42, 46, 74–76, 84
Dikani, Ishmael 124, *picture section p.5*
dismissals of employees at Bosasa 115
Dlamini-Zuma, Nkosazana 240–241
Doctors Without Borders 127
Dube, Benedicta 88, 94
Du Plessis, Carien 8, 48, 51, 54–56, 59, 61, 63, 77–78, 85–87, 89
Dutton, Frank 89, 182
Dyambu Holdings and Dyambu Operations 18, 23–38, 71, 126, 169, 205
Dyambu Trust 28

Economic Freedom Fighters (EFF) 227
Edelstein, Farber and Grobler Attorneys 225
'EFG2' account 225
elections xvii–xviii, 7, 21, 207–208, 210
Employees Trust 12, 38, 111, 114
Empowerdex 44
Engelbrecht, Freddie 41

Falcon Oil and Gas 201
farming
    aquaculture farm 200
    at prisons 49, 159
    SeaArk 13–14, 233
fasting 108
fencing 58–62, 83, 184
Ferrari cars and memorabilia 179, 223, *picture section p.6*
fist-fight 3–5
Fivaz, George 57
flights, payments for 74–75, 84
forced removals 131
Foresight Advisory Services 57
fracking 200–201
Fraser, Arthur 146, 232
Fraser-Moleketi, Geraldine 135, 139, 146, 149, 162, 165–166
Frolick, Cedric 213, 219
functions sponsored by Bosasa 199–200, 206, 207, *picture section p.1, 3–4*
funding of political parties 7, 209–210, 226–227, 239–241

Gamble, Pat 148–149

INDEX

Gauntlett, Jeremy 94–95
Gevisser, Mark 241
Gillingham, Patrick xiii, 17, 20, 39–47, 60, 78–83, 140, 143–144, 155, 159–160, 164–165, 189–193, 196, 224, 233, *picture section p.5*
Ginwala Commission of Inquiry 165
Gouws, Lindie xiii, 98–107, 111, 113, 119, 124, 225, 234–235, *picture section p.2*
Greyling, Geoff 83
Guardian, The 241
Guardiar *see* Betafence
Gumede, Joe xii, 85, 91–92, 106, 117, 121, 189, 201–202, 216, *picture section p.3, 5*
Gupta family 26, 56–57, 181–182
Gwebu, Brian 71, 163–164

Hani, Chris 11, 21, 22–23, 52
Hani, Limpho 11
harassment *see* threats
Hawks 46, 81, 173, 193, 201–202, 233, 244
Helmand, Johan 67
Hlabanzana, Sinoxolo 127–128, *picture section p.2*
Hofmeyr, Willie xiii, 64, 77, 79, 109, 194–195
Hogan Lovells 234
Hogg, Alec 91
hostels 16–17
hunting trips 22

Investec Securities 62

Jack, Mkhuseli 'Khusta' 14
Jacob G Zuma Foundation 199–200
Jacobs, Suad 77–78
Jaganda 61
Jali Commission 53, 77
Jiba, Nomgcobo 73, 192–193, 194, 196, *picture section p.5*
Johnson, Dudley 136
Jones, Buang 122–123
Jumbo Liquor 108

Kagiso Cemetery 127
Karoo, fracking in 200–201
Kebble, Brett 10, 70, 72
Kgwerano Asset Finance 162–164, 184
Kgwerano Financial Services 71, 161–164
Khoabane, Pinky 179
Kievits Kroon gala dinner incident 143–152, 166
Kirsten, Johan 234
Kotzen, Arthur 13–14

Larkin, Ken 108–109
Laufer, Stephen 88–89
leaked documents 65, 67–68, 74–75, 80, 82–84, 86, 196
Leigh, Russell 62
Lekota, Mosiuoa 27, 143, 146, 151
Lepinka, Jackie 72–73, 194, *picture section p.5*
Le Roux, Richard 203, 211
Leshabane, Papa xii, 41, 89, 91, 95, 106, 108, 117, 121, 124, 189, 200, 212, 216, *picture section p.3–5*
Leyds, Jackie 106, *picture section p.5*
Lianorah Investment Consultancy 53–54
Lindela repatriation camp 16–19, 24, 29–30, 39, 71, 126–128, 174, 184–185, 216, *picture section p.4*
liquidation of Bosasa 231–232, 243, 246
Little Falls Christian Centre (LFCC) 106, 109
Longworth, Margaret 225
Louis Vuitton handbag 199, 203
Luckett, Syd 133

Machiavelli, Niccolò 114
Madonsela, Thuli 26
Mafolo, Titus 70–71
Magwenya, Vincent 228
Mahumapelo, Supra 225
Mail & Guardian 74, 82–83, 86, 88, 94–95
Maimane, Mmusi 226
Makhanya, Mondli 122
Makoko, Thandi 106, *picture section p.3, 5*
Makwetla, Thabang 211–212
Malaysia 7
Malumbu, Irene 127
Mamoepa, Ronnie 71
Mandela, Nelson 20, *picture section p.1*
Mangcu, Xolela 122
Mansell, Danny xii, 13, 17–18, 39–41, 44, 60, 83, 101, 117, 187–188
Mantashe, Gwede 201, 211–212
Manuel, Trevor 139
Manyatshe, Maanda 22
Mapisa, Siviwe 22
Mapisa-Nqakula, Nosiviwe xii, 21–24, 28–30, 32–33, 38, 46–47, 78–80, 168, 173–174, 194–195
Maqetuka, Jeff 57
Maseng Viljoen 224, 234
Mathe, Ananias 150
Mathenjwa, Trevor 117, 203, *picture section p.5*
Mathwasa, John 227

273

Mawela, Calvo 212
Mbeki, Thabo 7, 27, 65, 70–71, 77, 142, 165–168
Mbete, Baleka 21, 29, 33, 38, 140, 168–169
Mbokodo 21, 56
Media24 87
'media consultants' 88–90
Mela Womans Investments 12
Meritum 16–18, 39–40, 126, 205
Meritum (later Mogale) youth hostel 17, 39, 184
Mhaga, Mthunzi 81
Mineral and Petroleum Resources Development Act 201
Miotto Trading and Advisory Service 225
Mitchells Plain Youth Movement 132
Mkele, Archie 11–13, 61, 62
Mkhize, Zweli 209–211, *picture section p.3*
Mkhwebane, Busisiwe xviii, 239–241
Modise, Zach 192–193
Mogale (was Meritum) youth hostel 17, 39, 184
Mogale Lodge 119
Mokonyane, Nomvula xii, 18, 21, 29, 38, 112, 198, 204–207, 211, 233–234, 245–246, *picture section p.4*
Molatedi, Grace 150–151, 153–154
Momberg, Vicki 120
money, influence of 115–116, 178–179, 183–185, 223, 236
'Monopoly money' 186
Moraba, Itumeleng 71, 85
Moroka Consultants 225
Motlanthe, Kgalema 168–169
Motlatsi, James 239
Motseki, Teboho 155, 158
Motsoeneng, Hlaudi 224, 225
Moyane, Tom 173–174
Mpako Investments 12
Mqobi, Tozama 143–144
Mrwebi, Lawrence 73, 192–193, 194, *picture section p.5*
Mti, Linda Morris 'Richman' xiii, 11, 21, 41–42, 46, 51–55, 58–60, 63–66, 69, 71–76, 80–81, 84, 189, 193–198, 224, 233, 244–245
Muntingh, Lukas 169
Murray, Cloete 231–232
Myakayaka-Manzini, Mavivi 21, 23, 28, 30, 33, 36
Myeni, Dudu xiii, 198–203, *picture section p.5*
Myeni, Thalente 199
My World 99, 103–104

Naspers 87
National Intelligence Agency (NIA) 56, 86
National Intelligence Coordinating Committee 53
National Party (NP) 3, 21, 87, 131
National Prosecuting Authority (NPA) 46, 73, 78, 81, 173, 193–197, 202, 244, 246
National Treasury 126, 159
Ndude, Hildegarde (Hilda) Nikiwe xii, 20–21, 23–38, *picture section p.1*
News24 89, 91, 122, 210
Njenje, Bulelwa 61, 62
Njenje, Collin 56
Njenje, Gibson xiii, 56–57, 61, 72, 74, 198, 213
Nkobi, Thomas 'TT' 7
Nocanda, Geoffrey 11
Nqakula, Charles 21, 22–23, 25, 56
Ntsimbintle 120–121
Nzunzo Investments 12

Oak Ridge Trading 114 cc 45
Oberholzer, Lizel 201
Oellermann, Clinton 77, 79–80
Oliveria, Munirah 12–13
Olivier, Natasha 225
O'Quigley, Phillip 201
O'Sullivan, Paul 227
overweight employees 114–115

paranoia 115
Passenger Rail Agency of South Africa (Prasa) 184, 199
People's War, The 21
Perry, Tony 18, 38–39, 53–54, 62, 187–188
Petersen, June 130, 132–137, 139, 141, 143–146, 150, 154, 167, 169–172
Petersen, Vivian 'Vernie' Patrick xiii, 38, 53, 59, 71, 82, 130–172, *picture section p.8*
Phalatse, Seth 71
Phezulu Fencing 5, 58–62, 75, 184
Pikoli, Nozuko 'Girly' 21, 23, 28–30, 33, 36, 61, 71–72
Pikoli, Vusi 9–10, 69, 71–73, 165
Police and Prisons Civil Rights Union 172
Post Office 22, 27, 185
prawns 13–14, 200, 233
prayer meetings 6, 106–112, *picture section p.3*
Pretorius, Paul 182–183, 187
Pretorius, Willem 140
Prinsloo, Jurg 3
prisoners, as hitmen 183
prisons
  catering services for 39–41, 49, 58, 64, 82–83,

140, 158–161, 164, 172–174, 184, 218–219, 232
  CCTV equipment for 58, 65, 67–68, 184
  compensation fund 81
  farming at 49, 159
  fencing for 58–62, 83, 184
  television sets for 6, 8, 48, 58, 164, 184
Protected Disclosures Act 162
Public Protector (Busisiwe Mkhwebane) xviii, 227, 239–241
Public Protector (Thuli Madonsela) 26
Public Service Commission (PSC) 64, 73, 147
Putziger, Philip 219

racial tension, in Bosasa 216
racism 86–87, 120–124, 179, 222
Radebe, Jeff 194–195
Radhakrishna, Aneel 200–201
Ramaphosa, Andile xiii, 225–229, 239, 241
Ramaphosa, Cyril xviii, 182, 200, 207–208, 224–227, 239–241
Ramsingh, Odette 147
rape 125–126
recordings 121–123, 188–189, 197, *picture section p.6*
religion 6, 55, 98–112, 116, 177–178, 236, 243, 246, *picture section p.3*
robbery at Bosasa office 101
Rodenburg, Michael 83
Roode, Ryno 74–75, 106
Routledge Modise 234
rugby 9–10

SA Fence & Gate 83
safes 185–189, 192, *picture section p.6*
salaries, at Bosasa 104, 124, 232
Sangweni, Stan 73
Sasol 27, 185
Schreiner, Jenny 46–47, 66, 78, 80, 140, 145–147, 173
Scorpions 63, 70, 73
Scott, Leon 131, 139
SeaArk 13–14, 233
security services 27, 49, 58, 65, 67–68, 184, 203, 206, 211
Selebi, Jackie 70, 71, 72, 117
Selfe, James 8, 59, 169
Seopela, Sesinyi xii, 57, 75, 199, *picture section p.3*
Sergeant, Barry 89–91
sexual assault 125–126
sexual promiscuity 118–119
Shabalala, Val 144, 148, 149

Shaik, Moe 56–57
Shaik, Schabir 6–7, 48, 70
Shanduka 227
shareholding structures of Bosasa 12–13, 38–39, 70–72
Shilowa, Mbhazima 27
Sibeko, Xoliswa 169, 172–173
Simelane, Menzi 194–195
Simmer & Jack Mines 61–62, 72, 91
Singh, Gavin 228
Singh, Nadira 144
Sithole, Khulekani 53, 172
Smalberger, James 143, 144
Small Business Development Corporation (SBDC) 17–18
Small-Smith, Ian 47
Smith, Jurgen 16–19, 27, 43–44, 75, 124
Smith, Vincent 59, 121–122, 211, 213, 219, 234, *picture section p.5*
Sondolo IT 5, 44, 48, 58, 70–71, 184
sources 55–56, 93–95
South African Human Rights Commission (SAHRC) 122–123, 127
South African National Editors' Forum (Sanef) 94–95
South African National Institute for Crime Prevention and the Reintegration of Offenders (Nicro) 135
South African Police Service (SAPS) 39
South African Revenue Service (SARS) 224, 232, 233, 242–243
Special Branch 133, 153–154
Special Investigating Unit (SIU) 41, 45–46, 57, 64, 70–71, 73, 75–81, 139–140, 164, 172–173, 194–196
Star, The 145, 146, 149
state capture 6, 26, 67–68, 179, 181
State Security Agency (SSA) 56–57
Stoltz, Jason 91, 121, 123–124, 236–237
Sun International 18
surveillance 56, 83

Tambo, Adelaide 21, 28
Taverner, Mark 39
taxes *see* South African Revenue Service
television sets, for prisons 6, 8, 48, 58, 164, 184
tender process 50–51
Thoka, Israel 225
threats 56, 85–92, 133, 136, 139, 153–155, 183
Trengove, Wim 94–95
Trump, Donald 113–115

275

Tsoka, Moroa 93–95
Twitter 47, 179

Ulloa, Félix 210
uMkhonto weSizwe (MK) 11, 52

Van der Bank, Gerhard 74–75
Van der Merwe, Retief 40, 104, 106–113, 115–117, 120, 246
Van der Merwe, Riaan 228
Van Dyk, Joan 127
Van Tonder, Andries xii, 44, 61–62, 74–76, 100, 103–104, 106, 108, 187–189, 219, 233
Van Zijl, Fanie 15–19, 205
vehicles 42–46, 54, 161–164, 179, 206, 231, 243
Vela Phumelela horse racing 36–37
Venter, Peet 104, 224–227, 230–231, 233
Viljoen, Ryno 107–108
violence, at Lindela repatriation camp 127–128
Von Solms, Basie 67
Vorster, Frans Hendrik Steyn xii, 12, 16–18, 39–46, 205–207
Vorster, Paulus (Oom Vossie) 16, 39–40
Vulisango 61, 72, 91

Wakeford, Kevin 61, 62, 89–91, 105, 245
'Watson Corporate University' 116
Watson family 9–14, 52–53, 62, 72, 198, 232–233
Watson, Bobbi 9
Watson, Dan 9
Watson, Daniel (Cheeky) 9–14, 62, 213, 217
Watson, Gavin Joseph
  Angelo Agrizzi and 215–223
  background of 9–14, 181–182
  'black books' 191–192
  Bosasa 38–40, 43–49, 60–64, 71, 80, 83–84, 120–121, 176–179, 199–212, 224–225, 230–235, 239–243
  death of 109, 243–247, *picture section p.8*
  destroying of evidence 42, 46, 74–76, 84
  Dyambu Operations 17–19, 22–38
  health of 113, 115
  Lindie Gouws and 98–102, 104–105, 119
  management style of 113–117
  media and 85–87, 90–91
  'Monopoly money' 186–189
  photos of xii, *picture section p.1, 3–5*
  plausible deniability of 80, 124, 187–188

racism 120, 123–124
recordings of 188–189, 197
religion 55, 106–112, 116
Watson, Jared 62, 104, 121–123, 222–223, 232, 243
Watson, Leigh-Ann 100
Watson, Lindsay 121–123, *picture section p.5*
Watson, Luke 10, 62, *picture section p.2*
Watson, Ronald (Ronnie) 9–14, 21–25, 27, 56, 62, 91, 174, 222–223, *picture section p.2*
Watson, Roth 121–123
Watson, Sharon 9
Watson, Valence 9–14, 61–62, 72, 91, 198, 222–223, 242, 245
Weeder, Michael 132–133, 153–154
Wesbank 162–164
Williamson, Kristin 10–11, 13, 14, 52, 198
Wills, David K 13
'witdoeke' attacks 142
Wolela, Manelisi 54, 145–146

xenophobic attacks 142

Yengeni, Tony 45, 133
youth centres 17, 125–126, 184

Zapiro cartoons *picture section p.7*
Zondo Commission
  background to 26
  Gavin Watson and 113, 246
  impact of 233–235
  Jumbo Liquor 108
  testimony of Adriaan Basson 89, *picture section p.8*
  testimony of Andries van Tonder 44, 188
  testimony of Angelo Agrizzi xvii, 12, 22, 32, 38, 44–45, 47, 53, 57, 60–61, 72–76, 80–81, 83, 88–91, 124, 172, 178–190, 192–194, 196, 199–207, 213–214, 216
  testimony of Clinton Oellermann 79–80
  testimony of Dennis Bloem 59
  testimony of Frans Vorster 39–41, 43–46
  testimony of Richard le Roux 211–213
  Watson family and 232–233
  Zapiro cartoons on *picture section p.7*
Zondo, Raymond 184–187
Zuma, Jacob 7, 26, 56–57, 63, 70, 165, 168, 173, 181–182, 197–207, 241, 246, *picture section p.4–5*

www.ingramcontent.com/pod-product-compliance
Lightning Source LLC
Chambersburg PA
CBHW070837160426
43192CB00012B/2221